COMMUNICATION AND HUMAN RELATIONSHIPS

COMMUNICATION AND HUMAN

RELATIONSHIPS

The STUDY of INTERPERSONAL COMMUNICATION

Gerald M. Phillips
The Pennsylvania State University

Julia T. Wood
The University of North Carolina at Chapel Hill

Macmillan Publishing Co., Inc.
New York

Collier Macmillan Publishers
London

Photographs by: Marc B. Levey, pages 7, 29, 30, 43, 49, 71, 75, 91, 103, 131, 134, 142, 162, 170, 196, 208, 215, 219, 221, 240, 254 and 282
and Juli Barbato, pages 2, 20, 38, 62, 82, 114, 148, 178, 236, 270, 294 and 300
Cartoons by Esther Szegedy

Macmillan Publishing Co., Inc.
866 Third Avenue, New York, New York 10022

Collier Macmillan Canada, Inc.

Library of Congress Cataloging in Publication Data

Phillips, Gerald M.
  Communication and human relationships.

  Includes bibliographical references and index.
  1. Interpersonal relations. 2. Interpersonal
communication. 3. Sex role. I. Wood, Julia T.
II. Title.
HM132.P468 1983   302.3′4   82-9956
ISBN 0-02-395240-7   AACR2

Printing: 1 2 3 4 5 6 7 8   Year: 3 4 5 6 7 8 9 0

ISBN   0-02-395240-7

DEDICATION

We dedicate this book to our spouses

To Nancy Phillips . . . "For thirty-two years I argued each case with my wife, and the muscular strength that it gave to my jaw has lasted the rest of my life . . ."

And to Robbie Cox whose ongoing commitment to effective intimate communication has greatly enriched the second author's life.

PREFACE

Three features distinguish *Communication and Human Relationships: The Study of Interpersonal Communication* from other books about interpersonal communication: its unique perspective on communication, its reliance on case histories of ordinary people, and its focus on sex-roles as a primary issue in contemporary relationships.

This book differs from many others in how it views interpersonal communication. Our approach is based on the premise that humans are symbol-using animals. Our facility with symbols allows us to think, to establish values and ideals, to reflect on ourselves, to remember the past and plan for the future, and to make considered choices about our attitudes and actions in relation to others. Humans *choose* how to define themselves and each other, how to deal with one another, and how to manage their association.

With these choices come responsibilities. We are accountable for our conduct and its impact on others, both to society and to the people with whom we come in contact. Our choices may be wise or foolish, productive or self-defeating, prudent or radical, safe or risky. Whatever they are, if we violate public rules of social conduct, society exacts its penalty, and if we violate the private agreements we have made with others we lose their affection and trust. Since informed choices tend to produce the most desirable results, a major goal of this book is to provide you with information to help you to choose wisely. Such information is both theoretical and practical. Most of all, it is personal.

It is our belief that good theory is eminently practical, and conversely, that effective practice contributes to theoretical understanding of new and unfamiliar events. By mastering both theory and practice, you increase your chances for a rewarding relationship life. In *Communication and Human Relationships* we blend theoretical and practical materials so that they contribute to each other, and so that together, they expand the bases for your choices.

Human behavior is, of course, influenced by what happens around us, but in virtually every case, we have the opportunity to choose among different courses of action. This book is designed to help you make the best use of that latitude of freedom.

A second feature of this book is our reliance on people's reports of their experiences to supply primary information about the pragmatics of interpersonal communication. We conducted hundreds of oral and written interviews in order to present to you real interpersonal issues that confront people like you, and to let you see how different people handle these issues (See Appendix A). We provide you with short descriptions of experiences reported by our interviewees. We use these sketches to amplify research findings. For the most part, the situations we present are the normal, average, common ones that comprise interpersonal communication in everyday life. Few vignettes stand out as unusual. Reliance on real life experiences of ordinary people gives this book an inherently practical flavor. On the other hand, our respondents' words illustrate the drama of everyday relationship life, with all the temptations, the hopes and dreams, and the hard work necessary to make things come out all right.

The sketches do not prove theoretical points, nor do they represent probabilities or norms. Instead, they allow us to glimpse the *possibilities* in human conduct. We learn what different people consider important, how they define themselves and their relationships, what goals they seek, and what problems they face. We get a panoramic view of interpersonal issues and, thus, we discover not *the* answers, but a wealth of alternatives against which to consider our own personal positions and values. We predict that the reports we include will provoke both thought and self-reflection. Consideration of the varied experiences, concerns, and goals of others should lead you to reflect on your own activities and choices. We can testify that both of us reconsidered, and in some cases modified, our own ideas as a result of the views expressed by our respondents. The people you will meet in the following pages will offer you that same opportunity.

A third feature of this book is our attention to the changing roles of women and men in our society. The 1980's in America is a time of confusion, revision, and new options in sex roles. The turmoil caused by breakdown of traditional modes of behavior permeates all dimensions of interpersonal life. Men and women of this era need to discover alternative ways of dealing with each other as colleagues, acquaintances, friends, and romantic partners. To address this complex issue, we listened to women and men of various ages and occupations representing various values. We asked them to share with us their views on friendship, work, and expectations from the other sex and to tell us what it means to them to be a woman or man in contemporary America. Chapters 9 and 10 are the result of these interviews. Chapter 9 reports the men's perspectives, while Chapter

10 describes women's views. We emphasize that these are *descriptive* chapters in which we present the ideas our respondents offered us. We do not agree with everything they said; in some cases we disagree quite strongly. Nonetheless, we present their ideas so you may discover how others deal with current changes in sexual definition and their impact on personal, professional and social communication. We think this is certainly one of the major social issues of our time, and thus, that it merits attention in the classroom as well as in any comprehensive treatment of interpersonal communication.

We hope you will find this book both interesting and useful. To enhance readability, we've minimized unnecessary technicalities and provided a wealth of examples to clarify complicated ideas. To enhance utility, we present alternative views of interpersonal issues, hoping this approach will encourage you to choose what is appropriate for you after reviewing the range of options. If you find the book useful, we have achieved our goals as authors. It was stimulating for us to write it, for it led us to consider perspectives other than our own and to expand our understanding of our fellow humans. That is always enriching.

Julia T. Wood
Chapel Hill, North Carolina

Gerald M. Phillips
State College, Pennsylvania

CONTENTS

10   THE WOMEN TESTIFY   237

11   HUMAN COMMUNICATION AND HUMAN RELATIONSHIPS: SUMMING UP   271

COMMUNICATION
AND HUMAN
RELATIONSHIPS

1

INTRODUCTION TO INTERPERSONAL COMMUNICATION

Read any popular magazine today and you will discover that people are very interested in how to get along with one another. Classes in interpersonal communication flourish at most universities and programs like sensitivity training, EST, and assertiveness training promise people they can improve the way they get along with one another. Instruction in interpersonal communication now competes for attention in college and university departments with the traditional classes in public speaking and group discussion. In fact, some authorities believe that interpersonal communication is the basis of instruction for all communication training.

Modern study of informal communication began with the work of Kurt Lewin, a pioneer in the social sciences. The group dynamics movement, which he launched, initiated intensive study of how communication is used to form and maintain human relationships. This interest is currently pursued by many academic disciplines including speech communication, social psychology, sociology, psychology and linguistics.

This book reflects the perspective of speech communication. Therefore, we will examine how communication influences the formation, maintenance, and dissolution of human relationships. We assume that communication is the primary means by which people define themselves and their relationships and by which they attempt to keep their relationships on constructive courses. To elaborate this point of view, we will address five major issues in this book.

1. How do trends in contemporary society influence the goals, quality, and form of interpersonal communication?
2. What theoretical position best advances understanding of how and why people talk to one another?
3. How do people build relationships, sustain them, and end them?
4. What special issues characterize relationships between men and women?
5. How may committed individuals evaluate and improve their own relationships?

This book is not a training manual for personal improvement. Too little is known about interpersonal communication to warrant general prescriptions or recipes for success. The self-help books flooding the current market tend to treat topics superficially and are not based on systematic study, so the advice they offer should be regarded with appropriate skepticism. The primary reason why general advice is inappropriate is that people use communication to achieve a variety of goals, and what is effective in one situation for one objective may be totally ineffective in another setting for a different goal. The nature of effective interpersonal communication must be decided on a case-by-case analysis. Thus, in this book we argue that individuals must define for themselves what is effective in each situation they encounter and what means will assist them in achieving what they consider effective behavior. Further, we believe that judgments of effectiveness are most sound when they are informed by existing research and by a mature perspective on the process of human communication. This book will summarize a great deal of research relevant to your judgments of what is effective behavior and how it can be achieved, and it will offer you a way of thinking about the complex issues that comprise interpersonal communication. Further, it will introduce you to the views of a variety of people whom we interviewed in researching this book (see Appendix A).

Over the last few years, both scholarly and popular writers have devoted their attention to problems in personal relationships. People naturally are concerned about whether they will be able to make and keep friends, build satisfying relationships with the opposite sex, and maintain productive contacts with their fellow workers, their neighbors, and the people with whom they carry on day-to-day business. The study of relationships has been characterized by a struggle for an understanding of the motives and goals people have in their relationships with one another. There have been a number of reports of growing discontent and malaise with relationships in contemporary society. A number of suggestions have been made about why this is, ranging from "narcissism" on one hand to "separation from God" on the other. A middle-of-the-road view is that people often have unsatisfactory relationships because they do not understand the possibilities open to them, and they are not skilled in the techniques that make their relationships satisfactory. This book takes this middle position. It argues that successful interpersonal relationships begin with an understanding of what possibilities exist for interpersonal relationships. Once people are able to choose goals from a wide range of options, they need to understand how they may proceed effectively to seek those goals. Finally, they need to practice oral communication to acquire skill in interpersonal communication. This book emphasizes understanding of possible goals and awareness of a variety of communicative means for achieving them. Our primary purpose is to increase your ability to manage your own relationships in a satisfying and responsible way.

The Communication Focus

Our emphasis is oral communication—talk. The comprehensive study of relationships, of course, includes many topics in addition to communication. A great number of social psychologists, sociologists, anthropologists, and psychiatrists have been working assiduously to discover the personal and social motivations for human interpersonal behavior. We will refer to some of their findings when pertinent, but it is important that you understand this is basically a book about how human talk is used to create and define relationships. It is based on three fundamental assumptions about the nature of human communication.

First, we assume oral communication exists on a continuum where the two extreme points are *expression* and *rhetoric*. Expression is communication to release emotion; its goal is to ease personal tensions. Rhetoric is planned communication which seeks to convey information or attitudes, present ideas, advocate for a point of view, or give directions. It is addressed to particular people with whom the speaker wishes to accomplish some purpose.

Expression is spontaneous. It often takes the form of emotional outbursts, such as crying, shouting, or cursing. Its impact on others is hard to predict. Rhetoric, on the other hand, is planned to a greater or lesser degree. Planning may be nothing more than specifying intent and forging ahead, or it may take the form of preparing, memorizing and rehearsing lines to deliver in particular situations. The main distinction between these two forms of communication is that expression generally focuses attention on the speaker's concerns while rhetoric emphasizes the interests of the listener as well as the speaker.

Our second assumption is that speech is a complex, conscious, human act. What distinguishes human communication from that of other animals is that humans can master the most sophisticated symbolic processes and thus can use symbols to store ideas and to create a history and a future for themselves.

To demonstrate that symbolic communication is a conscious act, consider that it requires coordination of mind, lungs, vocal mechanism, mouth and resonators to produce specific sounds, called words, which humans agree refer to things and ideas. Furthermore, communication demands a mastery of rules to arrange words according to patterns recognizable by everyone in a language community.

Finally, we assume that mature speech depends on the ability of one person to identify with the problems, needs, and wants of others. Aristotle, commonly regarded as the founder of the art of rhetoric, said, "the fool tells me his reasons, the wise man persuades me with my own." An effective communicator must understand that all humans have common needs: to stay alive, to be comfortable, to find pleasure and avoid pain, and to be respected by others. The ability to link your values and objectives to those that other people find important is the criterion for effectiveness in rhetorical speech. Attaining skill requires self understanding. As Socrates put it, "the unexamined life is not worth living."

Why Interpersonal Communication Is Important

Skill in interpersonal communication is directly linked to the quality of our lives. Interpersonal communication helps us to form an identity and to find a place to fit in with others. It enables us to employ the rules of social behavior to help us seek our personal goals. The process of interpersonal communication is the basis of our relationships.

Identity

Concepts like "identity" or "self" are hard to define; they are not physical entities or parts of the body. "Self" is an abstract term, not a concrete one. It is a concept that is useful in helping you understand your relationship world. "Self" refers to a repertoire of behaviors a person has for the people and social situations he or she encounters. The American philosopher George Herbert Mead believed that people learned who they are and what was expected of them by

Human relationships are the basis of society.

communicating with one another. Mead observed how children at play assumed identities like fireman, nurse, mommy or daddy, and proceeded to try them out on the people around them. When others confirmed a role, the children retained it to employ on other occasions. Once children discover that they must get approval for their behavior from others, they can begin to build their personality or "self." The process is life-long; it never stops.

Harry Stack Sullivan refers to personality as the relatively enduring social behavior that people use in their interactions with others. Speech is important because it is the way you identify yourself to others and motivate them to help you seek your goals. By remembering what worked before, you can select behaviors to fit new situations.

Social fit

When people communicate effectively, they find others with whom they regularly associate and with whom they fit in. They develop identities, such as friend, lover, colleague, boss, neighbor, family member, etc., which help others know what to expect and regularize relationships. When people cannot communicate effectively, they do not fit in well enough to be confirmed by others. As a result, they become lonely, bored and ineffective, frustrated by their inability to fit with others in a satisfying way.

Loneliness is being afraid, knowing that no matter where you look there is no one on whom you can rely. George Cukor once said, "after your mother dies, nobody cares all that much." All of us seek relationships with people who care about us and provide affection and support when we need it.

Corinne T. To go back to my room and sit alone was more than I could handle. Night after night I would leave work and go back there and sit and watch TV and wait for something to happen. I was afraid to go next door and knock on the door. I knew another girl lived there, but I couldn't bring myself to introduce myself. I wondered why she did not come and meet me. There is nothing worse than being alone in a new city trying to make it in a new job, and there isn't anything I fear more than having to go through that again. My days of loneliness taught me how important it is to keep in contact with others.

Boredom is not having anyone you care to do anything with. Everything seems the same. Nothing is exciting. People need people to help them solve the problems of living, and find excitement and pleasure. Boredom is associated with loneliness. There is a difference between being alone and being lonely. Being alone is a choice that people make when they have something pleasant or important to do in which others cannot share. Being lonely is being involuntarily separated from others. Boredom comes from being lonely too often and for too long. Once boredom becomes a habit, it is very difficult to get involved in activities or to become excited about anything. Your sense of fun atrophies and your ability to handle company withers. Boredom is a prelude to depression. Depression is an emotional disorder which often comes from the chronic inability to make lasting and rewarding relationships with others.

Ineffectiveness is another penalty for the inability to communicate well. When people cannot motivate others to respect them and to collaborate with them, they feel powerless. Although we do not have complete control over our own lives, there is a great deal we can influence when we are skillful in interpersonal communication. When we have the ability to motivate others to collaborate in goal-seeking with us, we can feel potent, and less bored and lonely as well.

Goalseeking

Most of us live part of our lives in fantasies and daydreams. Sometimes we think about how we would like the world to be, but most of the time we know the difference between our dreams and reality. When we think about reality, we think about the people whose cooperation we seek to achieve our goals, and what we must offer to get it. However, if we do not recognize the difference between what we would like to happen and what is possible, we face the possibility of frustration in our goalseeking, and from there, it is an easy slide into neurosis or at least chronic dissatisfaction.

Through effective interpersonal communication we can enlist the aid of others to help us accomplish our goals. People who communicate well with others can work for the common good. Civilized societies thrive when people cooperate to improve life through governments and social relationships, as well as they support each other in personal goalseeking. Interpersonal communication is the basis for cooperation.

We can rarely get what we seek without the support of others. Alfred Adler believed working for the social interest was innate in all of us and adjustment is the ability of people to relate to one another so that everyone's interests are considered. Seeking personal goals without concern for others was a sign of maladjustment. Furthermore, Adler believed courage was required to seek one's needs by seeking to serve the social interest. He regarded those who ignored the interests of others as they pursued their goals as "spoiled." Today, we refer to such people as "narcissistic" and "sociopathic." Our society has encouraged narcissism by promising people they could find true happiness and fulfillment alone. People have been advised to look out for themselves as their top priority. The message seems to be "there is not enough to go around so be sure you get yours!"

Daniel Trevor, M.D., Psychiatrist. People these days seem to be willing to trade almost anything for a little human contact. Karen Horney, who did so much to release women from socially enforced neurosis, pointed out that women often trade sex for social contact. Most women seem to have gotten over that, but there does seem to be a general state of doubt about how much you can trust people. Some folks seem to despair of ever forming a satisfying relationship. Narcissism keeps people apart. They have been encouraged to seek too much and they get dissatisfied even when they have a great deal. People get discouraged too easily. They are so intent on getting that they cannot think of giving and as a result, they compete with each other when they really ought to be working together.

The realities of today's declining economy mean it is not possible for everyone to get all they want. A survey taken in mid-1981 reveals that people have replaced preoccupation with world peace and the plight of the wretched of the earth, with concern about whether they will be able to make a living. The goal of actualization has been replaced with the goal of survival. When it is difficult to accomplish personal goals, people need to cooperate to realize their objectives.

The late Wendell Johnson referred to the problem that results when people want what they cannot have as IFD Disease: I for "idealization," F for "frustration," and D for "demoralization." People acquired IFD Disease, Johnson believed, when they could not specify what they wanted, so they could not know whether they had it. When people said things like, "I want to be poised, successful, and popular," they really had no way of knowing whether or not they ever made it. They could convince themselves that they were unsuccessful in the face of the most impressive counter-information. Since they could not prove to themselves they had succeeded, they became frustrated and eventually demoralized. They stopped trying and removed themselves from social contact.

IFD also applies to expectations you have for others. When you expect people to deliver more than is possible for them, you not only impose an excessive burden on them, but you deceive yourself into believing that the impossible can happen. Expecting too much from other people is a direct path to frustration, demoralization, and unsatisfactory relationships.

Successful goalseeking starts with a specification of your desired outcomes so specific that you cannot help but know whether you succeed or fail. Furthermore, you must take into account that other people are also seeking to accomplish goals and that all of you can do better, if you work together. Skillful interpersonal communication helps you find ways to accomplish the goals you seek, while you help others do the same.

Some Contemporary Myths

Relationships are seriously affected by myths. For example, the old adage about "love at first sight" has been translated into the contemporary myth of the "vibe". When you feel good "vibes", according to this myth, you can expect a rewarding relationship, and you should take care to avoid people who give off bad "vibes." Unfortunately, a "vibe" is nothing more than a transference response. In simple terms, this means that people tend to classify unfamiliar things or events in terms of their similarity to familiar things. For example, you order steak in a restaurant because you have had good experiences eating steak before. This leads you to bet on another good experience. It is unreasonable to believe that people who look alike will act alike. However our tendency to believe that people whom we see as similar will act alike leads to another serious problem, stereotyping. For example, we often expect everyone of the opposite sex to act the same way. Here's what was said by one of the people who responded to our research questionnaire.

Shirley T. People act like the word "woman" is a disease. My doctor associates "woman" with all kinds of diseases. My husband associates it with all kinds of weaknesses. I think I do the same thing with "man." For a long time I was startled when "a man" did not enjoy football. I guess we have to be careful to apply generalizations only where they fit. "Woman" or "man" refers to biological properties, and really has nothing to do with personality.

Another entrenched myth is that disclosure has real value in relationships. Unfortunately, the notion of "letting it all hang out" sometimes has precisely the opposite effect of what people who advocate it intend. In the first place, many people become annoyed or bored when someone dumps feelings on them; they usually prefer to avoid people who reveal personal details of their lives. People expect consideration and a reasonable exchange from others; they do not react well to demands for complete acceptance. This does not mean that you should misrepresent yourself to others. It means that you must modulate your demands and disclosures so they are appropriate to the nature of the relationship you have with another person. Furthermore, you become vulnerable when you disclose your secrets and weaknesses to those who do not respect this information. Such behavior in relationships is egocentric and has very low payoff. The most effective way to get attention and cooperation from others is through an exchange that is based on commonly accepted social rules that consider the convenience of everyone.

Understanding social rules

Interpersonal communication is important because it helps us identify and follow rules of social interaction.

Andy R. I don't seem to be able to figure out what to do when or where or with whom. I mean, I go to places and I think I know what's going on and then I say the wrong thing to someone then I think everyone is laughing at me. Or sometimes I show up wearing a suit and tie when everyone else is in jeans and sometimes I come in jeans and everyone is all dressed up. I was once invited to an informal dinner and I came in jeans and a T-shirt and everybody there looked like they just stepped out of some fashion magazine.

Andy has a problem with learning "rules." Human relationships are governed by rules. We have procedures for who can talk with whom, about what, when, where, and how. We establish rules about who is successful and who is not. Our language is put together with rules of grammar. Our society is governed by formal rules, called "laws." Rules are reliable generalizations that guide our expectations and help evaluate others. People reject those who violate rules consistently. We call them criminal or emotionally ill and we either imprison them or send them for treatment.

Learning interpersonal skill means discovering what rules exist in various situations, what we can gain from following the rules, and how we are punished for breaking them. We need to know what can be talked about and what cannot be mentioned. We need ways to identify who is friendly, who is hostile, who wants someone to talk to, and who would rather be left alone. We must know how to dress appropriately, how to ask questions, and how to say "hello" and "goodbye" properly in a variety of social situations.

Effective communicators adjust their talk to fit the requirements of situations. We know, for example, that different rules apply in the home and on the job. We do not regard our bosses as if they were parents, nor our friends as siblings. Inappropriate choices about how to speak to others can cause a great deal of confusion.

Marilyn Gardner, Ph.D. I just completed my dissertation on the effects of "transference" in ordinary social life. The psychoanalysts really didn't know what a powerful idea they had. People need to have some certainty when they meet strangers, and the easiest way for them to do it is to ask silly questions like, "who do they remind me of?" That's the worst possible way to do it. There is absolutely no evidence to show that people who resemble each other physically act alike. In fact, you can get into real hot water. Children have to learn this early. They have to learn that their teacher is not their mother, and that they have to develop categories that make more sense in order to deal effectively with others.

Effective communication equips us with what David Riesman refers to as "internal radar" which helps us discover how to adjust our behavior. Our society, Riesman believes, is "other directed." Skillful people learn to adapt and adjust in order to fit into various groups. Those who choose to march to their own drummer must take the consequences of possible ineffectiveness or rejection by others. Most of us want to find ways to be effective regardless of the situation.

It is important to be effective at interpersonal communication because:

1. It helps people form and present identities.
2. It helps people fit into society and, thus, ward off loneliness, boredom and ineffectiveness.
3. It assists in accomplishing one's goals with others.
4. It helps people to identify and to follow rules of social interaction.

Communication in Contemporary Life

Skill in interpersonal communication has taken on an ever-growing importance in recent days. In fact, some authorities regard communication as the most vital human skill. Consider the following comment:

Lane Jennings, (*Futurist*, June, 1981, pp. 7–15.) Though people spend much of the waking hours talking or listening, the status of spoken language as a reliable medium of communication seems to be declining throughout the industrialized world. The problem may be that we are losing our memories—and with them, our faith in one another's 'word'. Studies of cultures where few people read and write suggest that . . . as literacy improves, the ability to remember information conveyed by sound . . . declines. The ability to listen and report accurately what was heard without using pictures or writing may be on the "endangered skills" list as this century ends.

Fewer . . . important exchanges of information take place by word of mouth alone. Business deals are almost always based on written contracts so complexly worded that even those who sign them prefer to let their lawyers do the actual . . . interpretation. Rarely does a government leader venture a policy statement without a written text . . . Even at press conferences, reporters depend on written notes or machine recordings to keep their facts straight. And while the words "Will you live with me?" are probably still most persuasive when spoken, modern couples often make the answer "Yes" conditional on a written agreement spelling out responsibilities and expectations.

Decreased emphasis on teaching children such skills as careful listening, persuasive rhetoric, entertaining conversation, and even story-telling may have made reading and writing appear more necessary to education than they really are. But without some special effort to teach better speaking and listening, the average citizen of the future may be an 'oral illiterate.'

Lane Jennings is correct in his claim that the consequences of neglecting communication skills are serious.

Alvin Hookway, M.D. Psychiatrist. The people who seem to be wiped out are those who can't handle cooperating with others. It seems that most of our therapies these days are designed to help people become more effective in talking to each other. I don't think the problems are any greater today than they were ten years ago. And most important, I think we know today what we have to do to help people who are 'out of it'. We need to help them learn how to talk effectively with one another because relating is built on talking and happiness is built on relating.

Daniel Yankelovich, in *The New Rules*, and Alvin Toffler in *The Third Wave* suggest that new alternative life styles are optimistic trends. They believe society is in transition from the life style typified by a family consisting of an employed father, a stay-at-home mother, two and one–third children and a house in the suburbs, to a life style typified by people who have options about who works and who stays home, and about whether or not to have children. Working out new ways of living with each other requires considerable interpersonal skill. People must be sensitive to the needs of their partners and find creative ways to share what is available in a world characterized by diminishing resources. Any adjustment period is difficult, and so, according to both Yankelovich and Toffler, we need to be patient as people find their own ways.

The family, for example, must adapt to new concerns like increased opportunities for women to work, the problems of sustaining a decent standard of living with only one member of a family working, and changes in how children are integrated into society. The rise in single living does not mean that people prefer to live alone; accelerating divorce rates imply that many did not choose to be single. Still, people must adapt. They need to build new relationships, and to discover new methods of social exchange.

Young people, furthermore, must make decisions about the effects of an intimate relationship on their career. When the decision to marry is delayed, the possibility of building a family is reduced. People who live alone, whether by choice or necessity, need to find creative ways to build new kinds of relationships which take their needs into account.

In this kind of uncertain society, lack of interpersonal skill is a real handicap. For example, employees must be able to communicate their value to supervisors. In turn, supervisors must involve employees in decision making in order to compete effectively with the Japanese system of participatory management. In the community, citizens must make vital decisions about what to do as the federal government withdraws much of its previous financial support to states and localities. Solutions to major problems like public education, welfare, ecology, and law enforcement must be discussed and decisions made. In contemporary society understanding and effective practice of interpersonal communication are more important than ever before. The urgency people feel to improve their interpersonal relationships is the impetus for serious study of interpersonal communication undertaken in this book.

Developing Communication Skills

Many people believe effective interpersonal communication is a gift: some people are born with it and some are not. It is true that some people are quick to learn technique just as some people seem to have aptitudes for music or sports. But everyone can learn the basics of interpersonal communication.

- *Effective communication depends on the recognition that it is more useful to plan your talk than to depend on luck and spontaneity.* Most people can improve their interpersonal skills by avoiding purely expressive communication, by learning to consider the feelings of others, and by practicing under criticism.
- *Effective communication is goal-centered.* Goals must be adapted to particular situations. Formal occasions require formal preparation. Interpersonal communication requires understanding of various situations and a repertoire of effective behavior appropriate to them.
- *Effective communication requires that you be able to understand the requirements of various social situations and adapt to them.* This means you must be able to adjust the means by which you seek goals in order to meet the approval of the people around you, and sometimes you must modify your goals to take into account the desires of the people around you.
- *Effective communication requires that you understand what others are seeking and that you adapt your requests to it.* Effective interpersonal communication is characterized by letting other people know what you can do for them in exchange for what they can do for you.
- *Effective communication requires that you cue others into understanding what goals you seek and how you can assist them in return.* You must be able to specify your understanding of human nature in each particular case.
- *Effective communication involves skill in identifying your own suc-*

cess. A communicator becomes more effective by discovering what works and what does not and thus acquiring an extensive repertoire of behaviors suitable for a great many situations, as well as a means of criticizing and improving his performance.

Interaction and Transaction

There are two basic kinds of interpersonal communication: *interaction* and *transaction*. These two words are often used as synonyms. However, the differences between them are very important. When we use the word *interaction*, we refer to informal talk in public where people are bound by rules of etiquette. It is the kind of talk carried on in a business office, in a store, or among friends at social gatherings. Public communication is bound by rules to protect the participants.

The word *transaction* refers to private talk between committed friends, lovers or family members. Transactions focus on the concerns of the particular parties. There is no need for people to conform to public social rules when they are conducting private business. When people are alone they have the privilege of acting as a small society that generates its own rules and norms. Transactions are unsuitable in public because they mystify and offend outsiders. It is important to understand the difference between these two terms in order to maintain propriety in social relationships.

People sometimes impose excessive social rigor on their intimate relationships. They are unduly formal and interact when they should transact. Thus, they prevent the kind of communication that would result in mutual accommodation. Examples of such behavior are numerous: a husband who comes home from work and treats his wife as if she were an employee, a wife who acts as if her husband is a child. These kinds of errors in propriety can have serious repercussions in relationships, for people often behave according to the roles they are expected to assume.

The reverse is characterized by people who get excessively intimate in public situations; these people share their private lives and demand that others reveal their secrets as well. When people violate public norms, they alienate others and imperil their chances of making successful relationships. Most relationships start through interaction and move gradually into transaction. Interaction protects people while they try to discover how intense they want their relationship to be. Transaction affords the privilege of private talk to people who wish to build a private relationship.

Both interaction and transaction are purposive. In interaction, people persuade each other to act within the acceptable range of social norms in order to accomplish public business. In transaction, people persuade each other to share goals, support each other, and confirm personal identities. Although interaction and transaction differ conceptually, sometimes one may affect the other. Consider the following case.

The Hagen-Clark Relationship. The Shelton Company had a long-standing policy of division heads participating in decisions about company policy. Each month the Chairman of the Board reported about issues facing the company and solicited opinions about how to handle the various problems. The chairman had, over the years, become very responsive to the advice given him, and the division heads knew that a major criterion in their advancement in the company was their participation in the monthly meetings.

Bill Hagen of Logistics and Fred Clark of Receivables had been close friends for many years. Their families socialized regularly and they had taken several summer vacations together. They supported each other's ideas at meetings. In the eleven years they had been with the company no one could recall them disagreeing in public.

At a recent meeting, however, Clark spoke for automating Logistics. He felt automation would help shipping and give Hagen more authority and make his job easier. Hagen, however, felt automation would cost the jobs of several people he supervised. He objected to automation on those grounds.

This was the first time the two men had disagreed. They debated furiously. It seemed the more they spoke their positions hardened and the less willing they were to compromise or end the dispute. Finally Hagen accused Clark of supporting automation as a lever to get his own department automated thus increasing his authority. Clark said he would never stoop to such a thing. The men began to call each other names.

The division heads supported Hagen and advised the chairman not to automate. From that point on there was a marked change in the Hagen-Clark relationship. Disagreement became their norm. They argued bitterly about everything. They did not speak to each other except in the line of duty. Their private relationship deteriorated. Their wives continued to get together, but they no longer socialized as families. Gradually the dispute permeated their lives; the chairman felt one of them had to go to preserve the integrity of the company. Clark was transferred to another locale.

Clark and Hagen permitted interaction to permeate transaction. They were not able to adjust to their public disagreement and no longer preserved their private goodwill. What they had going for themselves in private was a sense of confidence and trust which should have permitted them to disagree and remain friends. However, the dispute broke that feeling of trust, and once they discovered that it was possible for them to argue, both brought up slights and insults from the past. Their private relationship was not as strong as they thought it had been. It may have been discontent with the private relationship that led to the public dispute.

Ben Parkhurst, Management Consultant. I advise people to avoid making close friends on the job. It gets in the way of work and work gets in the way of friendship. It makes a good deal more sense to make your friends off the job so that one doesn't affect the other.

In formal organizations, relationships are regulated by the demands of work and by the ways people agree it ought to get done. Private relationships, however, often complicate professional ones. Further, it's hard to predict the formation of private relationships. Consider the following:

Fred A. I first met Al at the orientation dinner for trainees. We sat next to each other and we began talking about how we had been recruited. He made some jokes and so did I and we kind of passed notes during the formal part of the dinner. Al had just gotten married and I had only been married for a year so we got along together real well. So did our wives.

About the second week of training we decided to get together for the first time. We discovered we lived only two blocks apart. We talked sports while my wife, Anne, and his wife, Mary discussed their future plans for work and children. When Anne got pregnant, Mary took her to the hospital and when Anne went back to work Mary was baby sitter. When Mary had her miscarriage, Anne backed her up.

We've known each other five years. I suppose one of us will be transferred sooner or later, but it's really like having family to know Al and Mary. I hope we can keep it together. Consider, for a minute, the chances of our meeting if we hadn't accidentally sat together at dinner. I'm in product testing and he writes PR releases for the president of the company. There are 5,000 people employed at this location. Our friendship is just some kind of lucky accident.

Many relationships begin as lucky accidents. Those that endure, however, turn out to be delicate fabrics of experience and agreements. The process by which they are built is difficult and requires consummate skill. Most people are not terribly skillful and many people have serious problems in their relationships.

Chapter Summary

This book offers a description of the process from which you can develop your own plan for personal growth in interpersonal communication. As we've seen in this chapter, through effective interpersonal communication you can declare your identity, enlist the help of others in your goal seeking, assist them with theirs, improve your effectiveness in the community, and have better control over your public and private life. Much of what we've discussed so far supports the premise that effective interpersonal communication can be learned. The understandings and skills that comprise effective interaction and transaction are not ephemeral. Rather they are very pragmatic, and mastery is simply a matter of personal commitment and effort. The first steps in learning how to communicate effectively are to understand the nature of our contemporary world and how this society influences our dealings with others. We will focus on this topic in Chapter 2.

REFERENCES FOR CHAPTER 1

A. Adler, *Understanding Human Nature.* Garden City, N.Y.: Doubleday Publishing Co., 1927.

R. Hart and D. Burks, "Rhetorical Sensitivity and Social Interaction," *Speech Monographs.* 30. June, 1972. Pp. 175–91.

R. Hart, R. Carlson, and W. Eadie, "Attitudes Toward Communication and the Assessment of Rhetorical Sensitivity," *Communication Monographs.* 47. March, 1980. Pp. 1–23.

K. Horney, *Our Inner Conflicts.* New York: W. W. Norton, 1945.

W. Johnson, *People in Quandaries.* New York: Harper and Row, 1946.

R. Mager, *Goal Analysis.* Belmont, Calif.: Fearon Publishing Co., 1972.

G. Phillips and N. Metzger, *Intimate Communication.* Boston: Allyn and Bacon, 1976.

D. Riesman, N. Glazer, and R. Denney, *The Lonely Crowd.* Garden City, N.Y.: Doubleday and Co., 1950.

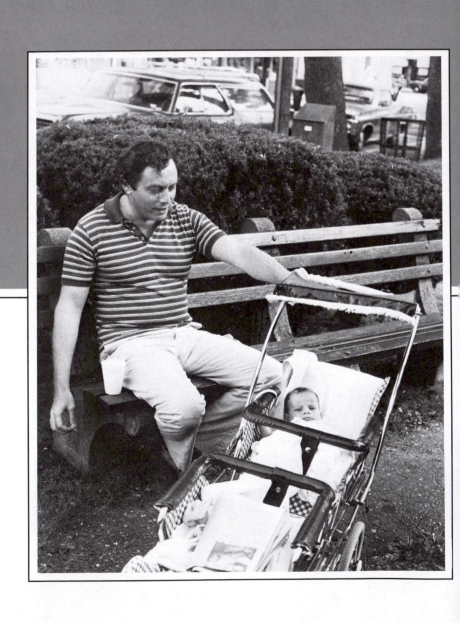

2

OUR RELATIONSHIP WORLD

In this chapter we will discuss contemporary society and how it affects and is affected by interpersonal communication. American life in the 1980's is a life of change and contradiction. Many traditional social values are no longer accepted without question by the majority of the people. Our patterns of family living have changed drastically in the past two decades. Not only has the typical family decreased in size, but a great many people have elected either to have childless marriages or to remain single. The extended family, once a mainstay of American society, exists only in a few pockets. In most cases, family members are scattered over so wide an area that they no longer can provide each other with substantial support.

Racial minorities are no longer legally excluded from participation in society, although discrimination and bigotry remain serious barriers to their acceptance in the economic mainstream. However, in many of our urban areas, ethnic minority groups predominate. The fact that these groups are beginning to assume a major role in government as they increase in number presents the society with new issues that must be addressed.

One of the most significant changes of our time is the role of women in our society. Within the past two decades, occupations and professions once regarded exclusively as "man's work" have opened up for women. The nation has begun to use the varied talents of fifty–two per cent of the population which had previously been relegated to hearth and home and to a few designated occupations. Because of these changes, women have been able to make new choices about their lives which have concretely affected the way interpersonal relationships are conducted.

As a nation, we have begun to decline in power as our natural resources dwindle and we have come to rely more on other countries in order to maintain our standard of living. Transportation and housing have become so expensive that the suburban dream of the 1950's is now denied to many. New housing arrangements have meant new problems in social relationships.

Our manufacturing products no longer dominate world markets. The confrontation between our economic system and that of the Soviet Union continues. In a tight economy, the stresses of inflation and unemployment put severe stress on normal patterns of living. Taxes are high, inflation is rising and credit is harder to get. Many Americans are finding, for the first time in decades, that they cannot afford the basic possessions and economic goals they had assumed were possible. All of this means that most of us will make major changes in life style in the coming decades, changes that will require us to accommodate other people in new and unexpected ways. All of us will be called upon to change our life styles and objectives.

These trends have placed a new importance on the way we carry on relationships with our fellow human beings. The way we adapt to new arrangements with others in order to solve our problems will determine how successful we will be in our social and intimate relationships in the decades ahead.

For example, if this book had been written ten or fifteen years ago, we would have devoted a great deal of space to explaining how interpersonal communication can be used to intensify our relationships with other human beings so that we could learn to understand one another, share our feelings, and be open, trusting, and authentic with one another. The dream of being actualized and fulfilled has been replaced by contemporary preoccupation with individual and community survival. Surveys published recently in popular magazines point out that people today are personally concerned about whether they will make it through the economic hardships ahead, whereas ten years ago they were concerned about whether they would be all they could be.

As we approach a general scarcity economy, what there is to go around will diminish and people will either have to decide to share smaller portions among themselves or to compete more fiercely to decide who gets what. The trend in housing, for example, is that landlords wish to avoid the pressure of increased taxes and turn their apartment buildings into condominiums, where the more desirable units are available only to individuals with high incomes. Since high credit has reduced the number of housing starts, and taxation discourages building multi-unit dwellings, people in the middle income ranges are denied good housing. How can people decide who is to get what housing unit? How can people decide on ways and means to provide adequate housing for all?

   This means that everyone has a personal stake in the survival of all. We can no longer afford to concentrate exclusively on accomplishing our personal goals. Maintaining the general welfare seems to be the essential part of sustaining oneself. Thus, it is in the personal interest of all of us to seek greater understanding of other people and their needs through greater skill at communicating with them to solve our mutual problems. In this chapter we will examine some of the issues that we will face together and some of the problems that will arise as we try to deal with them.

Social Issues and Interpersonal Communication

Productivity in an expensive society

America has traditionally valued productivity. People were trained to take pride in what they produced. As the society became industrialized, production became anonymous, the assembly line subverted pride in workmanship. Paul Goodman, in his book, *Growing Up Absurd*, argued that it was terribly important for people to find useful work to do. In our society, idleness has traditionally been regarded as a vice, and unemployed people have been viewed as drones and drains on the economy.

   Most of us talk a lot about the work we do. When you ask people to identify themselves, they usually refer to their occupation or employer. In the days ahead, the work people are called on to do will change drastically, and this, in turn, will change how people define themselves.

   In industry, for example, the computer and word processor have reduced the number of minor administrative positions available. People who operate high technology machinery in industry are seldom considered part of the managerial class. Theirs is a kind of new blue collar work. Thus, the identity that comes from holding a minor bureaucratic post is denied a great number of people. The question is how can people adjust themselves to the new kinds of jobs they have, or how can they find some substitute identity for that formerly acquired through their job? Service occupations will predominate, and many of the minor administrative jobs in which people once took pride will be replaced by the "new blue collar" jobs, such as attending to computers and word processing machines. People will need to find new ways to identify themselves, and new activities in which to take pride.

Individualism vs. conformity

We have traditionally encouraged people to be both independent and conformist. Our literature honors the hero who succeeds against the odds, despite opposition. But our media also honor people who are good neighbors, good friends, and good family members. The backpacker and the host at the barbecue earn equal credit.

We need to learn to identify ourselves both by our uniqueness and by our commitments to common goals. Maintaining satisfactory self-esteem requires the ability to make independent contributions to the general good. David Riesman's book, *The Lonely Crowd*, described three types of socialization. Tradition-directed people do whatever has always been done without questioning the process. Inner-directed people follow their own ideas regardless of consequences on situations or on others. Other-directed people are responsive to the people around them; they are able to adapt to public social rules so expertly that they belong to diverse groups without appearing to deviate from the norms of any group. The other-directed person characterizes our society today. This person develops multiple group memberships to fulfill a range of personal, professional, social, and intimate goals. More than in previous eras, people need to learn how to interact with a broad range of people for diverse reasons.

Cooperation vs. competition

In the professional world, there is immense pressure to get to the top. Although it is important for fellow employees to cooperate with one another, in the final analysis, everyone is after a slice of a pie that has a limited number of slices. It is very difficult to maintain the balance between being a team player and an individual winner.

Jungletime. Professor W.'s son arrived with his family and his little terrier, Horace. Professor W. had a slightly larger terrier named Rodney. Mrs. B., the wife of the violinist next door was very fond of her Chihuahua, Princess. The W.'s had a good dinner, and the prime rib materialized two good sized bones. To keep Horace and Rodney from fighting, Horace was tied outside with his bone and Rodney was kept indoors with his. Princess smelled Horace's bone and came over to where he was tied and made an attempt to get the bone. Horace attacked with such force that his rope snapped, and he and Princess became a snarling, snapping, mass. In the midst of it all, with

Professor W. pouring water on the dogs trying to separate them, and his son hitting them with a broom, Mrs. B. came into the backyard and began to scream at Horace's owner, "around here," she yelled, "we all learn to share."

Philip Slater pointed out in *The Pursuit of Loneliness* that we all find it hard to survive in a "scarcity economy." Because winners have what other people want, people try very hard to become winners. Nevertheless, they must demonstrate that they are also cooperators. In fact, winners tend to be those who can convince others to assist their personal goalseeking and who demonstrate a reciprocal willingness to assist others. This is the essence of team spirit that does not diminish individuality. It all means that relationships are not necessarily zero-sum games in which there is one winner and one loser. By working together, people can win together.

Violence

There is a fine line between competition and violence. Though our society has rules to keep people from hurting each other when they compete, there is a tendency to honor people who can violate the rules and win. We have our folk heroes who step outside the law but do so well that they rise to the top. The late John Wayne illustrated this when he faced his hecklers at Harvard University by driving a tank into the Harvard yard and using it as a platform from which to lecture his harassers on patriotism.

All of us are tempted from time to time to threaten to use force, to display tears, to blame, to wheedle and to bribe. We are constantly tantalized by possibilities to take advantage of others. We are also advised to control our aggressive tendencies, but to do so often jeopardizes success. Psychiatrists like Alfred Adler and Harry Stack Sullivan believed that the ability to find socially acceptable methods of seeking power and control was a sign of mental health. They believed that people who competed unethically needed treatment. Reconciling the intense pressure to compete with the urgency to cooperate represents one of the truly difficult problems in interpersonal communication. This problem is especially complex in intimate relationships where both partners have careers. It is sometimes difficult to keep competitiveness under control in transactions.

The pursuit of pleasure

Traditionally, men in America were supposed to be strong enough to withstand pain and adversity. Those that actively sought "soft" pleasures and comforts were regarded as "sissies" or worse. Women, on the other hand, were permitted the luxury of enjoyment, but denied the challenge of struggling with adversity. Today, the picture has changed drastically. Both men and women pursue many of the same goals.

Sigmund Freud pointed out that it is a human tendency to seek to maximize pleasure and minimize pain. Contemporary media emphasize the search for pleasure. Most of us devote a good deal of energy to it.

We seek pleasure in our social relationships. We try to find people whose company we enjoy, who can entertain us, or provide us with the kind of support we need. Most people do not hold formal auditions or try-outs for potential friends, but we do make choices among our contacts based on our estimate of how much pleasure they can provide for us. The problem of developing sustaining friendships is complicated by the mobility of contemporary life.

Many people have jobs that require them to move around a great deal. As a result, they may not be in one place long enough to build supportive friendships. People who are used to moving know how to begin socializing in their new community, but seldom do they have the time to get to know one another well. They tend to stay together with people very much like themselves, those who work for the same company or those who do the same kind of work. At least they can talk shop. That is why communities seem to be built very much like one another, even with remarkably similar home designs. It is so people get the idea that they have not left home. The Holiday Inn slogan "the best surprise is no surprise at all," is very important, for security is provided to some extent by familiarity. At least if rooms and houses look familiar, people do not need to spend a great deal of time adjusting to new scenery. However, mobile people have a hard time establishing connections with old residents. One of the respondents to our research questionnaire wrote of this issue:

Shirley T. They come and go. Back when the company first settled here in town, most of us were interested in meeting the new people, and we made every effort to get to know them. But their style is different. They don't value the things we do. It takes time to get to know them and just when you think you are getting to know them, the company moves them on. It doesn't seem to bother *them*, but it bothers us. My husband and I were trained not to make new friends every other week. So we stopped bothering to meet the new folks. Many of their companies encourage them to get into community enterprises, and we let them do some things, but the permanent people control the way things happen around here, and the way the company is now we take the taxes from the new folks and leave them pretty much alone. The people who benefit the most are the moving companies and travel bureaus.

The need to make friends is universal, but the ability to do so is restricted to those who have the time and technique.

We also seek sexual pleasure. A major theme in the popular media is that men and women should be able to find fulfilling sexual relationships, in order to be well-adjusted. The quest for "good sex" has become a preoccupation for a great many people. This, of course, contradicts an older value that sex is legitimate only in marriage. A great many people have become seriously distressed at what they see as their failure to accomplish sexual goals. A great many others have broken off fulfilling relationships because of their pursuit of mythical sexual accomplishments. Some regard sexual contact as the primary means of communication between men and women. Learning to communicate effectively with words is an important issue in relationships between the sexes.

Segregation

Despite legal advances, ours remains a generally segregated society. In addition to men and women being suspicious of one another, we tend to distrust people whose race, age, religion, politics, and social status differ from our own. Furthermore, we tend to keep people apart; we isolate the young in schools, the elderly in Golden Age communities, and the various ethnic groups in their ghettos. While we give lip service to integration and understanding, we continue to act as if "our kind of people" are the only kind of people. In the decades to come, it will no longer be possible to keep apart from one another, unless we are willing to face a kind of civil war between segments of society. We are already fighting that war politically through the formation of single issue political units which seek their own goals regardless of consequences to others. We are also fighting that war on the streets of our cities as deprived people are forced to turn to crime as the only source of income. Just as we will need to talk individually to each other in order to solve major social problems, we will need to find people who can talk from group to group to reduce polarization of our society.

Social paradoxes

It is important to understand that our culture is paradoxical in the sense that it sometimes presents us with different and incompatible demands or expectations. It is often hard to figure out a personal point of view because we owe loyalty to so many different groups. For example, our economic orientation may lead us to favor tax cuts, but our social orientation moves us to be concerned about needy people who will be deprived if tax money is not available. We are all members of various reference groups. We strive for our own self-interest, to protect our loved ones and family; we are loyal to our occupational grouping, to our town and country, to our religious point of view, to our social values, and to our ethnic heritage. We become involved in our hobbies and community concerns. Sometimes our loyalties conflict, and it becomes very difficult for us to decide where we stand and how we can express that position to others. For example, if we examine generalized beliefs in society we discover that:

- Despite public commitment to the idea that minority groups should be "equal" many people persist in making jokes about them, not to mention excluding them from socialization and economic opportunity. The same person who signs a petition to protect the rights of blacks and Chicanos in the morning may spend the evening enjoying a round of Polish jokes.

- Many people, both female and male, tend to believe that a woman's place is in the home; however, they also expect her to do her fair share in the economy, although for lower wages than men are paid (since men are supposed to be heads of families). Furthermore, when a woman seems to be making it at work, she is still expected to be able to handle her traditional responsibilities in the home and to defer to her spouse.

- We believe in the sanctity of marriage, but we also believe that people ought to have the right to an easy divorce when the going gets rough. We continue to oppose adultery but we condone cohabitation as a prelude to, or substitute for marriage.

- We believe in the right to make choices that affect our bodies, but we believe it is wrong to take human life. Therefore, issues like abortion and euthanasia confuse us terribly.

- We believe in law and order and the need to punish criminals, but we sometimes also believe that it is more important to protect the civil rights of the innocent than it is to punish the guilty.

- We believe that the poor and needy should be cared for but we oppose handouts and respect people who can pull themselves up by their own bootstraps.

- We extol the importance of respecting our elders and of maintaining family ties, yet many older parents find themselves in old age institutions because their children will not invite them into their homes.

- We believe that we must do everything in our power to preserve the peace, but we also believe that this may require a strong military posture.

- We believe in democratic societies, but we support dictatorships when it is politically expedient.

There are no easy answers to these dilemmas. They represent some of the major sources of conflict and anxiety for people of our

Segregation in society.

time. While a great many people manage to avoid these kinds of conflicts by becoming insensitive to some of the major issues in society, most of us are perennially confused by these paradoxes. Our confusion is one of the reasons that people are so unpredictable in what they believe and in how they respond to competing demands.

The most serious stress of all

One of the main sources of stress and emotional illness is the notion that we should be able to solve most of our personal problems ourselves, without help and without training. What the schools offer is often too little, too late, and too simple. Sex education, for example, provides instruction about fertilized eggs to people who have become sexually active years before, or at least sexually educated through private talk that is not always accurate. Virtually no schools pay attention to training children to socialize, to respect the rights of others, and to communicate with others to solve problems. Although learning to communicate orally is not widely recognized as basic to survival, some authorities regard communication skills as the cornerstone of our social and personal well-being.

Robert Maynard Hutchins. (*Center Magazine,* January/February, 1973). The barbarism, "communication skills," which is the contemporary jargon for reading, writing, figuring, speaking, and listening, appears to have permanent relevance. These arts are more important in a democratic society than in any other because the citizens of a democratic society have to understand one another. They are indispensable in a world community. Without them the individual is deprived; and the community is too. In a technical age these are the only techniques that are universally valuable; they supply the only kind of vocational training a school can offer that can contribute to vocational success. They are the indispensable means to learning anything. They have to be learned if the individual is to expand his individuality or if he proposes to become a self governing member of a self-governing community . . .

Using leisure time is also a problem today. Back in the 1920s, use of leisure time was a major preoccupation of educators. People

Solitary activities are on the increase.

worked long hours back then but enlightened educators looked forward to the time when innovations in industry would shorten the work day and people would have leisure time. Today there is almost too much time, and there is a wealth of devices and distractions that encourage people to spend it alone. Television computer games and movies are not conducive to meeting new people, making friends, or engaging in conversation. Activities like jogging are best conducted alone. The trend to solitary and narcissistic activities may be a symptom of universal problems in making and sustaining human relationships.

The Interpersonal Fallout from Social Strains

Because a great many of our interpersonal problems resist solutions, the rate of emotional illness in society has increased. We have already shown you that the main elements in interpersonal success are understanding the nature of the social situation, the people in it, and your own goals. We have shown you that our society is characterized by confusing paradoxes which complicate the choices you make about the people you meet. Our choices are vast and conflicting and it is difficult to decide what and whom to believe. People who cannot make these choices sometimes decide to align themselves with a leader or a cause, so that they can be spared the agony of making individual decisions. The spectacular histories of Charles Manson and the Rev. James Jones exemplify the perils in store for people who cannot make their own choices.

Ken T. I am about to graduate and start medical school and what I have learned so far is that I can solve all of the problems of life, provided that they come to me in multiple choice form. Seriously, doc, how am I supposed to know what is right. Should I be a doctor dedicated to the care of the needy, or should I make a buck? Do I want to contribute to society through research or do I want to contribute to society through skillful care? And what should I do with my money? And what do I owe the community? And most important of all, sixteen years of school never taught me who to trust and how to pick my friends. I suppose you don't even know!

We have limited control over how and with whom we form relationships. In the first place, we cannot conduct auditions. We work with the other people who have been hired, we live with our neighbors or the other people on our floor. We can only make contact with the people around us. Computer pairing never really worked well because only a small number of people ever signed up. Furthermore, there is no reason to believe that the kinds of coding used in computer pairing will guarantee relationships that are any better than those we form at random. At this point we know too little to be able to say what the criteria are for selecting a person with whom to form a relationship. It seems to help if you are physically attractive, well dressed, have some status in the community, and some money in your pocket. However, most people have even become suspicious of those popular criteria. There does not seem to be any simple answer for anyone.

What we do know is that there are some basic skills that seem to be effective in building relationships. Ability to sustain conversation is one of them. Ability to get the other person to talk about his or her interests is another. Also valuable is skill in expressing your own ideas in an interesting way. Being a good listener is very important as is responding thoughtfully.

We learn how to present ourselves to others by modeling our behavior after important people in our lives. Our parents were very influential in molding our behavior patterns. We tend to imitate the way our parents and other significant role models related to other people. Many people offer us rules and some present us with examples of politeness and consideration. Others, however, may display selfish and egocentric behavior. Some of us learn to take turns and share, for example, while others go through life taking and grabbing whatever they want. Harry Stack Sullivan defines clear stages in development of social skills. He points out, for example, that it is very important to have a very close chum in early adolescence with whom to check things out. "Consensual validation," according to Sullivan is a way of discovering whether other people are living in the same world you are. If you are bewildered by something, it is important to check with someone else to find out if (1) they are also bewildered, or (2) whether they were bewildered by it once but figured out a way to handle it. This is the way peers help each other grow. Consensual validation is equally important for adults. We need people whom we trust enough to talk to about issues that perplex us.

But, in order to validate, it is necessary to disclose. Disclosure is very risky because it usually involves telling other people about our weaknesses, confusions, and fears, thus providing them with knowledge they can use against us. During the early days of the humanistic psychology movement people believed that it was useful to disclose private matters indiscriminately, for they assumed that if everyone was completely open then people could deal with situations honestly. The hazard was that some people used their knowledge against other people. Clearly some disclosure is useful, for we cannot make a firm relationship with another person without sharing some private information. Some people "hire" counselors, psychologists or psychiatrists, for the purpose of disclosing. A trained professional who guarantees confidentiality provides a safe opportunity for disclosure, and even for validation. But a counselor is really not a substitute for a friend. People who cannot share their ideas and feelings with anyone tend to become isolated. They withdraw or join movements. Many of the followers of Rev. Jones were people who had isolated themselves from others.

People express their distress in various ways. Here are some samples written anonymously by students asked to describe their relationships.

Bert T. I remember, I did something really cute when I was a sophomore. I turned in a computer card to my composition teacher and I wrote on it, "do not spindle, fold, or mutilate because I am a human being." She didn't like it much, but I was thinking about that story by Oscar Wilde, *The Picture of Dorian Grey*, where the guy didn't change but the picture did, and I thought maybe I will never change, but if someone puts a spindle through my computer card, I'll die.

Sally S. I really got a shock when I discovered that they had form letters written by computers for all possible situations. When I got the first letter from the credit card company that told me I was behind in my payments I got really upset. I had visions of them coming to my apartment and taking away my furniture. I wondered why a company as big as that one would take the time to come after me for a matter of $115. I was new in town, you know, just graduated, and I was trying to make it in the company, the only female engineer there, and I didn't want to admit to anyone that I couldn't keep up my payments. Then I noticed on the bottom, the encouraging words, "if you have already made your payment please disregard this notice," and I thought, heck, I'm just one of a million people who were a little late this month. Then I had the horrid thought that it might have been a little better if I could have believed that somewhere in that company there was a little guy who was thinking, "what can I do to get Sally to pay up!"

Cornelia W. The first time Edna yelled at me I almost came unglued. Edna was so damned immaculate she didn't look like the kind of person that ever yelled, but there she was standing at the door to my office calling me all kinds of names and threatening me with mayhem if I ever underestimated a job like that again, and she didn't even give me a chance to answer, she just stormed out. I sat there shaking. After two years with the company I still didn't know anyone well enough to ask them about her peculiarities. So I took the bull by the horns and walked into the office next door where Greg fiddled with some strange-looking keyboards. I didn't even know what he did, that's how isolated we were in the company. I said, "Greg, I don't know you well enough to tell you this but . . . ." He finished the sentence for me, ". . . Edna just yelled at you." He smiled. He'd been with the company for years. "She does that once or twice a year to someone. I guess it was just your turn. It means the balance sheet didn't come out right and she had to blame somebody. Is there anything you'd like for your office?" "Huh?" I said. "Wait til tomorrow and go in and ask her for something expensive for your office. She'll feel so guilty she'll authorize it. That's how I got this computer." And that's how I got this new desk.

Generally, the first symptom of interpersonal distress is having something to talk about and no one with whom to talk about it. A second symptom is having someone to talk to but nothing interesting to say.

Shirley N. When me and my guy get together and we go and find some movie and then decide we really don't want to see it, then we go back to his apartment or mine and he says, "time to crank up the old tin lizzie," and I say "let's get a pizza," and he says, "after," and then we are in the sack and we do it and then we get up and maybe blow some grass and then we go get a pizza and then we go to some club where the music is so loud we can't talk anyway and then we go home. My life is all sex and small talk. Damn, I'd like to have an argument with somebody about something some day.

Boredom tends to push people into taking risks. They may experiment with drugs, alcohol or sex, or get involved in some kind of activity like listening to loud music or running long distances that keeps them apart from people. There is only so much a person can do alone. Contact with others is a major source of excitement, but only if people are willing to get excited.

Eleanor N. When I was a little girl I liked to go off by myself for a long time and I'd read and think about things or draw and then I'd come downstairs and talk to Mom or Dad or my sister, Ethel about it. I could come downstairs anytime I wanted to and there was always someone there to get excited with me. I've been in this city for six months now and I've spent whole weekends where no one knocked on the door and the phone didn't ring. I can go shopping on Saturday and walk around on Sunday, but I can't go out at night they tell me. I don't know a soul in the apartment house. I've watched every rerun of the Mary Tyler Moore show and I'm not sure I'll ever get to toss my hat in the air and listen to people sing about how I'll make it after all. I could go to a singles bar and wrestle for a few hours but that wouldn't be any better than sitting alone. I think I'll pour myself another drink.

Risks like Eleanor's reliance on alcohol tend to increase when we are not content with our interpersonal lives and when we do not take the initiative to improve the state of things. Thus, learning more about interpersonal communication is a foundation for general balance and quality in how you live your social life.

Chapter Summary

In this chapter we've identified some of the special problems and possibilities that characterize the era in which we will live and build our relationships with others. Central to our personal and collective effectiveness, even survival, will be our communicative skill. We will close this section with a very important statement about the condition of human beings in the eighth decade of the 20th century. It is a powerful statement that sums up this chapter and the general condition of contemporary society. It is from a book called *The Dying Self* by Charles Fair.*

> . . . If my analysis of the human . . . condition is close to the truth, it follows that man is unique among creatures in being condemned from the outset to long milleniums of turbulence and discontent, even under the best of external circumstances, or when his adaptive success has minimized the more obvious causes of his distress. Properly understood, the "sense of sin" is perhaps the beginning of his awareness of his own psychic predicament, a discrepancy gauge which tells him the fearful distance that lies between the self as it is and as it might be.
>
> The quest for happiness then becomes really a quest for "grace." And if sin is taken to mean not this or that specific offense, but the cardinal offense of trying to live simply as a supremely proud, supremely crafty animal, the "darkness of sin" may for vast numbers be a literal reality—a state of torment and blindness that are natural features of the I half-formed. Sin in the more sophisticated sense is the refusal to admit that there may be anything wrong with this program, even though a distant voice, the uneasiness of the aborted soul, tells us otherwise. This stubbornness in the face of one's own misery, as it acts in fact to perpetuate and even to worsen the conditions that produced it, is the essence of what the older moralists called the state of damnation. We have given it other names (neurosis, alienation) without, I think, really understanding it.

*Copyright © 1969 by Wesleyan University. By permission of Wesleyan University Press.

Following the overt destruction of Victorian standards (long ago covertly destroyed by the Victorians themselves), we have entered an era of libertinism the results of which, in the light of our realistic *ideés fixés*, are puzzling. The lifting of sexual repressions, the easing of conflict which Freud and others evidently expected to come when men stopped taking extreme idealist positions and began to "accept" themselves, should by now have eventuated in a more relaxed, more human and permissive way of life. In fact we have become somewhat more humane and permissive, for instance, in the treatment of children or of rebellious minorities at home, but that may be mostly due to the lingering influence of the Christian past. The ease of spirit and improved psychological health for which we hoped have *not* come, even with the unprecedented affluence . . . Our crime rates continue to rise, and in our sex lives we appear to be bedeviled by odd abnormalities and a widespread jadedness.

The resort to promiscuity or in the extreme to orgiastic sex games, which is a feature of modern life, although one not easy to document statistically, has, I think, a definite meaning. It is not simply that we are indulging ourselves sexually as never before; we are also in the process depersonalizing an act that our highest tradition has made intensely personal and private. Essentially, perhaps, we are submerging ourselves, using drugs or alcohol or free-wheeling sex to overwhelm what is left of the I, drowning the self that discriminates and chooses in the Id, which is no respecter of persons, oneself included. Better no "me" at all than the shapeless, doubt-ridden, anxiety-vexed one that most of us adults find ourselves to be. Better the Dionysian abandon of the romantics than the grey vacancy of conscious life as we are obliged to live it. This, fundamentally, is the ground of our anti-intellectualism. Like the Germans of three decades ago, we are turning against mind because the further promises of rationality have not been fulfilled; because as the I dies, all that was once clear and beautiful to it becomes opaque and ugly . . .

It is all the easier to despise intellectuals too when so many have become the *reductio ad absurdum* of their species. But these are simply used as a stick to beat the real enemy, a way of destroying a once noble ideal by associating it with the effete and niggling and mean spirited . . . The same civilization that becomes orgiastic in its old age is apt eventually to kill those who will not join the party. This is the point that, I believe, we are now approaching.

We believe that this quotation deserves the most intense study. It is difficult to understand but it presents us with some of the choices we might have to make about our relationships in the decades ahead. If we are to escape loneliness and boredom, to feel effective in our social lives, and to contribute to each others' lives then we must learn what people expect and need from one another and work out ways to live together that make us all interpersonal winners. As you consider theoretical material about interpersonal communication in the next chapter, test it against your own life. See if it helps you understand and solve some interpersonal issues confronting you. When you finish the next chapter, reread the above quotation. It should be clearer by then.

REFERENCES FOR CHAPTER 2

C. Fair, *The Dying Self*. Connecticut: Wesleyan Univ. Press, 1969.

E. Fromm, *The Anatomy of Human Destructiveness*. New York: Holt, Rinehart and Winston, 1973.

P. Goodman, *Growing Up Absurd*. New York: Vantage Books, 1960.

L. Lofland, *A World of Strangers*. New York: Basic Books, 1973.

V. Packard, *A Nation of Strangers*. New York: David McKay, 1972.

D. Riesman, N. Glazer, and R. Denney, *The Lonely Crowd*. Garden City, N.Y., 1950.

P. Slater, *The Pursuit of Loneliness*. Boston: Beacon Press, 1970.

A. Toffler, *Future Shock*. New York: Random House, 1971.

A. Toffler, *The Third Wave*. New York: Morrow Publishing, 1980.

D. Yankelovich, *New Rules: Searching for Self-Fulfillment in a World Turned Upside Down*. New York: Random House, 1981.

3

RHETORIC: AN INTEGRATING PERSPECTIVE ON HUMAN RELATIONSHIPS

The purpose of this chapter is to offer you a perspective on human relationships—a way of thinking about what's involved when people interact and transact. Understanding of interpersonal relationships comes from the work of scholars in a number of fields who have proposed a variety of theories to describe and explain how and why humans relate. We will not survey all of those theories here, but we want you to have the option of learning about them on your own. We invite you to consult Appendix B of this book. In it we identify major approaches to interpersonal relationships and recommend references for each of them.

Each of the theories discussed in Appendix B provides valuable insights into interpersonal behavior, and we will draw upon these in presenting our own perspective. Yet each theory also neglects some important dimensions of human behavior, so we'll need to extend the collective wisdom found in those theories. To achieve our goal we'll first introduce a rhetorical perspective and explain how it synthesizes other views and also fills in gaps in their coverage. Next, we'll identify rhetorical premises that demonstrate the pragmatic implications of this perspective for our choices in relationships. In the final section of this chapter we'll examine how our rhetorical approach blends with and differs from other approaches to interpersonal behavior. After reading this chapter you should have a firm understanding of the rhetorical position and a general grasp on the importance of theory in the study of human relationships.

Introducing the Rhetorical Perspective

Rhetoric offers us a broad and powerful perspective on relationships. While this approach does integrate the best insights of other theories, it also makes unique contributions to our understanding of how and why people form relationships and how they act within them. The unique thrust of the rhetorical perspective emanates from questions it addresses that are neglected by other theories. For instance:

1. How much choice do individuals have regarding their own actions in relation to others?
2. To what extent do relating individuals control each other?
3. To what extent should individuals be held responsible for the quality of their relationships?
4. What responsibility do we have towards those with whom we form relationships?
5. To what extent can one person understand another person's perspective?

These questions are central to how we think about and participate in relationships, yet they are not adequately answered by theories from the psychological and sociological perspectives. Therefore we need a perspective that deals with these essential issues.

Rhetoric, which has a heritage spanning over two thousand years, offers a powerful and broad perspective on human communication activity. Plato, Aristotle, Cicero, Quintilian and other philosophers applied rhetorical theory exclusively to oratory. Contemporary scholars have applied it to informal and private talk, and found it enriches our understanding of conscious, responsible human discourse.

A rhetorical viewpoint begins with a fundamental assumption about the nature of human beings. The rhetorical position is that human beings are defined by their ability to use symbols, to be aware of themselves and to make choices.

Symbolicity

The core of our humanness is our ability to use symbols in thinking. A symbol is a word, sound or gesture used to represent a thing, event, person, process, situation, or idea. We use symbols to note, define and give meaning to our experiences. We also use them to think about phenomena that are not part of our present situation; this enables us to dream, remember and imagine.

Other animals do not seem capable of the highest forms of symbolic thought. Even advanced animals such as chimpanzees have been able to learn only very limited symbolic functions, despite years of dedicated instruction. Animals tend to think "signally" which means they usually respond relatively automatically to events in their environment. Signals request attention to tangible things. Symbols, on the other hand, are often complicated and abstract. For example, to a trained dog, the word "dinner," means food to be eaten, while to a human it can evoke images of various restaurants, dim lights, soft music, romance, and a myriad of other associations. The dog reacts in a relatively predictable way to the word; it is a signal that food is available. For humans, however, the word "dinner" is a symbol which presents a wide array of possible interpretations. It can mean that food is ready now. It may also mean a decision must be made about where to eat, when and with whom. It may evoke images of "Big Macs" or quiche. To a human being, the meaning of the word may go far beyond mere eating. This array of meanings is possible because people create symbols which they use to interpret and give meaning to their actions.

Human relationships would not be possible if we were not able to use symbols. Not only do we use our symbols to engage in relationships for the reasons that other animals do (protections from predators, territoriality, mating and teaching of the young), but also to identify ourselves and each other. Without the ability to use symbols, the best human beings could do would be to become very sophisticated in pursuing goals dictated by instinctual drives.

We form relationships partly to fulfill our biological drives. However, because we are human beings, the meaning of our relationships go far beyond that. Even when our motive is to gratify some drive such as sex, we tend to invest our behavior with all kinds of values beyond physiology and hormonal tension. Sexual engagement may be defined as an expression of love, a demonstration of liberation, a cheapening of self, a rebellion against some authority figure, proof of sexual prowess, an act of violence, and so forth. Humans are unable simply to act. It is nearly impossible for us to respond to our drives unthinkingly. We must contemplate our actions and attach meaning to them. We use symbols to think about our actions, to plan them and to evaluate their outcomes. We use symbols to attribute significance to ourselves, others and the relationships in which we participate. Our penchant to invest our relationships with meaning is what makes them *human* relationships.

Symbolic capability is a two-edged sword. We've suggested some of the ways in which it enriches our relationships, but we should also be aware of how it may damage them. Because we are symbolizers we can think about things we have not experienced, imagine ourselves in unfamiliar roles and situations, and yearn for people and sensations we've never known. In our minds we can create elaborate fantasies, in which we star as irresistible lovers, intrepid heroes, or anything we choose. When we see other people that we find desirable, we imagine what it would be like to form relationships with them—or at least to have contact. Sometimes our fantasies do not stay inside our heads. We try to turn them into realities and pursue relationships with the co-stars of our dreams. The only problem with this is that even if we are successful in realizing a particular fantasy, we may not stay satisfied for long. Along comes the next imagined relationship, the next object of our longing, the next vision of who we might be. Our symbolic imagination is both a blessing and a curse: It is the source of efforts to expand ourselves and our relationships, but it is also the root of much of our dissatisfaction with what we have. Dogs never entertain visions of themselves as superdogs, and neither do they go through mid-life crises or leave perfectly good owners because they find someone younger and more attractive.

Bruce W. We'd been married about ten years when it happened. I guess you could say the novelty had worn off. There was nothing particularly wrong with our relationship. Jean is intelligent, attractive, and a first-class mother to our two boys. No, nothing specific was wrong. All I knew was I was bored. About that time I got a new assistant at the office. Her name was Eleanor, and boy was she a knockout! A real go-getter if you know what I mean. One thing led to another. For a while we saw each other only at the office and lots of hints were exchanged. Then we had to go out of town together to do a consultation with a branch office, and we decided to sleep together. Pretty soon I was seeing her after work and before I knew it I promised Eleanor I would divorce Jean and marry her. I did it too, and now I've been married to Eleanor for almost three years. The only problem is that I'm starting to get a little bored.

The quest for meaning is intrinsic to human nature. We cannot accept things at face value. We seem compelled to think about them and envision alternatives to them in order to decide what they mean.

We interpret our own activities and those of others because we are driven to find some meaning in what we do and in what is done to us, and in our relationships. Thus, our symbolic activity is directly relevant to human relationships: without the ability to think symbolically there would be no *human* relationships.

Self-reflection

Self-reflection is the second key term in a rhetorical definition of human nature. Self-reflection refers to our ability to think about ourselves and our activities. Human beings can and do reflect on who they are and what they do. In fact, Morris Rosenberg's exten-

Self-reflection is central to human nature.

sive research on self-hood led him to say that while most creatures can reflect to a degree, humans alone can reflect on themselves. Self-reflection presupposes symbolic activity. Because we can make and use symbols, we can symbolize ourselves and think about ourselves just as we do the other things and activities about which we make symbols. Self-reflection is a process whereby we take note of our own attitudes and actions and then attach meanings to them to tell ourselves who we are and what we are doing. George Herbert Mead described self-reflection as the ability to view the self-as-an-object. What he meant was that we observe and evaluate our own actions much as we do other objects of our experience. We are objects of our own consideration. Mead believed this ability to be the hall-mark of humanity because it gives us the power to control many of our actions. Humans reflect on possible courses of action and their probable consequences. Then they act and reflect back on the action.

Because self-reflection allows us to control our attitudes and actions, it is directly pertinent to our relationships. We can plan ahead and anticipate the impact of our behavior on others. Prior to communicating with someone, you conduct dress rehearsals in your mind, casting yourself in various roles and trying out different scripts. You evaluate each role and each bit of dialogue, then make some final adjustments before you ever actually talk to the other person. Because we can engage in this kind of "inner speech" we are spared from reacting to whatever impulses hit us at the moment.

Self-reflection is not restricted to anticipation. It is an ongoing process. People *monitor* (that is, observe a process as it occurs) their actions as they talk with others. For instance, in a conversation you may notice your voice sounds impatient, so you remind yourself to slow down, to show interest, to increase your eye-contact with your listener and to soften the tone of your voice. Because you can monitor your actions, you can control the way you appear to the other person. Monitoring is such a natural process for most of us that we are seldom aware of doing it. Nonetheless, it is extremely important since it helps us keep our behavior in line with our own objectives.

Self-reflection takes place after our contact with others in addition to before and during communication. With all-too-keen twenty/twenty hindsight we look back on interactions and judge ourselves. Sometimes our judgments are positive. "I really pulled that off smoothly." "I think I helped him work out his problems." "I did a good job of leading the meeting." "I really let her know where I stand." Other times we evaluate our performances less favorably. "I was too abrupt with him." "I wish I hadn't said, 'I told you so.'" "Boy did I ever blow that interview!" "Now I know what I should have said when he said I was selfish!" We seem unable to resist appraising ourselves. You can check this out by trying not to observe and criticize yourself for a day or so. You'll find it's impossible.

The judging process in self-reflection is very important, because it helps us to recognize mistakes and to minimize their chance of reoccurrence in future situations. More important, self-judgment assists us in our efforts to become the kind of person we want to be. This happens when we reflect on particular encounters ("I really should have made time to talk with her since she was so upset.") and use that as the basis of a self-evaluation. ("I am an inconsiderate person.") The implication is that we must change. When we approve of one of our behaviors, we continue to behave that way in subsequent human contacts.

Human beings can feel pride and shame, tranquility and anxiety, self-righteousness and humility, satisfaction and guilt, joy and remorse. The experience of such feelings goes to the very core of our being. We attempt to avoid acting in ways that result in feelings of shame, anxiety, guilt, embarrassment and other emotions we would like to avoid, and we try to act so that we feel pride, peace, and joy and so forth. We use our personal feelings, the results of our self-evaluations, as the bases for the future choices we make about how we will deal with others.

Furthermore, self-reflection helps us to avoid the hazards of overly expressive communication. Totally spontaneous, unreflective behaviors generally lead people to evaluate themselves as childish, selfish or mean. When we are able to plan, monitor and evaluate ourselves, we can become thoughtful communicators whose actions reflect awareness of our impact on others. This type of awareness is integral to rhetorical communication and to its use in building effective human relationships.

Will

The third key term in our rhetorical definition of human nature is will. Will arises from our ability to make symbols and to think about ourselves. It refers to the human capacity to decide to conceive and pursue individual goals. Human ascendence over other life forms is due largely to our ability to make decisions about events, situations, other persons and ourselves. We do not see ourselves as pawns of fate or simple, conditionable creatures trying to fulfill our biological urgencies. Human beings constantly attempt to reshape their world. For us it is never a given which we must accept unquestioningly. Because we were dissatisfied with extremes of climate, we invented air conditioning and heating; because we wanted a constant source of power, we invented electricity; because a small band of English citizens envisioned a new way of living, they colonized America.

We can imagine alternatives to our present conditions and we can then act to bring about desired changes. Other animals have substantially less control over events that affect them. Even animals as intelligent as the great whales can do nothing about human depredations except to try to avoid them as best they can. Humans need not always accept bad situations. Instead such situations can become an impetus for change. We need not resign ourselves to accept tension between ourselves and someone we love. Rather, we can plan and act to improve the situation and to preserve the relationship. Because we can imagine what an improved relationship would be like, we can motivate ourselves to act. The possibilities that we imbue with value become our goals. We organize our actions to advance the goals, monitor our effectiveness, evaluate our impact and plan the next step. Thus, we use will to impel ourselves toward whatever goals we seek.

Clearly there are limits to human will. We do not believe that people have complete control over their lives. Such an unqualified view of will is dangerously naive. There are many things that we can do nothing about, no matter how much we want to. We cannot will earthquakes not to happen, terminal diseases not to result in death, or other people to like us. In many ways, we are prisoners of our biology and the laws of nature.

In other areas we can have only limited and indirect influence. For instance, though people can exert some control over corporate policies, government taxation and social trends, no one, not even the head of state cannot control them entirely. In our interpersonal relationships, we can exert will only over our own behavior. It is impossible to manipulate other people or to will how they act. It is only possible to appeal to them rhetorically, to convince them that what we intend for them is desirable in their own scheme of values and to will our own actions toward those others in ways that invite them to respond with reciprocal respect toward us. So *will* cannot be regarded as an "all or nothing" capability. Instead, it is a continuum of more and less. People who do not understand the limits of their powers often become frustrated. They attempt to control things beyond their power to control and become frustrated and demoralized. IFD disease, which we discussed in Chapter 1 frequently results from being unable to distinguish between what is desired and what is possible.

Will is most important in interpersonal relationships and personal behavior. In these areas an individual has considerable control over what happens. You can decide how you want another person to see you and you can then work to achieve that self-definition. You can decide what kind of relationships will satisfy you and figure out what investments you must make to realize them. You can also decide what kinds of relationships and actions are unacceptable to you and act to avoid those. Even in such areas there are limits. We cannot make another person love us or be our friend. We cannot will ourselves to be geniuses if our genes don't cooperate; we cannot all be physically "hunks" or "dishes." Despite these limits, however, we can do a great deal to control how we will present ourselves to others in order to achieve the kinds of relationships we want. Our relationships could be greatly improved if people recognized how much control they had over them and put that knowledge to constructive uses.

We have now taken a preliminary look at a rhetorical perspective based on a definition of humans as symbol-using, self-reflecting, willful agents, able to decide on many of their own attitudes and actions. These three human qualities are the bases for human relationships and for efforts to improve them. In the next section we'll explore what they imply for relationships with others.

Rhetorical Premises About Human Relationships

Our definition of humans as rhetorical beings is not abstract. It is the foundation of our entire theory of human relationships. From the definition we can derive three broad premises about our relationships:

1. Human communication is purposive.
2. Effective interpersonal communication requires a dual perspective.
3. Individuals are responsible for the choices they make in communicating with others.

Human communication is purposive

We've already introduced the concept of will which underlies this first premise. Human communication seeks to accomplish objectives. We do not act without a reason. Freud was one of the first to call attention to the purposive nature of human behavior. According to Freud, all behavior has a cause. It is never accidental or random. Every act of communication has a reason, sometimes a hidden one. So, Freud said, a slip of the tongue (saying "government snoopervision" instead of "government supervision") is caused by an underlying, sometimes unconscious, belief or need. Our style of communication reflects our previous experience. Even disturbed communication is purposive. It is a visible symptom of some less visible need or problem. For example, a person obsessed with cleaning and washing herself may be communicating that she has "unclean thoughts" which she keeps trying to wash away. A man who develops laryngitis each time he has to give a presentation may be communicating his fear of speaking in public. Freud believed all communication serves a purpose and reveals something about the communicator.

In recent years other authorities have broadened Freud's idea by identifying communication as a cause as well as a symptom of human behavior. For instance, avoidance of speech may symptomize an individual's fear of failure (Freud's view), but it may also reflect the individual's previous experience with others' responses to communicative efforts. If a person's early efforts to talk were met with constant interruptions and disapproval, (communication as cause) then silence (symptom) may be an adaptive response to others' communication. The way others respond to you shapes the way you communicate with others; this in turn, influences how they see themselves and, therefore, how they communicate. Many of the people who responded to our questionnaire gave examples of how others affected their views of themselves. Consider this comment by an undergraduate student:

Marjorie T. About a year ago I went to the university counselling center and enrolled in an assertiveness program. I really want to learn how to stand up for myself and what I want, because I'm tired of being stepped on by everyone else. But it's going to be a long haul for me. One of the first things I had to do in this program was to figure out why I was not very assertive—amateur analysis. I know I haven't put all of the pieces together yet, but I have realized a big part of my problem comes from growing up in my family. I have three brothers and very traditional parents. I was brought up to "act like a lady" if you know what I mean. I was taught not to speak up much and certainly not to argue with others or disagree with them—especially with males. "Women should know their place" was my father's favorite saying and mother believed it too. She always was quiet, and she never opposed father, even when she really wanted something different from what he did. Once my brothers got to be about thirteen or so, she even deferred to them. My counsellor says that I learned to be unassertive because I got rewarded for not asserting myself and punished for trying to assert myself. The more I think about this the more I agree.

We can clarify the idea of purposiveness by pointing out that our communication is inevitably persuasive. When we talk, there is no way we can avoid influencing others and ourselves. Sometimes we try to influence someone to accept information from us, sometimes we want them to accept our opinions or ideas, and sometimes we want them to do something. Much of the time all we want is for the other person to accept us.

The primary persuasive purpose of our communication is self-confirmation. When we talk, we declare who we are, and we try to convince others to accept this identity. If others confirm our identity, we feel satisfied and secure for the moment. If others fail to confirm our identity, we may modify our communication and try again for confirmation.

Social conversation helps us understand others' perspectives.

By the same token, the way we talk to others is our response to *their* declarations of who they think they are. We confirm or reject their efforts to persuade us to see them as they wish to be seen exactly as they confirm or reject our efforts. For example, suppose you're in a group meeting and one person outlines procedures for the discussion and assigns research tasks to other members. If you go along with the suggested procedures and agree to your research assignment, then you confirm that person's declarations of an identity as group leader. If, on the other hand, you argue for alternate procedures or refuse the research assignment, then you reject that individual's declaration of leadership identity.

A similar process operates in relationships. A husband could declare himself liberated from traditional male roles by spending time caring for the baby. A young woman could reject a man who displays his muscles and so deny his declaration of masculinity. An employee of a woman could reject the boss' identity by refusing to accept orders. If the wife of the husband providing child care rewards him with affection, she confirms his declaration of the role of non-traditional man. If, however, she constantly finds fault with his activities, she may push him back into a traditional role.

We are not always aware of confirming or rejecting people's roles. Sometimes, in fact, other persons misinterpret our response. In the final analysis, it is how we interpret the reactions of others that is crucial in shaping our personality. Actually, we are all constantly involved in negotiating our identities. The process of declaration, confirmation, rejection and modification continues throughout our life. We can, therefore, "make or break" our relationships through our decisions to act and respond as we do.

Dolores J. My friends are telling me to ditch Kurt right now, but I want to give him a bit more time before I do anything drastic. After all, we've been going together for nearly two years, ever since my first semester as a freshman. We have a good relationship in a lot of ways, so I don't want to throw it away just because we're having problems right now. But, boy! Do we ever have a problem! I feel uncomfortable almost anytime I'm with Kurt these days. When we first started going together I was really your typical insecure freshman and he was a pretty with-it junior. I didn't trust my judgment on anything, so Kurt helped me pick out courses, decide what activities to participate in, even which sororities to rush. He always decided what movies, concerts, restaurants we'd go to. We went along fine like this my whole freshman year and even some of the first semester this year. But then things started getting rougher. I've done very well in school so I'm getting more confident of my abilities. A few months ago I was elected president of my sorority, so others recognize my leadership potential too. I'm changing a lot. Now I have my own idea of what I want to do, where I want to go, what courses I want to take. But Kurt seems to resent these changes in me. He says I'm trying to change the way our relationship has always been. I guess I am, but I've changed and the new me doesn't really like the old rules. I don't think our relationship is going to survive unless Kurt starts accepting me as I am now.

We declare ourselves to be different people at different times. It depends on the situation, the other people present and our own purposes in relation to them. We, the authors, declare a range of identities in our daily lives. To our students we try to be seen as teachers; to our colleagues, as competent researchers and scholars; to our friends, as dependable companions; and to our intimates, as loving and lovable life partners. To confirm these identities, we expect our students to learn, our colleagues to respect our publications and seek our advice about their work, our friends to enjoy spending time with us and do us favors, and our intimates to love us as much as we love them.

Just as we vary our declarations of who we are, so do our expectations of confirmation. We don't want our students to act like our lovers, or our spouses to behave like colleagues. Furthermore, each of us has a different idea of what behavior is acceptable to confirm our expectations. Thus, we aim to evoke what we expect from others, for their responses to our declarations are the data on which we evaluate the success of our interpersonal lives. In each situation we declare who we are and respond to how others define themselves. We seek and give confirmation. If we are effective at adapting our talk we will receive enough confirmation to be satisfied (and perhaps enough rejection to keep us challenged).

Our communication is purposive and persuasive. We act toward others as we do in order to achieve a variety of human goals in relation to other people. By far the most constant and the most important purpose of communication is self-confirmation. No matter what other goals we pursue, we are constantly engaged in a quest for others to confirm our declarations of who we are. Every communication has a "validate me" dimension, a tacit request to be confirmed.

Effective interpersonal communication requires dual perspective

A perspective is a viewpoint; a dual perspective is a double viewpoint. When we use the term dual perspective we refer to one person recognizing another person's viewpoint on events, experiences, situations or things, and blending that perspective with his or her own. An individual with dual perspective understands that other people have personal values and commitments that are important in their lives and which guide their behavior. To use dual perspective requires that you take this into account when you speak to others. If you want other people to participate with you in seeking your goal, you must be able to commit yourself to help them seek theirs. Understanding another person's perspective does not imply agreement with it. You may consider others' viewpoints silly, distorted or wrong. Nonetheless, you must understand and respect their viewpoints in order to adapt your actions effectively to theirs and in order to expect reciprocal respect from them.

Dual perspective enhances interaction because it helps you understand whether you have anything in common with your listener. You can get a sense of what the other person agrees with and what might offend him or her. You can plan your communication with the other person's point of view in mind. Acquiring dual perspective begins with the understanding that a great many people share your ideas. People in your culture agree on many values. Therefore, what injures you might also injure them, and what might reward you might reward them. Later on you may discover some of the subtle differences between people by examining differences in economic means, acculturation and belief. The more you grasp of the other person's perspective, the better you can adapt what you say and how you say it so that your ideas are understandable and persuasive. We're not suggesting you alter your beliefs to suit the other person, nor are we advising people to misrepresent their ideas. We are merely suggesting that consideration should be given to the ideas and beliefs of your listener. If you do not believe that it is possible to be compatible with a particular person, prudence advises that you do not try. If you must be compatible with a person with whom you have some deep disagreements, dual perspective is a way to discover and stay within whatever neutral middle ground exists and, perhaps, to expand that ground over time.

Relationships are not solo trips. Two individuals, or more, make up a relationship. They are interdependent. The relationship cannot last unless both parties employ dual perspective. Even when people are very close, there will be differences between them. Each partner, therefore, must confirm the importance of the other by understanding and appealing to the other's basic values, beliefs and ways of seeing the world. For this reason, time must be taken in the formation of relationships. People who communicate egocentrically with each other cannot build an ideally satisfying relationship. They will stay together only so long as their surface values coincide or conditions require them to interact. Sooner or later one will interfere with the other and there will be no basis for repairing the relationship. The ability to employ dual perspective is the one important quality on which relationships can be sustained.

Although dual perspective is an ethical mandate for interpersonal communication, it's not entirely altruistic. Adopting dual perspective tends to enhance your effectiveness in seeking your goals by involving your relationship partner. If, for instance, you want a friend to tutor you in statistics, you must identify some way to make the act valuable to your friend. The fact that you need help will not be persuasive to your friend. Although friends rarely say it out loud, they will ask, "what's in it for me?" every time a request is made. You must find something your friend values: good seats at the game, or an introduction to a desirable person; you may make the promise that he or she might cash in on a favor from you at some later date, or you may accept the help as repayment of a favor he or she previously performed. The point is that to be effective, your request for assistance cannot reflect only your purposes. You must somehow tie your goals to the goals and values of your friend. Remember, the fool tells me his reasons, the wise man persuades me with my own!

Tony B. A lot of people have said I have a knack for leadership. They say I'm just a "natural leader." Well, they wouldn't think so if they knew of some of my early disasters as a leader! But I am good now. I can make almost any group work well and enjoy doing the work. It's no "knack" though. It's skill, and I've worked hard to develop it. I've learned that before I can lead other people well I have to figure them out. I need to psych out each person and find out what makes them tick. When I can figure out what a person likes doing and thinks she or he does well, then I know how to lead that person. And it's not like imposing my will on them or anything. The thing I do is find a way for others to enjoy doing what I want done. Everybody benefits. I think most leaders don't understand this. They start where they are—what they want out of a group, and that's all they can see. You have to understand what the other people want and then find a way of working that in with your own objectives.

Dual perspective is a way to promote reciprocal behavior; if you demonstrate respect for others' viewpoints, they usually respond in kind by respecting yours. Use your own experience to verify this claim. When you talk with people who try to impose on you, chances are you resent it. You either ignore them, or get irritated, or try to impose back. None of these are productive alternatives. In contrast, when you talk with someone who seems aware of your values, you are likely to want to cooperate and be sensitive in return. We tend to treat others as they treat us; by the same reasoning, others tend to act toward us as we act toward them. In that sense, dual perspective is the Golden Rule of interpersonal communication.

Closely associated with the concept of dual perspective is *reciprocity*. Relationships are based on reciprocity; they consist of exchanges between people. Each person in a relationship expects reciprocal treatment. We may not ask for it explicitly, but we expect it and we become discontented with a relationship where we do not get it. When we do not get what it is reasonable to expect from others, we seek equity. We may try harder to make it clear what we think is fair, or we try to get "even" or break off the relationship. Thus, reciprocity, which grows from dual perspective, is a crucial factor in any relationship. Time is so valuable to people that most will not waste it in relationships in which they are not rewarded adequately. Reciprocity is based on a principle of fair-play in human relationships. To deal reciprocally with others we use dual perspective in order to understand their viewpoints and help them understand ours.

We acquire dual perspective gradually in our contact with others. The more intense our relationship with a person, the greater our awareness of that person's unique viewpoint. What we learn in the home helps us begin to make relationships with the new people we meet in the neighborhood and at school. When we first meet new people, we have almost no knowledge of them as individuals. We must start our relationship with public kinds of acts, the kind that we know people approve. We are courteous and we allow time for others to present themselves. In initial encounters we must rely on norms to help us get to know another person. Learning to interact effectively is important; otherwise, we could not get to know anyone well enough to form an intimate relationship in which we could transact. We expect others to fit within the basic norms of our shared culture, and we expect them to evaluate us, initially, on shared public criteria.

For instance, polite but superficial talk is appropriate in first meetings. By staying with neutral topics for a while, people have a chance to size each other up. By listening carefully, each can discover something about the beliefs and values of the other. Most important, you can find out how the person identifies himself or herself through their talk about their social roles.

We generalize about others on the basis of social roles. When we discover what role others are playing, we generate some expectations about their behavior. We expect students to be interested in classes, campus causes and the home team; we expect businesspersons and professionals to talk shop; we avoid profane language around ministers. Sometimes our role stereotypes get us into trouble. For example, we may expect older people to be more conservative than younger people, or mothers to be truly interested in their homes. When people identify themselves by their religions, nationalities, races, or regions, all of our basic prejudices come to the front. Sometimes our generalizations don't fit particular individuals so we have to adapt very quickly. But our broad generalizations must do until we get more details. Awareness of dual perspective helps us pay attention so we can find those details. In fact, the superficial knowledge we acquire through casual contacts is generally sufficient for most relationships. It helps us make pleasant conversation and keeps us out of trouble. We need a more individualized understanding of those people we choose to know better. We want to appreciate these people as unique individuals who do not fit so neatly into cultural and social generalizations. Therefore, we seek to acquire knowledge of them based on personal observation and interaction. The more we interact with them, the more we understand how they construe experience, what they value and why they act as they do. We learn their perspectives on particular things and after a while, we comprehend their orientations toward life. Thus, dual perspective grows by degrees and accumulates over time. The more intimate our relationship with another, the more finely tuned our ability to attain dual perspective in our communication with that person.

We are responsible for the choices we make in communicating with others

This final premise establishes an ethical baseline for interpersonal communication. We deal with this idea last because it is a summary proposition, pulling together all we've covered in this chapter.

Because we can symbolize, self-reflect and exert our *will*, we can control much of our interpersonal behavior. Aside from involuntary responses and physiological reactions, our actions are seldom the *only* ones we could have selected. We choose from a range of possibilities. We decide whether to ignore an acquaintance who is having problems or take the time to talk, whether to seek further contact with a person, whether to respond to an insult with silence, physical violence or a retaliatory insult, and whether to accept another's attempts to dominate us, end the relationship, or negotiate for equity. In each case we can choose not only what to say, but how to say it. If we are skillful in our use of voice and gesture, and if we have a good vocabulary, our possibilities for response are almost limitless. In fact, a great many people do not do well in relationships because they lack the skill to employ some of the possibilities for response available to them as human beings. We can use our symbolizing ability to visualize alternative goals and alternative ways of pursuing a given objective; because we are self-reflective, we can conceive different versions of ourselves, we can accord value to each option, and we can imagine how each might affect other people. Because we can exercise will, we can choose which goals to pursue, with whom and how, which identities to declare for ourselves, which to confirm for others, and what type of impact we seek to have on others. Our ability to make choices arises from our human nature as symbolizing, self-reflecting, willing beings.

The capacity to make choices is not a freedom without cost. In a sense, it is liberating to be a choice-maker, for it frees us from the primitive responses of instinct and reflex. By the same token, each act we direct toward other people is constrained by the necessity to assume some responsibility for the consequences of it. When we choose to form a relationship with another person, we are obligated to deal with that other person for a while, even if our choice was an error. If we choose to get angry, we cannot wave off the anger we get in return. If we choose to act subserviently, we cannot blame others totally for dominating us. Because our actions are chosen rather than inevitable or necessary, we shoulder blame or earn credit for them.

It is not always easy or pleasant to accept responsibility. Many people prefer to blame their defeats and disappointments on circumstances or others rather than accepting them as consequences of their own unwise choices. Excuses may be comforting, but often they are evasions of responsibility. Failure to take responsibility has a nasty way of catching up with us. If we deceive ourselves into believing we are not responsible for what we say and do, then we tend to repeat our mistakes. We're also less likely to reflect on the consequences of what we do before we do it because we often think we can avoid the penalties of careless choices.

A distinguished psychiatrist, Richard Rabkin, makes the case that people wish to avoid responsibility for their actions toward others and try to do so by claiming to be ill. Recent studies of shy people show that most of them want to overcome their shyness by seeking a psychological cure rather than by learning skills of effective interpersonal communication. Many people use emotional illness as an excuse for their inept behavior toward others. It is our contention that regardless of a person's emotional state, he or she can improve interpersonal relationships by learning some communication skills. But one has to choose to do so. The learning does not come easily, and for many people, it is simpler to wait for someone to come up with a miracle cure for troubled relationships than to take personal responsibility for improvement.

Nowhere are the twin issues of choice and responsibility more critical than in our intimate relationships. Because intimacy is private, it is not governed by social conventions. We have considerable freedom in how we fashion our intimate bonds, and we must assume primary responsibility for the choices we make. Intimate partners regulate their own conduct and ways of acting toward each other. Their personal values and interpersonal agreements are the driving forces of the relationship. In their private time and space, partners are not bound by social norms and conventions, although they may choose to abide by them. If you abuse or hurt a friend or lover, no officer will appear on your doorstep, nor will there be a sentence to serve. If you permit yourself to be bullied there is no arbiter to protect your rights. Intimacy is the part of our lives least regulated by public rules and most subject to individual choices. Thus, the quality of our intimate relationships is largely within our control.

Because we have choices in how we design our intimate relationships, we assume considerable responsibility for them. There is no escape from personal accountability. Responsibility emerges as a central issue because our choices have such power to affect others. To our intimates we reveal our private dreams, hopes and fears, we admit our weaknesses and inadequacies, we disclose our failures and share our goals. This in-depth knowledge makes intimates supremely vulnerable to one another, because each person recognizes the other's weak points and knows all too well how to inflict harm. We depend on our intimates to support us, and when they fail to, we are deeply hurt. What our intimates say and do counts more heavily than what is said and done by all of our other acquaintances combined. The motto of the 1960's, "Do your own thing," cannot apply to intimate relationships because it implies a disregard for how doing our own thing may affect another human being with whom we have a commitment.

Leonard C. "Independence." I'm starting to hate that word! All this talk about independence is just great *until* you try it. Take the three guys I share an apartment with. Two of them are real slobs— I mean the genuine articles! I wouldn't mind if they kept their mess in their rooms, but that's not what happens. I come home and the living room is usually draped with several pairs of jeans and shirts and dishes from whatever they had for dinner the night before. The bathroom is always filthy because they don't pick up their clothes or put their shaving stuff back in the cabinet. I have to clear a space on the sink and wash it out before I can shave myself. I've tried telling them that I resent their behavior. You know what the answer is? "Hey, Lenny, you do your thing and let us do ours. If you want to be so neat, that's fine with us, but we're not that way. It's no skin off your back!" Well, pardon me, but it *is* skin off my back. I live there too. What they do affects me. You aren't ever really independent as long as you're involved with others, and I'm tired of suffering the consequences of their "independence"!

Because intimate partners interweave their lives by choice, what each person does necessarily affects the other. Linking of present and future is a characteristic of intimacy. We cannot be close to another person without risking being vulnerable or without accepting the fact that what happens to them will have consequences for ourselves.

Our definition of human beings as symbolizing, self-reflecting, willing agents has implications for interpersonal conduct. Three of the primary implications are that human communication is purposive, effective interpersonal communication requires dual perspective, and individuals are responsible for the choices they make in communicating with others. These three premises form the foundation for effective, responsible communication in relationships with others. We turn now to a final section of this chapter in order to wrap up some of the ideas in our examination of interpersonal communication theory.

The Relationship of the Rhetorical Perspective to Other Interpersonal Theories

Many of the theories about interpersonal behavior such as those surveyed in Appendix B are complementary to one another because they consider various aspects of human relationships. Collectively they add up to an understanding. However, we are concerned here with a single important aspect of human relationships—interpersonal communication. Therefore, we use rhetorical theory to tie the others together. For instance, we can consider exchange theories of how people determine what they consider to be fair to discover what relationship partners seek to persuade each other about. We can examine theories about rules to discover how our talk conforms to social expectations. Study of situations helps us to understand how to analyze and prepare our talk. Psychoanalytic theory leads us to consider private and hidden motivations for actions, as well as to recognize some possible errors in the choices people make. Sociobiology, which stresses the urgency to preserve the species and be safe and satisfied brings us back to the origins of human relationships. Our understanding of human beings as symbolic creatures, who are aware of themselves and consequently able to exert their will, shows us how we have developed the ability to transcend a major part of our own biological nature. Consideration of behaviorist theory guides us to an understanding of how we may influence others and be influenced by them, and study of systems theory shows us how we can influence events and events can influence us. A rhetorical view synthesizes several of these theories to provide a powerful and comprehensive perspective on human relationships. In this sense rhetoric is entirely compatible with many other contemporary approaches and may be fairly regarded as an integrative and interdisciplinary perspective.

Despite rhetoric's alliance with other theories, there is an important way in which rhetoric diverges from standard views of interpersonal behavior and relationships. It addresses the crucial issue of individual responsibility, which must occupy a central role in our thinking about human conduct. Theories that focus on internal and external determinants of behavior provide little basis for an interpersonal ethic that might improve our ability to build and sustain satisfying relationships.

By contrast, the rhetorical point of view is *fundamentally* concerned with ethical issues. Because the rhetorical perspective emphasizes our ability to make choices and manage our behavior, it forces us to consider consequences and their impact on others. The ethics suggested by rhetoric are not ephemeral. They are very practical. If we do not choose our behaviors well, we will not attain our goals and we may injure others in the process. We may be partly constrained by biological limits and membership in particular a society, but even so, we are free within those limits to make choices based on awareness of consequences.

The moral fiber of a rhetorical position grows out of its starting point. Since rhetoric begins with a specific definition of *human* nature, it permits us to focus on human characteristics. Sociobiology may help us understand the human as partially limited by biology, equity and exchange may help us understand the possibilities of our economic nature, but rhetoric directs us to consider our human identity and enables us to take the fullest advantage of our human capabilities.

What life form is not limited by its genetic pre-wiring and the environment in which it lives? Humans are to be sure, but so are horses, cats and green peas! Let's take another example. Exchange and equity theories describe humans as interdependent animals who barter their services and feelings. True enough, but exchange is also characteristic of ants, spiders, packs of wolves, and symbiotic relationships between mistletoe and trees. To take a third example, consider rules theory which focuses on how humans develop and use rules (agreed-upon conventions) to regulate their interaction. No one would argue that we do this, but so do most animal tribes and insect colonies. In fact, ants and bees have developed highly sophisticated rules that coordinate their behavior in very complex ways. These examples should be sufficient to establish the point that the understanding about human relationship behavior we seek can only be found through an approach directed toward understanding what is fundamental in human nature. *We have, in offering this perspective, ANTHROPOMORPHIZED the study of human behavior. Instead of considering humans as animals, we have considered them as humans and we therefore are able to examine their behavior in light of exclusively human issues.*

We have presented a viewpoint that considers human beings and the way they deal with each other. Only a point of view that begins by probing the nature of humanity has the potential to offer us a full understanding of what we are capable of achieving in our relationships. So we look to the rhetorical perspective as our baseline. Rhetoric recognizes the ability to use symbols, to be self-aware and to exercise will as the *sine qua non* of humanity.

Chapter Summary

Throughout the rest of this book we will explore the implications of our definition of humanity. This chapter introduced a rhetorical view of human relationships. The rhetorical position begins with a definition of human beings as symbolizing, self-reflecting, and willing agents. From this definition we elaborated three rhetorical premises about human relationships. First, we discussed the purposive nature of human communication. We communicate to achieve goals in relation to others. By extension, communication is invariably persuasive, a process by which we attempt to influence others in a variety of ways. The most important and constant kind of persuasion centers on gaining confirmation of the identities we declare for ourselves.

The second rhetorical premise states that effective interpersonal communication requires dual perspective, which combines a personal perspective with an understanding of how another person views things. When we grasp another person's way of perceiving we can take their perspective into account as we plan and enact our own communication. We can adapt what we say and how we say it to their values and frames of reference, a process which makes communication more effective and satisfying for all participants. Dual perspective in relationships tends to be reciprocal. The more respect we demonstrate for others' viewpoints, the more they are likely to respect ours. Dual perspective is also something that occurs in degrees and that tends to enlarge as a direct consequence of interaction. The more intimately we know others, the more fully we can adopt and act on dual perspective in our communication with them.

The last rhetorical premise states that individuals are responsible for the choices they make in communicating with others. As we deal with others, we make choices about what to say and not say. Further, we make choices about how to express our ideas and how to seek our goals, including the primary goal of self-confirmation. We choose how to respond to others, most importantly whether to confirm their declarations of identity and how to deal with their responses to our own declarations of identity.

The fact that we are capable of making choices gives us considerable freedom. At the same time, however, it constrains us with the uniquely human burden of responsibility. Especially in our intimate relationships, which are largely immune to public rules and conventions, we are responsible for the choices we make. If you wish to deal ethically with others, you must begin by accepting responsibility for your conduct, your part in building relationships, and your impact on others. There is no excuse for and no escape from irresponsibility in human relationships.

We regard the rhetorical position as the most comprehensive, insightful, and humanistic of those currently available. *Its essential premise is that despite limitations on human experience, whether physical, social, physiological, or psychological, situations can always be made better by using self-awareness and will to improve the use of symbols in interpersonal relations.* In the chapters to come we will build on the ideas we have presented in this chapter by offering you generalizations about the way people initiate their most intimate relationships, how they develop and alter those relationships and how they deal with problems encountered in relationships, and how and why some relationships come apart.

REFERENCES FOR CHAPTER 3

H. Blumer, *Symbolic Interactionism: Perspective and Method.* Englewood Cliffs, N.J.: Prentice-Hall, 1969.

E. Cassirer, *An Essay on Man.* New Haven: Yale University Press, 1944.

E. Fromm, *Escape from Freedom.* New York: Holt, Rinehart and Winston, 1941.

R. Hart and D. Burks, "Rhetorical Sensitivity and Social Interaction," *Speech Monographs.* 30, June, 1972. Pp. 175–91.

R. May, *Love and Will*. New York: W. W. Norton, 1969.

G. H. Mead, *Mind, Self, and Society*. Chicago: University of Chicago Press, 1934.

G. Phillips, and N. J. Metzger, *Intimate Communication*. Boston: Allyn and Bacon, 1976.

N. Postman, *Crazy Talk, Stupid Talk*. New York: Delacorte, 1971.

R. Rabkin, *Inner and Outer Space*. New York: W. W. Norton, 1970.

M. Rosenberg, *Conceiving the Self*. New York: Basic Books, 1979.

H. S. Terrace. "How Nim Chimpsky Changed My Mind," *Psychology Today*. November, 1971. Pp. 65–91.

J. Wood and G. Phillips, "Metaphysical Metaphors and Pedagogical Practice," *Communication Education*. 29. May, 1980. Pp. 146–157.

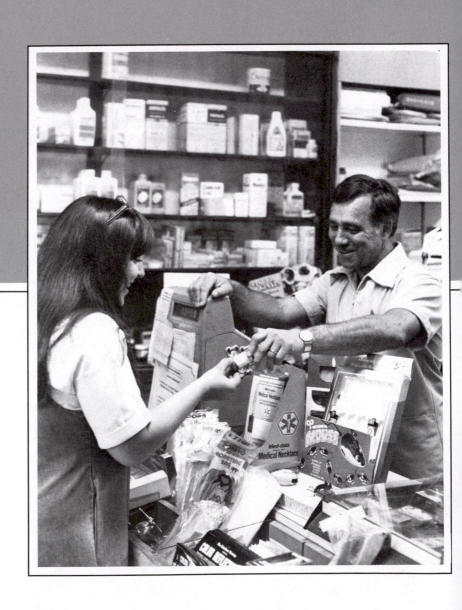

4

INTERACTION AND TRANSACTION IN EVERYDAY LIFE

Before we begin to consider the intense interpersonal relationships, including the male-female bond, we must examine how interpersonal communication is used in our daily life. It is relatively easy to analyze and understand our public interactions and transactions. By examining them, we will gain skill in viewing processes and components so that examination of our more intense relationships will be facilitated.

This chapter is about day-to-day interpersonal activity. In it, we will describe situations in which people relate to one another to accomplish tasks necessary for daily living. The chapter is primarily descriptive devoted to typical problems we encounter in familiar situations. Understanding your own behavior in such situations will help you decide whether, and in what way, you wish to alter your interpersonal communication behavior.

The information in this chapter comes from four sources: (1) formal research in interpersonal communication, (2) insights from the surveys and interviews conducted by the authors in order to write this book, (3) the accumulated experience at teaching interpersonal communication compiled by the authors and their colleagues, and (4) "folk wisdom" about relationships representing the expectations of society in general.

The issues in interaction and transaction we present in this chapter will help you examine your strengths and weaknesses and set your improvement goals. Personal improvement begins with understanding how and where interpersonal communication is used. It proceeds through goal setting and diligent practice with evaluation and criticism of an expert critic. In the final section we offer criteria for selection of improvement programs and relationship therapies.

Interpersonal Skill Is Important in Your Daily Life

The people around you

You must communicate with the people with whom you share space in the world: neighbors, tradespeople, and work-mates, for example. People cannot read your mind. People will judge you decent or indecent, interesting or dull, intelligent or slow, competent or ineffective, reliable or untrustworthy based on what and how you communicate with them.

Expectancies in social situations

There are expectancies in every social role. Your neighbors will expect you to act like a neighbor. Store clerks expect you to act like a customer, doctors and dentists require you to play a patient's role. Your effectiveness with friends and lovers depends on your ability to identify what is expected of you and to deliver it. Your relationship life is characterized by a continuing demand to assess situations and figure out how to act in them.

This is crucial on the job. It is not sufficient merely to be competent at what you do. You must demonstrate your competency by meeting task demands to present information fluently and accurately, ask the right questions, answer questions efficiently, give instructions, present and defend ideas, participate in group problem solving, make presentations in public, and use aids to communicate productively. Furthermore, in most jobs, people are expected to use communication to socialize and build "team spirit."

Some people are still intimidated by the telephone, for example, even though the next decade will see our communication on the job dependent on video interconnections, computers, and word processors. Our social contacts with others will adapt to our ability to connect vast distances and share incredible quantities of detailed information. It will require skill and alertness to use this equipment well and to maintain quality social contact.

Initial social contacts on the job and elsewhere are made through "small talk" which enables you to share time with a new acquaintance while deciding about future possibilities. Social communication is used as a source of pleasure in public and private. Casual conversation, joking, and discussion of ideas and opinions sustain both friendships and intimacies. We can earn a reputation as bright and interesting or dull and banal based on how well we handle social conversation.

Expectancies in intimate situations

Our friendships grow from our conversations. Others become interested in us when we discover and respond to their needs. Long lasting relationships are built when we discover how we can support each other and exchange information, services, and affection. Important and enduring friendships are based on communication that respects and responds to the needs and identities of others.

Marriage and family therapists look first to communication when they seek to help couples in trouble. We often take our loved ones so much for granted that we do not make an effort to communicate as well with them as we do with our more casual acquaintances. We justify our lack of consideration by saying "we need someplace where we can let our hair down." However this is counterproductive and should it become chronic, it can destroy our closest human relationships.

Exerting influence

Finally, skillful interpersonal communication can help you influence events important to you. Shy and silent people are often ignored. If you want your views to be respected and your ideas considered, you must communicate them willingly and well. Hardly anyone solicits opinions from people who stand by quietly. On the job you are responsible for saying your share. If you can't show your interest, people will believe you apathetic. You discover how important competent expression of opinion is once you have endured the frustration of seeing someone else credited for ideas you could not express.

There are many opportunities to speak in the community. Good government depends on communicating citizens. In addition, you gain the respect of your friends when you speak forcefully against statements you feel are bigoted or ignorant. Firm but un-belligerent answers to people whose ideas you oppose tends to generate confidence in you as a person.

The Components of Effective Interpersonal Performance

Attentiveness to others

Interpersonal competence starts with attention to situations, other people, and your own behavior. Effective communication is listener-centered, not egocentric. No one has to agree with you or support your ideas. The only way to win their cooperation is to provide something of value to them. Agreements are negotiated, not demanded, based on mutual reciprocal persuasion rather than coercion. Bargaining and sharing in interpersonal relations depends on mutual respect and consideration so people understand each other's priorities and everyone gets a fair share and no one gets it all. If you support others they will usually return the courtesy. It is easy to make people look stupid or foolish but it is hard to handle their retaliation. Disagreement should be directed toward ideas and issues, not personalities, for when conflict becomes personal, everyone is hurt. Even if you are not aware of it, bystanders evaluate what you say and do and their evaluations affect your reputation. Your conversation is the basis for their decisions about you. The more decency and fairness you will show, the more appeal you will have to others.

Goals for talk

Purposive communication seeks to accomplish personal goals. People communicate because they think they can gain from it. Goals can be simple and short term, "I want to pass a pleasant fifteen minutes at this party" or complicated and long range, "I'd like to make this person my close friend." When people discover common goals they develop a relationship designed to accomplish these goals. Goals are usually specific to people and situations: "I want Sandra to know this" or "I want Marlene to teach me how to run the machine." People have long-term goals for themselves, as well. Long-term goals like "I want to attend graduate school" or "I want to have a child by the age of thirty" help us define ourselves and guide our activities of the moment so they are consistent and productive.

You cannot force people to relate to you any more than they can coerce you to interact with them. If a person already has all the relationships he or she can handle, there may be no time for you. If your goals are not compatible, a friendship may be against your best interests and you risk being "used." Attention to your goals will help you assess a relationship's potential. Enlightened self-interest together with consideration for others afford the best friendship prognosis. A relationship is satisfying when everyone involved is rewarded by it. Sensitive monitoring of input and reward will help protect your interests. You owe others only courtesy, what your job requires, and obligations you have taken on yourself. Once you have allowed a person to count on you, however, your relationship can be broken only with considerable pain. Care in initial contacts can spare you and others discomfort later on.

Improvement and Criticism

The difficulty of self-viewing

It is difficult to watch yourself communicate. Some people believe they are fascinating conversationalists despite obvious cues of boredom from their listeners. Others misinterpret intense interest as hostility. Some are so intent on what they are saying they see nothing at all. Skill at interpersonal communication requires the ability to observe, interpret, and respond to other people's responses to you. The most effective way to learn to do this is to have a critic observe and guide you. You may choose a professional as your teacher, or you may rely on the comments of a trusted friend. The most important consideration is to be sure the criticism offers you a specific way to modify your behavior and provides a method to accomplish this. Unsolicited criticism is often not worth considering because it does not provide tangible advice for improvement. The ethics of criticism demand that a critic be sensitive to aspects of behavior that can be modified as opposed to those intrinsic aspects that are not amenable to change.

Judging advice and criticism

Before responding to criticism, you must discover what you'd gain if you were successful. If a critic explains you can be a leader, you must decide if you want to lead. The value of criticism depends on its ability to advance your own goals.

Once you have decided a criticism is useful, you must specify what you would be able to do if you followed it so you can judge whether you have changed successfully. Next you must decide how high on your list of priorities the change is. Finally, you must be able to specify what you have to do or learn to do before the change comes about. While we cannot change all aspects of our communication, we can make a careful selection from among possibilities and change what is to our greatest advantage to change.

Features Common to All Communication

Communication in relationships consists of both form and content. There is a purpose to what is said and a manner of saying it. Evaluation leading to improvement of interpersonal communication requires analysis of goals, motivations, topics, and style of presentation.

Effective goal-setting involves seeking something of advantage to yourself and to the other people involved. For example, if you are in a store, a reasonable goal might be purchasing something you need. The clerks are assigned to sell. If you give them an opportunity to try to sell you something, you serve their interests as well as yours.

Motivating means appealing to what you believe others need, want or value. Most people seek safety, rewards to self-esteem, amusement, useful knowledge, and ways to advance toward their personal goals. If you know specifically what other people seek you can appeal directly to them. Otherwise, you'll have to rely on general appeals to persuade other people to attend to you.

Topics may be transacted uniquely between relating partners. As we will point out in detail later on, every relationship, no matter how casual or intense, has a way of making decisions and carrying them out, and of settling disputes. People relating to one another can talk about what might be exchanged and how they wish to carry on their relationship, or they may discuss ideas of mutual interest, share amusing stories, and decide what they will do in the future. Making plans for future contact is one of the most important topics of relationships.

Finally, talk must be intelligible and interesting. Many people pay little attention to the way they communicate. We do not advocate that you train yourself as an actor. On the other hand, when your talk is monotonous, monosyllabic, marked by "and uhs," "y'know," and "like, I mean," your chances of sustaining conversation are very slim. To be regarded as an interesting person, your talk should be interesting.

Shyness and Related Problems

Most people suffer from shyness at one time or another. Shyness is not an emotional illness. It is simply an inability to communicate skillfully with others. Shy people believe they gain more from silence than from communication. They often become victims because they cannot defend their point of view. The person who cannot make his or her goals explicit to a partner is vulnerable to exploitation.

Shy people can become more effective with training in interpersonal communication. If shyness is not remedied, serious emotional problems such as loss of self-esteem may result. When people expect to fail, they fail, and thus surrender the ability to direct their own lives. Low self-esteem and anxiety can be helped by counseling, but communication skill is required to sustain competent performance within relationships. Inability to play a competent role in intimate communication can seriously impair relationships.

There are other kinds of communication problems resulting from inadequate interpersonal skill. Compulsive talkers, people with unpleasant vocal habits, egocentrics, and excessively argumentative people could improve their relationships by learning effective techniques of analysis and presentation. Emotional problems seem to accompany communication disabilities. We do not know whether communication problems arise from emotional problems or whether neuroses come from a lack of communication skills, but there is evidence to indicate that the two tend to go together.

People who are very fearful about participating in communication are referred to as "communication apprehensives." People are apprehensive when they understand what communication can accomplish in social situations but they either cannot figure out what to say or believe they cannot say it effectively. Their tension keeps them from participating. Communication apprehensives can be helped by training designed to teach them how to handle specific social situations. A very small proportion of them may need to learn techniques of relaxation so they can be desensitized to some of the situations that make them fearful. Communication competence demands that you be able to figure out what to say and be willing and able to say it.

Developing Communication Competence

To become a good conversationalist you should develop a repertoire of topics as well as the ability to recognize which topics are appropriate in various situations. The first step is to keep posted on current events, major films and books, and sporting and cultural events. The second step is cultivating skill in talking about your interesting experiences. Regular reading of newspapers and popular magazines will help. Rehearsing techniques of meeting strangers, cultivating a firm handshake and becoming adept at phatic communication (small talk) will support your efforts. It is also important to convince others that you are interested in them and in what they have to say. Conversational skill increases the number of people from whom you can select friends. If you convince people you are interesting, they will generally seek you out and be responsive to your overtures.

Acquiring competence starts with the observation of effective communicators. By observing how others communicate, you can make a decision about what skills you have and which ones you need to acquire. Becoming a skillful communicator does *not* require a total personality change. Mostly, it involves attention to how you affect others accompanied by decisions about what aspects of behavior you need to change in order to have more impact. Often, small changes, like acquiring more variety in vocal presentation, or becoming more orderly in the sequences of ideas you present are sufficient to make significant changes in the way your communication is received. It is the same on the job and with your friends. People cannot read your mind. The only way they can tell what you intend for them and what you seek for yourself is if you say it in an interesting manner in language they can understand.

Conversational competence is not a panacea. It will not, of itself, make you a desirable human being. But if you are a desirable human being to begin with, it will help bring that fact to the attention of the people whose attention you seek.

Nonverbal Communication

Your physical appearance, facial expression, eye contact and gestures influence others' impressions of you. Nonverbal communication refines and amplifies your talk. It may contradict the spoken word and plant the seeds of doubt or it may support what you say.

Nonverbal communication also identifies ethnicity. An Italian may wonder how an American man can talk all day with his hands in his pocket and a pipe in his mouth. The American may wonder how Italians can talk to one another without poking each others' eyes out. People who are familiar with one another develop gestures and expressions characteristic of their social group. Strangers are easily identified because they do not speak in the same manner. It is important not to judge people by their gestures and facial expressions, since such behaviors are intrinsic in their education.

Visual signs help you understand social situations and the peo-

We use nonverbal communication to respond to others.

ple who share them with you. The arrangement of furniture in a home reveals a great deal about the taste and personality of the people who live there. Dress also influences judgments about personality. People respond to physical appearances. Those who conform to standards of attractiveness are considered more acceptable than those who do not. Excessively fat, thin, short, or tall people are often rejected in initial contacts.

When you know someone well, their gestures, expressions and movements can give more information than their talk. For example, a smile does not always indicate pleasure. Some people smile in anger. Lack of eye contact does not mean lack of attention. Some people find they can listen better if they keep their eyes closed. It is impossible to understand these personal nonverbal behaviors in advance. Information comes only with extended interaction.

An interesting phenomenon takes place once you get to know a person well. Nonverbal behaviors that were initially annoying and confusing seem to disappear. If you like the person, disqualifying features like obesity, for example, or baldness, tend to disappear. On the other hand, when you find you do not like a person, unpleasant nonverbal behaviors seem more prominent.

Listening

People seldom feel obliged to listen. Whether you listen depends on how interesting the other person is and how well they take your interests into account. Listening is actually a sign of respect that is earned. Attentiveness can be very encouraging and rewarding to another person.

Failure to listen is not a social crime. On the other hand, it pays to listen because *you cannot tell whether something is worth listening to until you have listened to it.* But, if what is said does not appear useful, you need do no more than show ordinary courtesy. The burden is on the person who speaks. If they can make themselves interesting to you then it is worthwhile to listen. To evaluate talk requires taking the time to listen.

Some situations demand attentive listening. When doing business or seeking a particular goal, the other person's response can be crucial. You must listen in order to plan your next move. You can demonstrate you have listened attentively by asking good questions or making relevant comments.

How to listen

Effective listening requires a system. You must decide whether you want to understand the main points, master some particular details, or just pick up the mood. People seem to speak faster than it is possible to listen. Actually, if the speaker is organized, we can hear a good deal more than we expect. If we are so disorganized the listener must provide the order in our speech, we risk being misunderstood. Competent speakers try to provide a logical framework for listening in both public and private.

In formal and public situations, you can assist your memory by planned note-taking. You must decide in advance what you want from a presentation and avoid casual jotting. Note-taking is only useful if it helps you recall what was said. In informal situations, you must take advantage of your privilege to ask questions. You will not remember as many details, but your questions can help the speaker understand what is important to you.

Throughout this book we've emphasized that by helping others achieve their objectives, you earn their assistance in your own goal-seeking. If you listen attentively to others, they are likely to return the courtesy. If you watch impatiently for your turn to talk, you can alienate the other and worse, you may say something inappropriate. Effective listening helps you figure out what is important to others. It provides a basis for decisions about whether to make future contact and how to initiate it.

Skill with Language

Effective communication requires skillful use of language. Unfamiliar, overly technical, or excessively colloquial language and sloppy grammar will persuade people to stop listening. The reason you analyze your listeners is to increase the chance your talk will be intelligible and interesting to them.

People seem to expect others to understand them, no matter how sloppy or confusing they may be. Social conversation is often delivered in a kind of "stream of consciousness," with no visible effort to organize ideas. It is important to understand your listener has no way of knowing what is on your mind unless you make it clear. If your words and grammar confuse others, they will impose their own meaning which may be very different from yours.

Strategies in Interaction

Deciding when to speak

Interaction is guided by both public norms and your personal interest. To accomplish personal goals you must conform to social norms and the requirements of the situation. Mastery of phatic communion, the "hello, how are you?" type of communication, is a form of basic competence.

Techniques of social talk

A great speech teacher once said public speaking is enlarged conversation. Public speaking requires you to adapt your ideas to the sensitivities and needs of your audience. The same is true with social talk. Consideration and coherence are vital to sustaining attention on your talk. Willingness to take turns and making sure others get their turn is a sign of courtesy. At a social gathering, virtually everyone wants to talk, and good listeners are in short supply and high demand.

You must be careful about disclosing personal information. It is risky to tell secrets about yourself to people you hardly know. Information can be used against you, but more important, giving personal information to people who do not want it is a presumption. Disclosure is a sign of intimacy and is generally inappropriate during interaction.

Arguing

Public disagreements can be sticky. Most of us feel a bit threatened when we are contradicted. Our usual response is to try to get out of the situation. However, you need not submit to conversational bullying. Sometimes it is important for our ideas to be heard.

Focus your talk on ideas, not on you and the other person. By confining your comments to the issue, you demonstrate your fair-mindedness. If you launch a personal attack, you deflect attention from the issues to personalities, a state of affairs which is seldom productive. Even if you are attacked personally and unfairly, it is not necessary to respond in kind. If you are unwilling to engage in personal attacks, you may distract your opponent from such behavior. You may also earn the respect of your listeners for your ideas and your personal behavior.

It is time to break off when you find your opponent repeating the same arguments and you are tempted to do the same. Say "this has gone far enough, I'm sure everyone has made up their mind by now. Excuse me." You need not be silent while someone insults a minority group, misleads or exploits others, or presents a biased opinion. Those who speak reasonably against such practices win the respect of those who listen.

Speaking on the job

Social communication is a delicate aspect of work life. When people spend a great deal of time together they cannot help forming both friendly and hostile associations. Personal relationships on the job are risky because they are vulnerable to exploitation on behalf of economic gain. For example, promotions often result in aborted friendships. Closeness with a supervisor may antagonize fellow workers, and if the boss feels the friendship seeks personal advantage, he or she can be antagonized as well. There are political hazards as well. If you are friends with superiors, your fortunes are directly linked to theirs. When the president loses an election, the entire cabinet loses too. Furthermore, in hierarchical relationships, one person (the boss) has greater power and less dependence on the relationship than the other. In general, successful interpersonal relations on the job require careful analysis and restraint.

Issues in Transaction

Friendship

You may have friendships with many people for a variety of reasons. Casual friendships revolve around mutual interests or common activities: for example, the people with whom you exercise or play bridge, those who share your hobby, those you see from time to time. Casual friendships can also develop on the job among people who enjoy "talking shop" occasionally. Neighbors can be friends out of common interest in the locale and the desire for mutual protection.

Some friends will become intimate. You will spend a great deal of time together and share personal information. You count on each

Casual friendships revolve around shared activities.

other for special favors, emotional support, and sharing joy and victory. Intimate friendships are so demanding that most people will have no more than four or five of them in a lifetime. Intimate friends provide validation for each others' ideas; they encourage growth, confirm worth, and share sadness and joy. Attention to the needs of others is basic to successful friendships.

Sexuality

Once a man and woman have sexual contact, sexuality becomes part of the symbolizing process. Sex is more than a simple physical act. It heavily influences a relationship and reflects how partners feel about each other.

Men and women sometimes differ on the meaning of sexual activity but there is no way they can escape the issue of sexuality. Any time a man and woman come together they must agree on how to dispose of sexual issues. Both men and women must take care to recognize and resolve sexual issues so they are not surprised later on, if they emerge.

Rejection

You can't win them all. Sometimes the person you want most to like you wants nothing to do with you. It is unreasonable to demand that everyone accept you. People sometimes blackmail, bribe, and intimidate in order to get attention, but such attention does not last long. We need to know when to leave people who do not want to associate with us.

Furthermore, you need not admit to intimacy everyone who seeks it. You need only go to the limit of your personal interest. No matter what price the other is willing to pay for intimacy, you have the right to refuse. A great many people get trapped into painful relationships because they are afraid to say "no!" *Mutuality* is the essence of intimacy. You have the right to make your own choices of intimate partners.

Dependence

A degree of dependence on others is not necessarily bad. People cannot attain their goals without depending on other people. However, it is important to avoid pathological dependence in which a person cannot make personal decisions or be autonomous in any aspect of his or her life. Intimate partners must give space and privacy to one another, so they can make independent choices where necessary.

To prevent pathological dependencies, partners must earn each other's trust and must work out some reciprocal dependencies so that each counts on the other. They should realize the value of privacy, time alone, and time with others. Women sometimes fret when their husbands are out "with the boys," while husbands wonder what their wives do with their "girl friends." Both tend to become edgy when their mates deal with the opposite sex.

Furthermore, mates must be able to carry on without each other. Wives should understand finances. Husbands should be able to cook and clean. Spouses in stereotyped roles may become desperate in case of death or divorce. Both men and women need to be able to cope alone. It is important to have someone to bring you chicken soup when you are ill, but you must be able to make your own if no one else is around.

Intimacy and change

As people grow older, their values, needs, health, and interpersonal goals change. Each partner must accommodate to changes in the other. Skillful communication is required to handle major life changes. It is impossible to predict all of the changes that will be required in a lifetime, but couples can prepare to deal with some recurrent issues. For example, financial fluctuations, illness, moving, changing jobs, problems with children, new friends, and changes in interests crop up regularly. They can be anticipated and tentative plans made. The talk required to make these plans serves also to cement the relationship. As we describe the process of relationship evolution in detail in later chapters, you will discover that whatever problems occur in relationships, communication will be one major resource in solving them.

A Brief Consumer's Guide to Therapies for Relationships

It is possible to get into trouble while trying to get out of trouble. In these times, when relationship problems dominate the popular literature, promises of help are found everywhere. A couple in trouble can select solutions from primal screaming, role playing, massaging, meditating, encountering, hot-tubbing, asserting, consciousness-raising, behavior-modifying, sexual expressiveness, alternative life styles, exercise, special diet, artistic expression, and straight psychotherapy.

Universities have courses in interpersonal skills, conjugal and filial relationships, helping relationships, marriage preparation, and "open" communication. The health community offers psychoanalysis, Gestalt therapy, desensitization, cognitive restructuring, skills therapy, brief therapy, family therapy, and networking. Commercial offerings include "Lifestream," "EST," transactional analysis, conjoint family therapy, bio-feedback, and open marriage training. Furthermore, every religion—fundamentalist, oriental, and exotic— offers a "cure" for relationship problems.

Many who offer cures are untrained and unlicensed. Most states do not certify marriage and relationship therapists. Couples in trouble must exert caution when they look for help, for without government controls charlatans can be found everywhere. Licensed or not, therapists seek to make a living. Free therapy (like the kind you find on college campuses) is usually associated with someone's training or research project; this may or may not affect your confidence. In addition, you can buy books, magazines, film strips, home-study courses, cassettes, and movies designed to solve your problems.

Problem definition

Can you describe your problem precisely? Saying that you simply "don't feel well" or things are "shaky" is not helpful. Do you feel that you are not exerting enough influence on the relationship? Does your mate ignore your ideas? Is your partner "fooling around" with someone else? Do you feel a need for more fun in the relationship? Would you like to change to a career that gives you more prestige, identity, personal pleasure, a feeling of importance, or an outlet for your "creative" talents? It is not useful to seek help until you can identify a problem. Otherwise you risk allowing the therapist to define the problem for you. Therapists deliver cures. Most of them will try to persuade you that your problem is something they can cure. You must retain control over the definition of your problem.

Demand competence

How do you know a helper is competent? Inquire whether your state licenses therapists. If you are going to a clinical psychologist or psychiatrist, you can check credentials and background. The American Association of Marriage and Family Therapists maintains a list of people who are qualified for such counseling. Licensing does not guarantee competence but it provides protection against malpractice. Furthermore, most licensing agencies require a reasonable level of preparation.

If you seek help from the clergy, you can inquire about the kind of training in counseling he or she was given. Be wary of sex therapists who make outlandish claims and resort to bizarre methods. If you use a university-based service, check whether your therapy is part of someone else's research. Most such programs will require informed consent on your part. Community agencies can provide competent therapy, but it is useful to check track records with someone who has used the service previously.

Groups and disclosure

Does the therapy require you to disclose personal information in front of strangers? If group activity is required by the therapist, inquire about how the group is supposed to help you, and what you are to contribute to the group. Be particularly careful about groups associated with charismatics who ask you to "believe in them" or systems that require sensory deprivation.

It is virtually impossible for one partner in an intimate pair to solve relationship problems alone. Effective therapy usually involves both partners. A relationship is a living unit which cannot be treated in components. Relationship problems are best addressed when both partners consent to working out problems together. Some therapists have a tendency to polarize relationships by treating partners one at a time. An effective therapy should encourage partners to work together, both during and between sessions.

Second party payment

Is the therapist you selected eligible for payment by reputable health insurers. If the therapy is covered you have the assurance that it has been checked and found reputable. It is, of course, not a guarantee that you will be helped, but at least you know that the therapist is regarded as competent by other therapists. It is most desirable to work with therapists associated with major helping institutions, who belong to recognized associations, and whose services are covered by medical insurance.

Track record

Do you have any information about how successful the therapist has been with *problems similar to yours*. It is not helpful to go to a therapist who specializes in problems you don't have. Don't hesitate to ask around to see if other people have been "burned" in their search for a helper. It may be useful to remember the simple admonition we gave earlier in this book—do not criticize when you cannot provide a method for improvement. A helper should give you something more than a state of mind. He or she should take responsibility to provide you with methods for solving your problems. Most important, a good therapist will try to equip you with questions and methods you can use to handle your own problems in the future. A therapy session should be a learning experience that increases your personal skills.

Chapter Summary

This chapter surveyed the issues involved in interaction and transaction. Relating to others requires a synthesis of goals, analytical skills, and technique. In the remainder of this book we will describe regularities in relationships, the *probabilities* of which can be discovered and used as guides to action. We will also emphasize that relationships are unique experiences and the choices made about them must be guided by an assessment of *possibilities*. Building and sustaining relationships are enhanced by a combination of theory and practice. Theory provides understanding and guides your efforts. Practice applies your skill to building and maintaining relationships satisfying to you and to those with whom you relate.

REFERENCES FOR CHAPTER 4

R. Adler, *Confidence in Communication*. New York: Holt, Rinehart, and Winston, 1979.

C. Brown and C. Van Riper, *Communication in Human Relationships*. Skokie, Ill.: National Textbook Co., 1973.

J. McCroskey, "Oral Communication Apprehension: A Summary of Recent Theory and Research," *Human Communication Research*. 4, 1977. Pp. 78–96.

G. Phillips, *Help for Shy People or Anyone Else Who Ever Felt Ill at Ease on Entering a Room Full of Strangers*. Englewood Cliffs, N.J.: Prentice-Hall/Spectrum, 1981.

G. Phillips, *Communicating in Organizations*. New York: MacMillan Publishing Co., 1982.

C. Weaver, *Human Listening*. Indianapolis: Bobbs-Merrill, 1972.

J. Wilson and C. Arnold, *Public Speaking as a Liberal Art*. Boston: Allyn and Bacon, 1974.

J. Wood, *Human Communication: A Symbolic Interactionist Perspective*. New York: Holt, Rinehart and Winston, 1982.

5

THE NATURE OF HUMAN RELATIONSHIPS

What is the nature of human relationships? How would you describe them? The obvious response is that human relationships consist of two or more *individuals*. We're certainly not about to argue with that idea, but it's not a complete response. It doesn't explain very much.

We could try again and say that human relationships consist of individuals linked by *communication*. This improves on the first definition because it specifies how persons form relationships—through their communication.

As individuals communicate, they create something new—a relationship. The relationship is both formed by communication and defined by communication. That is, the individuals come together by communicating with one another, and what happens to them thereafter is the result of their communication.

To complete our definition we need to add two more features:

social systems and time. Both individuals and communication exist in *social systems* that influence how humans come together and how they present themselves to the world. Finally, to emphasize the process character of human relationships, we add the dimension of *time* to our view of relationships. Now the definition is that human relationships consist of individuals linked and defined by communication within social systems, all of which change over time.

Social systems constantly change. Thus, relationships that exist in social systems must change to accommodate the changes around them. The people who make up a relationship also change, and the relationship must accommodate that also. Relationships are subject to constant influences from the society outside and the individuals inside. One test of a good relationship is its ability to deal constructively with changes. Many relationship failures result from the inability of the relationship to adapt to change. Please note the interesting paradox: individuals change constantly, but sometimes they refuse to accommodate their own changes by permitting changes in their relationships. More about this later. Your own experiences should convince you that both you and your social milieu are constantly changing, and you must adapt to sustain yourself and your associations with others.

Now our definition has dynamic quality appropriate to the nature of human interactions. This definition fits virtually all of our casual to friendly relationships, but it does not capture the more specialized nature of intimate relationships which extend beyond our ordinary social relationships. To define intimacy we must recognize the private world developed by people who wish to become enduring partners in a very special way. We refer to this private world as a *relational culture* because it is unique, carefully tailored to the particular values, goals and identities of intimate partners. A relational culture is created as a pair of individuals communicate intensely to move beyond public norms to a special arrangement in which partners acquire and use dual perspective to deal with each other as unique individuals. In its ideal state it meets the partners' needs that are not accommodated in the general realm of interaction. It grows out of the transactions and the rules that the partners develop as they communicate over time. In this chapter we will examine each of these features in detail. Our goal is to make you aware of influences that shape and stimulate change in interpersonal relationships, and to show you how communication is used both to negotiate what changes are desirable and to bring about those changes. The five elements we've identified provide a comprehensive, yet economical description of human relationships.

Individuals

The structure and content of any relationship reflect the personalities, values, and goals of the individuals who form it. To analyze how individuals tailor relationships, we will consider how people define themselves and how these definitions establish standards for their relationships.

Self-definitions

The way people define themselves directly affects their choices of interaction and transaction partners, as well as their behavior toward other people in general.

A woman who views herself as highly independent may seek few contacts and may abandon relationships that even minimally constrain her autonomy. A man who defines himself as dominant may choose to interact only with people who will defer to him and may bail out of any relationship that threatens his self-image of power. Individuals who see themselves as liberated from traditional sex roles may seek romantic partners with congruent self-images. People who see themselves as rising superstars in their professions may emphasize interaction with others who can further their climb to the top and may avoid people who cannot assist their careers. We seek people who confirm our self definitions and avoid those who might challenge our self-images.

Josie K. They say dorm life is a "learning experience," and I'll vouch for that. I've learned a lot about myself by living in this dorm for the past year. When I first got to campus, I got my room assignment and went up to see who I'd be living with. Well, la de da, Miss Big City Sophisticate was my room-mate. I'm from a farm and my family doesn't have money—like, I'm only here because of two loans and a small scholarship. Denise and I just did not get along. She put down my clothes (I made them myself), and I thought that she was really stupid to spend what she did buying clothes. She made jokes about me because I dated "dormies" while she was going out with the members of the best fraternities. She wouldn't even consider dating men who were not in either one of the top two frats or on the basketball team. That's just the beginning. Denise and I disagreed on just about everything you could imagine—why we were in school, what we wanted out of life—everything. Anyway, we learned to avoid each other. Talking just created hassles. But I made friends with two other people in my suite. One of them is from a farm in another state and the other is a big mover in 4-H. We have a lot in common and I like spending time with them.

Self-definitions influence more than initial choices. They reverberate throughout human relationships. Because people communicate to gain confirmation of their identities, the first step in building a relationship is to negotiate roles. They must agree on who they are in relation to each other before they can create a workable relationship. If they cannot negotiate mutually satisfactory roles, they usually abandon the idea of serious involvement. If they are forced to interact, they tend to limit their association as much as possible because it is uncomfortable when roles remain unsettled and unsettling.

When individuals confirm each other and reach agreement on who they are in relation to each other, they have a minimum social relationship. Because they have defined who they are in relation to one another, they know how to act towards each other. As long as they continue to confirm each other, they can sustain a relationship. But things are not always so simple. If one person projects an altered identity or a new aspect of self to the other, then negotiation begins anew. Sometimes it is easy to adjust to identity changes. We may even welcome them. At other times we may reject a redefinition because it compels us to redefine ourselves in ways we may find unacceptable or threatening.

Alex R. In my family dad was always the authority figure. That was all he knew how to be. He made all of the family decisions and ran all of our lives. For the first two years I was in college dad would veto certain courses I wanted to take and he told me what organizations to join and all that. What's really amazing is that I let him. I guess old patterns are hard to break and I'd spent 18 years following his orders without question. Dad had told me to major in Business because there would be a market for me there. So I started that curriculum, and I did okay in it.

The only problem was I didn't like it, and the more courses I took, the more I knew I didn't want to spend my life in that field. So I braced myself for an explosion and went home to tell dad. At first, like always, he didn't listen to me. He just told me he knew best and I should stick with Business. Then I told him I wasn't asking his advice or permission—I was telling him that I was not going to major in Business. Well, I was pretty sure the roof was going to cave in on me, but we wound up having the first real conversation we'd ever had. Since that talk four months ago I'd have to say we have an entirely different relationship. It's like dad now sees me as an adult and he respects my right to make my own decisions. We argue, sure, but now he's more like a friend than a dictator.

Unilateral redefinition of relationships presents serious problems. It is very difficult to sustain a relationship if only one person seeks to redefine its focus radically. We may feel secure in a friend-ship with someone who would be unthinkable as a romantic part-ner. If the other person seeks to change the relationship to a sexual liaison, we could easily be scared off. The reverse is also true. It is extremely difficult to redefine what has been a serious dating rela-tionship as "just friends." Some satisfactory marriages fall apart when the birth of children requires the couple to redefine the rela-tionship as a family. By the same token, some marriages come apart when the children leave home and the definition of family no longer fits.

Janet N. A lot of people think it's strange that we divorced after 22 years and three children. To tell the truth, I wouldn't have predicted a breakup even five years ago, and neither would Herb. Everything seemed fine as long as the family stayed together. Then four years ago our oldest went to college, and we missed him, but were still okay. The next year the twins left for school, and that's when the problem became clear. Herb and I had nothing to talk about unless there was a letter from one of the kids or something we needed to deal with regarding them or the house. I'd come to see him as a very fine father and us as a good family, but I didn't see him as a close friend or a lover. He felt the same way about me—I was a mother, not his companion and lover. Maybe we had kids too soon after marrying and never really established ourselves as a twosome. All I know is that when it was just the two of us living together after all those years with the kids, there wasn't enough there to sustain the marriage.

We cannot assume individuals will remain the same when their relationships change. Dating partners differ from friends; lovers dif-fer from dating partners. People change as they change the defini-tion of their relationship because a relationship consists of individ-uals *in relation to one another*. When the nature of the relationship alters, there will be corresponding changes in each person's percep-tion of and attraction to the other. And, as the individuals change the way they define themselves, the relationship must either change to accommodate them, or come apart.

Individual standards for relationships

A second way in which individuals influence relationships is through the standards they use to evaluate interaction. It is useful to think of two broad types of standards: one for overall involvement and one for specific relationships.

Each individual has a standard for overall involvement. We can think of it as a basic "quota" for relationships. Some of us enjoy having a great many friends while others prefer only a few. Some people like to juggle several dating relationships simultaneously while other people focus on one at a time. While individuals vary in their preferences, each of us tries to maintain whatever is standard for us. How well-satisfied a person is about his or her present relationships influences his decisions about forming new relationships. If you are satisfied by the company of your current friends, you're unlikely to seek additional contacts actively. On the other hand, if you've just moved, leaving behind all of your friends, you might be especially receptive to new associations. The "rebound phenomenon" illustrates this point. The end of an intense relationship may create a void in the life of each partner, which may motivate a quest for other intense relationships.

We all have some level of relationships with which we are comfortable. Two few or too many make us uneasy. How well our quota is met at a given time influences our interest in new relationships. You might pause here for a moment and think about your own quotas. How many friends do you want? How many close relationships can you handle comfortably? How do your job and your current interests affect your desire to meet new people?

People often misjudge their ability to handle relationships. Most of us cannot handle very many close relationships at one time. They take great commitment and constrain involvements with other people and activities. Furthermore, we can only handle a reasonable amount of emotional commitment. Trying to manage too many close relationships can be very exhausting.

In addition to standards for overall involvement, each of us has standards to judge specific relationships. The social psychologists, Thibault and Kelly tell us we assess relationships by first comparing them to a subjective standard that is called a *Comparison Level* (CL). Our CL is based on our previous personal experiences in relationships as well as on our observations of others' relationships. The CL specifies what we can expect of an "average" relationship and how we identify good and bad relationships. The CL is a continuum which enables us to decide on the quality of each of our relationships. A person with considerable experience in rewarding, confirming relationships will have a high CL and, thus, will set high standards for an acceptable relationship. Someone who has experienced and observed unsatisfactory interactions will have a much lower CL and will have lower expectations for an acceptable relationship. Therefore, a relationship that one person considers excellent might be judged mediocre by another individual with a higher CL. Because the CL is based on accumulated experiences, it tends to be fairly stable. A single relationship has limited long term effect on the CL.

Ricky C. At first I just couldn't figure Stan out. I mean this guy went through more women in one semester than most guys do in four years of college. And I don't mean average women either.

I've never seen him with someone who didn't have a dynamite personality and knock-out looks. Like I said, at first I couldn't understand why he kept dumping these super women. Then I got to thinking about Stan. He's good looking, smart without trying, smooth, rich as the devil, and a hell of a nice guy on top of all that—one of those people who has everything going for them. I guess if I had that much on the ball I would be more choosy and I'd be used to the kind of women he chooses from. I think I could get used to his style.

The CL helps us judge the possibilities of relationships. Because we are able to decide on the quality of our relationships, we can make choices about what we do with whom, and when. But the CL alone does not completely explain our choices of which relationships to continue, which to intensify, and which to cast aside. Each of us probably knows people who cling to relationships that do not measure up to the CL's, while others end relationships that meet or even exceed their CL's in the hope of finding something even better. Their sense of risk may amaze us. It is very hard to understand how other people see the social world. Thus, while the concept of comparison levels is a useful starting point in explaining relationship behavior, it doesn't answer all questions.

According to Thibault and Kelley there is a second standard called the *Comparison Level of Alternatives* (CL_{alt}). It measures the worth of a particular relationship *relative to* currently available alternatives. Unlike the CL, the CL_{alt} is not necessarily stable. It varies according to situation and the visible options to existing relationships at a particular time.

Furthermore, there is no necessary connection between an individual's CL and CL_{alt}. Suppose that Jim and Dena have been dating for three months and he thinks she is the most intelligent, interesting and attractive woman he's ever dated. This relationship clearly exceeds Jim's CL. Then an even more engaging woman named Shelley enters the scene and seems interested in Jim. Suddenly Jim's CL_{alt} shifts dramatically. Though the relationship with Dena was more than satisfactory until now, Jim responds to Shelley by asking her out and thus ends the relationship with Dena. Jim sacrificed the known relationship to gamble on a higher potential. If things don't work out with Shelley, Jim might be willing to accept a relationship considerably less satisfying than the one he had with Dena, because of the altered CL_{alt}. CL_{alt} refers to all alternatives to a given relationship including the option of no relationship at all. Sometimes independence is the most desirable of all options.

The balance between CL and CL_{alt} may tip the other way, leading us to stay in an unsatisfactory relationship because there is nothing better around. To illustrate, let's look at a friendship between Mark and Cary who both joined the Conarton Supply Company at the same time. The friendship began naturally enough as an alliance between two men who were close in age and who were new to the company. Cary finds Mark rather boring and far too conservative politically, so the friendship fails to meet his CL. However in the small town where Conarton is based there are few young people and those who are there tend to be even more conservative than Mark. Therefore, Cary's CL_{alt} is lower than the quality of the relationship with Mark and he will stay in this basically unsatisfactory friendship because it is the best available possibility. If a more liberal person moves into town, Cary's CL_{alt} will change and he may not try so hard to maintain a friendship with Mark.

Each of us uses CL and CL_{alt} to guide our choices of whether to maintain, intensify or reduce our investment in various relationships. The concepts of CL and CL_{alt} may seem like rather harsh and mechanical ways of viewing human relationships. However, substantial research testifies to the fact that most people do indeed use these standards consciously or unconsciously in their decisions about interpersonal involvements.

Relationships reflect the individuals who build them. Their self-definitions shape the kinds of relationships they seek. Their experience guides them to set standards by which they judge their relationships. This in turn influences their choices about whether to stay put or to seek new arrangements. Through our self-definition and our standards for judging relationships, we define the range and type of relationships we form.

Social Systems

The second element in our definition of relationships is social systems, the context within which relationships develop. Social systems include our acquaintances, friends, neighbors, families, organizations, and professions. These are sometimes referred to as "reference groups." To belong to such systems, we must abide by the values and styles of behavior of the other people in them. Our participation in social systems shapes the public part of our identity. They both shape our public social activity and provide us with people from whom we can choose our private relationships. We will examine the impact of social systems on our individual development and then explore the ways in which they affect our interpersonal relationships.

The way we interact with society is complex. Although each of us is unique, we are also members of a shared culture. Through interaction with others we develop common beliefs and ways of thinking and behaving. Thus, our individual thought and action reflect "social overtones." Through years of social interaction we learn the rules and values of our society, and consequently, how to operate within it. In this sense, society teaches us to be human. Yet, we are more than social robots who refelct unthinkingly the cultural values to which we are exposed. We are individuals with unique experiences and perspectives; therefore, we sometimes interpret and respond to society in unpredictable ways.

The interaction between individuals and society was a primary concern of George Herbert Mead, one of the most provocative social theorists of this century. After years of thought about the delicate mix between individuality and socialization, Mead postulated that the human self has two complimentary aspects: the *I* and the *Me*. The *I* is the individual, unique self. It is not constrained by social conventions and expectations. The *I* is spontaneous, creative and impulsive, seeking to maximize pleasure and to reduce pain. The *I* responds to impulses of the moment and generates attitudes and actions independent of society. It is mostly expressive in its tendencies. It can be brash and careless, just as it can be innovative and imaginative. The *I* serves an important purpose, but it needs to be disciplined.

The ME aspect of self grows out of interaction with peers.

The second aspect of self is the *Me,* or the social self. The *Me* is the internalized attitudes of society. The *Me* understands and respects social constraints; it recognizes norms of behavior in situations and acknowledges the values and goals of others. The *Me* is reflective, analytical, deliberative, and socially sensitive. The *I* guides the *Me*'s goal seeking in social interaction. The *Me* controls the demands of the *I* to make them realistic in the light of social constraints. If we had only the *I,* we would be narcissistic and unrestrainedly impulsive. When the *I* is ascendant, we tend to want more than our fair share, we are not realistic in our assessments of situations, and we do not employ dual perspective in relation to others. The *Me* protects us by reminding us what is possible and acceptable in the social world. But if we had only the *Me,* we would be gray flannel imitators of the social norms with personalities like flavorless gelatin. The *I* and the *Me* complement each other. When the *Me* gains excessive ascendancy over the *I,* we are less effective in our personal and social goal-seeking. By integrating the *I* and the *Me,* we balance our public and private personalities.

The dialogue between the *I* and the *Me* can lead to sensitive awareness of social cues and subtle personal adjustment to maximize the supportive quality of private relationships. The skill that the *Me* cultivates in sensing proper responses from society-at-large can be applied to the intense task of sensing the needs and interpreting the responses of an intimate partner. As each partner's *I* adjusts to what the *Me* reports, the couple builds a mutually satisfying relational culture.

Andy G. Sometimes my mouth gets ahead of my brain. They don't call me "motormouth" for nothing! You know what I mean—I say something before I really think about it or how it will come across to someone else. Sometimes I come up with something pretty funny, like a wise-crack or real good come-back. That's okay I think, because it makes people laugh and nobody gets hurt or anything. But there are other times when I make someone feel bad because of something I say without thinking or because I let my temper take over. Like the other night my girl and I were having an argument and it got heated and I started fighting dirty. Then before I thought about it I said to her, "that's about what I'd expect from someone whose father is a mill-worker." Holy mackerel, I know how sensitive she is about that, and I didn't mean to say it. I just didn't control the impulse to strike back in the fight. I wish I could take that back, because I know it really hurt her a lot.

The *Me* can be thought of as an internalized, interpreted composite of all of our interactions with society; it represents our interpretation of the values, rules, meanings and expectations held by others in general. The *Me* picks up on the values of others, then reports them back to the *I* to figure out how to synthesize *I*'s goals with *Me*'s knowledge of social conventions. The *Me* is our *internalized understanding* of the social world at large. Even in a private relationship, the *I* must call on the social skills of the *Me* to be properly considerate of an intimate partner. When we build a private, intimate relationship, the *Me* must focus intensely on the goals and concerns of our partner.

There are no parts of the body or mind called the *I* and the *Me*. They are metaphors that help us understand how people make their choices and act on them. Mead believed we are not born with social awareness so he studied the process by which the individual is socialized. Social awareness is acquired through interaction with others. We learn what it means to be human, to think and act in human ways within a given society. As we interact with others we acquire an understanding of the social world and our own place within it.

For most of us the first and most significant context of social learning is our families. Our families help us acquire basic values about a range of attitudes. We learn what life goals are respectable, how much material wealth counts, how much value to attach to education, social status and appearance, and so forth. Our families teach us our first interpersonal values by word and deed: from them we acquire our basic attitudes about how couples should interact, the importance of monogamy, the place of children in a family, appropriate behavior for men and women, how children are to be raised, and what makes a "happy family." In short, families provide an initial design for interpersonal relationships. Our families give us our first sense of who we are. If our families treat us lovingly, we learn we are worthy of love. If parents tell us we are bright, we come to think of ourselves that way.

Gina R. In my family we learned early that "idle hands are the devil's playground." I mean we were expected to stay busy, to do things. Laziness was a capital crime as far as my folks were concerned. I still feel that way too. I just don't respect people who loaf around or who get by with as little work as possible. I like to be around productive people.

If parents imply we are constantly in the way, we come to view ourselves as unwanted. If they ignore our ideas and efforts in school and emphasize our physical attractiveness, we learn to regard appearance as more important than other aspects of ourselves. From our families' attitudes toward us, we learn how to act toward ourselves.

Randall W. The name of the game is winning. Good guys finish last. It's not how you play the game, it's whether you win. My dad drummed this into me since I was a kid. Even in pick-up games with my friends, dad pushed me to win, to compete, to drive, drive, drive. Now I see everyone else as competition. I'm afraid to trust someone or to get really close, because then they'd have a hold on me or something. God, I'm tired of doing combat with everyone I meet. Sometimes I think I'll change my attitude and so I try to consider someone as an ally or friend, but then I hear dad's voice in my head saying "If you don't step on them, they'll step on you. Look out for Number 1." I wonder if I'll ever break out of this.

Once our families teach us how to distinguish between good and bad, we enter into interactions with peers in school and in the neighborhood. Initially we carry our ideas about our identity to other children, and through interaction with them we find out how we measure up. Contact with peers becomes centrally important to our social development. We constantly compare ourselves to peers (our families often help with their comparisons, although sometimes we are not comparing ourselves to the same peers). Various standards, such as grades, social competency, possessions, where we live, whether we were picked first or last or whether we did the picking, appearance, talent, whether we travel in the right social circles, and athletic prowess can all be comparison points. So can negative qualities, like ability to break the law. Our cliques control many of our behaviors: so do the media. As children, we are especially responsive to the behavior of others; the *Me* gets so much exercise that it sometimes seems as if the *I* has retired early.

The adolescent years are particularly important. Harry Stack Sullivan advises that at this age, it is crucial to find peers whom we can trust so that we can validate ourselves and our ideas. During adolescence, we try out different roles, observe how others respond, and decide which roles to keep. We learn what others regard as our strengths and weaknesses. When we begin dating, we find a whole new set of criteria for judging ourselves: Do others respond to our indications of interest? Do we get asked out as often as our peers? Do our invitations get rejected too often? Do we ask out or get asked out by the "right" people? We learn whether we are desirable as women and men.

When we fail to make the transitions, our relationships are unsuccessful. Adults who retain the *Me* dominance characteristic of adolescence are social "chameleons," ready to be anything anyone wants. Worse, if a person's *Me* only imitates, but does not understand the needs and wants of others, that person can become socially exploitive. Crime, addiction, the urgency for power and other psychopathic orientations are the result of the inability to make the transition to a dual perspective that guides *Me* respectfully in its attention to others.

Interaction with peers never ends. We learn in adolescence that we must have people to validate us. It is important to form a few close friendships so we have a reliable source of information on how well we are doing in the world of interaction. Our public choices may vary as we move from group to group. We may emphasize athletics with one group, intellectual accomplishment with another, but somewhere along the way, we have to be close enough to someone to get information about how we are doing.

To interact successfully requires the ability to discover what is proper and improper in any given situation. You need not enter a situation if you feel uncomfortable about what is going on, but you cannot demand that the people engaged in interaction adjust to your biases. The situation is just the reverse in transaction. There, two people can develop what is most comfortable for them, and if they wish to stay together, they must both cooperate in changing.

Leigh M. Coming to college was a real downer for me. I'd been pretty big in my high school—president of my class, voted most likely to succeed, you know the whole success bit. Do you know what that amounts to here? Zilch! The big zero. My roommate is a National Merit Scholarship winner. The guy down the hall was class valedictorian. His roommate is an English major who already published a short story. Around here everyone is big stuff, which means everyone is nobody. I talked to my advisor about all of this once and she told me that I had to consider the fact that in my high school class there were 300 people in all and the freshman class here is about 2,500. I guess that makes sense, but it doesn't help a whole lot.

As we change the people with whom we interact, we alter the basis for judging ourselves. Interaction with others is the primary way we become socialized and refine our *Me*. Public norms provide us with information about how society operates in general as well as information about what people expect from others. Interaction is the way we find out what society values and how to act effectively in the world. From our interactions, Mead tells us, we generalize a sense of *other*. This *generalized other* represents our overall understanding and it guides how we behave in the public world. In addition to *generalized other*, we also draw information from significant *others*, people whose opinion we prize highly and whose support we seek. These plus our personal goals represent the tools with which the *I* and the *Me* work as they make decisions about our public and private behavior. We refer to our society to examine goal possibilities. Our evaluation of who is successful gives us a sense of strategy. Our sense of *other*, our dual perspective, informs us of the specific ways we can approach and deal with the people important to us. Thus, our public behavior is regulated in a relatively orderly way. In Mead's words, society has "gotten into" us. The *generalized other* represents our synthesis of the views modeled by the people with whom we interact. This informs us of acceptable ranges for our own behaviors in interpersonal settings.

The particular segment of society in which we participate helps us define our values. The great anthropologist, Wynne-Edwards, noted that humans are unable to deal with large numbers of their own kind. Roughly 1600 people was about all he felt we could handle. When our community gets too large to handle we become suspicious. We create an *us* and *them* dichotomy. We need a manageable segment of society in which to relate. Thus, we try to locate ourselves in manageable units; neighborhoods, clubs, social interest groups, cliques, work groups, teams. Those groups help us identify *us* and *them*. Once we discover who *us* is, we can get on with shaping our values. Some people develop their values after they have identified *us* and some seek a group that has values similar to theirs, with which it is convenient for them to affiliate.

Each of us reflects the social systems of which we have been part. Sometimes the reflection is positive; our values and those of the social group concur. Sometimes we shape our values so that they differ from groups or people we oppose. Normally, we do not like to think about enemies, but during our lives most of us will offend and injure at least a few people. Some of them will find us so distasteful that they will actively seek to hurt us. Other people, in groups of *them*, may dislike us because of our race, religion, or national origin, or because we affiliate with a group they oppose. We learn to adjust to this kind of hostility and to work with our ideas and values so that they do not bring us into the horrible dissonance of believing the things the "enemy" believes.

We communicate to make both friends and enemies. By communicating with others we define ourselves as members of specific groups in society, select transaction partners, and, at times, defines who our enemies are. Through communicative interaction we come to appreciate the viewpoints of specific *others*, various groups, and eventually society as a whole. Our relationship goals and the strategies we use to achieve them echo the social values that we have encountered as well as the unique aspects of our selves. Our social systems constrain our interpersonal attitudes and choices, and conversely, our personal choices shape broad social values. Thus, our individuality exists side-by-side with our social nature. The *I* and the *Me* become collaborators as we attempt to accomplish personal goals without violating social codes.

Communication

Communication is the lifeblood of human relationships. To explain the centrality of communication, we will discuss its two primary functions in interpersonal settings: defining relationships and coordinating interaction and transaction.

Communication defines relationships

We communicate to define ourselves and our relationships with others. Sometimes all that is needed is a general label like student or teacher, best friend, fiance, wife or husband, father and daughter. Conventional terms guide how we behave in the most public circumstances. We actually develop repertoires of standard behaviors which we can use in public, almost without thinking. But it is our private relationships that provide us with our most important and most emotional social sustenance. General labels do not define the personal values and unique behaviors of particular individuals on which private relationships depend. So we need additional ways of indicating who we are in relation to others.

Researchers who have studied the ways we use communication to define our identities in relationships refer to two levels of messages exchanged. The first level, called *content*, refers to information, the literal meaning of what is said. The second level, called *relationship*, tells us how to interpret the first level by defining how the communicator sees himself or herself and the person addressed. The second level defines each person to the other—the relationship.

These two levels co-exist in all interpersonal messages. For example, when Bob tells Marian "I'll pick you up at 6 on Friday. We'll grab a pizza at Jeno's, then take in the new Cheech and Chong movie. Dress casual," the content level of this message provides information about the sequence of activities for an upcoming date. But there's more to Bob's message than just this information. On the relationship level, Bob's message says he decides what he and Marian will do. Thus, Bob defines himself as the primary decision-maker in the relationship. If Marian agrees, she accepts Bob's definition of where the power lies. On the other hand, Marian might say, "I'm tired of pizzas. Let's go to the Deli," or "I don't like Cheech and Chong. I'd rather take in Alan Alda's new flick," or "I've got a late student government meeting, so I can't be ready before 7." The content level of these messages is simple. On the relationship level, however, Marian's messages argue that Bob does not have absolute control over what happens. The problem of working out rules for decision making is important in every relationship. So is the method of resolving the conflict that takes place in this negotiation. Bob and Marian need to work out how things are to be done. If Bob is used to getting his own way, Marian's unwillingness to accept his direction might set off a conflict between them. Attention to content and relationship levels in communication helps both participants and observers figure our what is going on in a relationship.

We can identify content and relationship levels in most of our communication. If a husband tells his wife, "You're spending too much on groceries. Cut down the excess," then he claims the right to decide on the budget. The statement implies that groceries are the cause of whatever financial problem they are having (not his membership at the Spa or his football tickets). If, however, he says, "we are running a little short this month; we need to figure out what to cut," then he defines his role as "investigator" and defines his wife's role as co-investigator suggesting the two of them should jointly define the problem and its solution. Some authorities classify relationships as complementary and symmetrical. A complementary relationship is one where one party has authority to direct the behavior of the other. In a symmetrical relationship, both parties are relatively equal in decision-making.

Relative symmetry is implied by a supervisor who says to a line worker "Production seems to be dropping. Maybe we should try to find out why." By contrast, a supervisor signals a complementary relationship by saying, "Production is down and I expect you to solve the problem fast!" In each case the content of the communication has to do with a problem, but the relationship comment is quite different. Very often the relationship level consists of nonverbal communication that affects our interpretation of verbal messages.

Donna F. I avoid my advisor like the plague. I get super uncomfortable anytime I try to talk to that man. It's not so much what he says that bothers me. I mean, he knows all the information about requirements and all that stuff. But I always get the feeling that he doesn't have time for me. He glances at his watch, drums his fingers on the desk, even looks out the window sometimes. If a phone call comes while I'm there, he takes it and just lets me wait. Once he was on the line for eight minutes while I sat there—I timed him! I feel that I'm taking up too much of his time or like he's just too high and mighty important to be bothered with me. That's the real message that comes through, and I don't need it.

We define ourselves differently in various relationships. We seek to convince our professional associates of our competence and authority, our social friends of our wit and friendliness, our followers of our leadership ability, and our intimates of our trustworthiness, fidelity and affection. We use our communication to define ourselves to others, to tell them who we think we and they are. This process requires extensive communication. People may negotiate about definitions at some length and may renegotiate definitions over time. Both parties must agree about each other, or a serious relationship cannot be sustained.

Communication coordinates interaction and transaction

In addition to defining relationships, communication coordinates the process within them. People are not automatically synchronized in their understandings and behavior patterns. Each of us has preferred ways to organize our own time and activities, characteristic response styles to topics, other people and situations, and specialized ways to show our feelings and assert our wants. If two individuals want a workable relationship, each must learn how to interpret the other. Together they must coordinate themselves into a functional unit.

They do this by communicating. They talk with each other to learn how they define themselves, what they believe, and how they behave. Initial conversations may be superficial, but as a relationship develops, people seek keener insights about each other. After a while they begin to understand each other's unique ways of thinking and acting. They develop a dual perspective and work out ways to accommodate to each other. The relationship takes on its character from their adaptations. They will eventually learn to predict each others' responses with relative accuracy.

It is rare to achieve genuine dual perspective. It comes only after a great deal of time, and it requires intense commitment by both partners. In most of our relationships we only get a glimmer of the other's point of view. This is sufficient for casual social coordination. However, in our most intense relationships we gain substantial insight into our intimates' ways of thinking and acting as a result of extended communication. We simply do not have the time and energy (or the need) to work out such closeness with everyone we meet. That is why we rely on the norms of interaction to carry us through our public contacts, and we confine our transactions to only a few people for whom we care a great deal.

Dual perspective is the foundation of coordinated transaction. We must first comprehend another's viewpoint before we can take it into account in planning our own communication. In intimate relationships, for example, each partner must understand how the other bestows affection and what she or he would recognize as affection. They must learn to recognize invitations, demands, put-offs, and rejections. They need to know what constitutes a betrayal, and how reconciliations can take place. This does not come easily; until we achieve this information, it is difficult to coordinate our activities properly. Many potentially good intimate relationships come apart prematurely because the partners did not take long enough to exchange important information that would have increased dual perspective.

Time

Time is the fourth feature of human relationships. Time is the format we use to describe changes in relationships, individuals, social systems and communication. Time makes very little happen, but it is a convenient way of looking at what does happen.

Time and individuals

Although it is obvious, it is nonetheless important to realize that individuals change over time. Age not only changes them physiologically but their experiences expand their repertoires of choices. Their self-definitions alter according to those with whom they relate. Young people often have difficulty getting a picture of themselves because they simply do not have enough experience to test themselves. As people encounter new groups and new values they expand the choices they can make about who they would like to be. When we are young, we are likely to define ourselves by our peers, what we own, and how we look. Beyond adolescence, we are more likely to define ourselves in terms of intended careers and life plans. Our self-definitions can be classified into long term and short term. "I want to be a useful, productive person," would be a long term definition. "I want to have fun tonight," would be short term. Long and short term definitions need to be generally compatible so that each small goal contributes to accomplishment of the broad one.

Our choices change to accommodate changes in objectives. People we found devastatingly desirable in high school may leave us cold seven years down the line. Conversely, those people we care most about right now might not have rated a second thought a few years back.

Many people redefine themselves in their middle years. When this happens, established relationships may no longer be viable. A dramatic illustration of this is the impact of the Women's Movement on some women's views of themselves and their relationships. Prior to this movement, most women accepted traditional home-making and child-rearing roles, and defined themselves primarily in terms of their husbands and children (Mrs. Don Smythe; Alice's mother). Exposure to Feminist thought led many women to see other possibilities for themselves. They redefined themselves and adopted behaviors appropriate to the redefinition. But this made changes, often traumatic, in the relationships they had with the people around them. Often, the men in their lives could not accommodate the changes. They were having their own problems. The male mid-life crisis revolves around the discovery that he has not accomplished all he aspired to in his life. He begins to wonder if he had sacrificed some valuable opportunities for relationships. He may be tempted to experiment in ways that jeopardize his long-standing bonds. Women, particularly those who had devoted most of their lives to husband and family, wonder about what they could have done in the world of work. They may enter the work force and discover that they can make it. The entry of women as competitors into the work force frequently causes tension both on the job and at home.

Our standards for judging relationships also undergo changes as a result of time and experience. The basic comparison level (CL) becomes more stable as we accumulate experience in a range of relationships. We refine our basis for assessing the worth of relationships, having a more discriminating and more solid basis at age 35 than we did at 22. The CL_{alt} also changes as we see more alternatives. When the middle-aged housewife discovers that she can learn word-processing and get an interesting and lucrative job, her view of what might be satisfactory changes drastically. It may become more important to her to have some work associates than to play bridge and attend coffee klatches. By the same token, a man might discover that he had put too much energy into his work; he may seek a life change characterized by travel, creativity and interesting new experiences with his intimate partner.

The standards we use to judge relationships, particularly CL_{alt}, change as we mature. Consider the following:

Frances S. Why did I marry Alan? Very simple—I didn't want to spend my life alone and I got tired of waiting for someone better. Sure, now I wish I'd devoted more effort to some of the relationships I had in college with really interesting men, but somehow making the BIG commitment didn't seem important then. There were always so many men around that it never occurred to me that there wouldn't be later. Then I got a job with the state government. Well, you can just imagine how many exciting people work there. Most of them are older, almost all of them are married, except for the *real* losers. Same story in my apartment complex. There were a lot of couples that were married or living together and a few men that weren't attached, but I could see why! To be real honest, Alan was the only decent male I met in the two years after college. At first when he started getting serious, I put him off. I guess I was still hoping someone better would come onto the scene. After a while, however, I realized it probably wasn't going to happen, and life with Alan wouldn't be a bad deal at all. I know it's not very fashionable for a woman today to admit she feels the need to get married, and I wouldn't unless this were anonymous. But the truth of the matter is I did want to be married, I was 25 years old and Alan was the best bet.

Frances' choice to marry someone she might not have considered an acceptable partner a few years earlier is not necessarily a bad choice, if Frances and Alan are willing to make the relationship work. Some people may prefer not to marry rather than settle for what they consider an average match. The rise of singles clubs and bars, and the relatively new phenomenon of advertising for dates and mates testify to the fact that it's difficult to make contact after the socially intense years of 16 to 23. Some people have to choose between entering the public dating market and immersing themselves in other activities in order to find fulfillment in other ways.

Alternatives to particular relationships may be further limited by choices we've made along the line. The most obvious example is the impact of choosing to become parents. Two people who exchange their status as a couple for that of a family reduce their freedom to abandon the marriage. Divorce is a less attractive choice once children enter the picture. Thus, a parent may stay with a less than good marriage even when a more desirable potential mate is available. Without children that same person might risk exploration of relationships beyond the marriage. Every choice we make potentially constrains choices we will be called upon to make later, exactly as every choice we make provides us with a new set of alternatives from which to choose.

None of us are the same as we were even a few months ago. A year from now, we will be different. The basic principle is that there is no way to escape the necessity to respond to change. Attempts to keep things as they always were are non-productive at best and neurotic at worst. We have pointed out before, and we will remind you again, that many of the problems people have with their relationships arise from their inability to change effectively.

Time and social systems

Social systems and the way individuals fit within them also change over time. As people learn the values, rules, and techniques of interaction, they assume different positions within the structure. Furthermore, social codes and norms change. Each small social system is part of a broader society. The effect is reciprocal. Changes in small systems add up to changes in the society, and changes in the society affect the smaller systems. Public problems such as fuel shortages and high interest rates have an impact on interpersonal relationships.

America has undergone a major transformation in its values about social and intimate relationships in the last forty years. In the 1930s, the ideal family consisted of a strong father, a hard-working mother, and clean-cut kids. During the depression, the influence of the father waned. During World War II, fathers became heroes, and mothers entered the work force. After the war, mothers, fathers and children prized togetherness. In the turbulent 1960s, many fathers grew long hair and mothers carried their babies on their backs, while American youth experimented with drugs and sex. In the 1970s, men and women became competitors in the world of work; relationships diversified in forms ranging from cohabitation to renewable marriage contracts. In the 1980s—who knows? Single person households, relatively casual live-together relationships, serious commitments without formal marriages, homosexuality, open marriage, and communes, are all possibilities that really did not exist even ten years ago. No relationship can remain immune to these choices. In the final analysis, in a good relational culture, it is your intimate partner that keeps you alert to possibilities. Success at intimacy requires both enough idealism to identify alternatives and enough realism to know which alternatives are possible.

Elsie D. Things have really changed. Frank and I were married for 34 years before he died, and they weren't such good years either. We had money problems and personal problems. In fact, I often wished we hadn't gotten married, and I think Frank did too. But we never thought about divorce. It just wasn't something you did in my day. Now my son just left his wife. They'd only been married about two years, so I wonder if they really made an all-out effort to make it work. I asked my son and he said they hadn't made as much effort as they could have, but neither of them thought it was worth the effort to work that hard. If the marriage didn't work out on its own, they'd rather leave. So he moved out and he's doing fine now. So's his wife (or is it ex-wife during separation?) Neither seems to have had any real trouble adjusting. It was like a minor inconvenience to take care of the legal stuff and logistical matters. Well, all I know is that I couldn't have done that, but I'm not sure whether my way or theirs is better.

Our mobile society influences relationships.

If futurists like Alvin Toffler are correct, there will be even greater changes in family structure during your lifetime. We will all have to adjust to the changes as they come along, learning to modify our values, expectations and conduct to fit shifting social norms. You might find it instructive to talk with your parents—better yet, your grand-parents—about the changes they have witnessed in interpersonal values and behaviors.

Think for a moment about your own vision of family life. What do you anticipate? Do you intend to marry? If so, do you anticipate that both you and your spouse will pursue careers? How will mundane chores of home maintenance be managed? What about children? Would you open your home to your parents or those of your spouse? What if the marriage doesn't meet your expectations? Is divorce an option? Would you hesitate to marry someone who had been previously married? What about extra-marital relationships—would you consider these?

Now shift your focus for a moment and think about professional relationships you might form in the future. What kind of person would you seek as a colleague or partner? How will you go about forming allies in your profession? If you're male, do you have any reservations about being subordinate to a female? If you're female, can you see yourself supervising men? What do you want to achieve from your career? What kind of assistance will you require from others to achieve it? How will you go about getting that assistance? As you respond privately to these questions, ask how your parents might have responded at your age. You might ask your parents and grandparents these questions in past tense to find out how they've accommodated change. As the saying goes, people who will not learn from history are destined to relive it.

The change in sex roles is probably the greatest single social change in your lifetime. The views men and women have of themselves and each other have changed drastically. Women see possibilities that they would not have dreamed of ten or fifteen years ago. Men find themselves competing for jobs with 51% of the world that had been barred previously. As we write this chapter, Mary Cunningham, accused of using her sexual powers to become vice president of Bendix Corporation is now safely in her position as Vice President of Seagram's. Sandra O'Connor became the first woman on the U.S. Supreme Court. Despite an impressive record including *magna cum laude* graduation from Stanford and a mind well-respected by colleagues in the Arizona State Senate, O'Connor would never have been considered for this post five years ago. At the same time, the Equal Rights Amendment was defeated. By the time you read this book, the concluding lines to these chapters of history may well have been written, and they will become part of your life.

Men's roles, too, have changed greatly in the past decade. Most men now have more than a few women as colleagues—as professional equals. Furthermore, most men are married to working women. Few families can survive in a hard economy unless both members work. Marriage to working women materially alters social and sex life, and men and women find themselves taking on new responsibilities in order to sustain old arrangements. Problems of child care complicate the picture. Increased longevity means that it is harder to reach the top, and that there is a class of potentially deprived citizens who must be provided for. All of these changes affect our closest relationships as well as the broader social systems in which we live, and we must change to meet the new demands. Every public change places demands for accommodations on private relationships. Public changes, on the other hand, are responsive to changes made in private. Large social systems, after all, are made up of individuals and private relationships.

Time and communication

Both content and relationship aspects of communication change with time. We learn new skills about interacting in our various social systems, and we learn to adjust to necessary changes in our private relationships by changing the way we transact. A couple of examples should clarify this point. At most modern campuses mixers are a popular way to make new acquaintances. Off campus, singles bars and clubs fulfill a similar function. In both situations an individual may introduce himself or herself to strangers and no one regards this as pushy. Not so many years ago, formal introductions by a third party were the only socially approved means of meeting new people. Polite men did not approach young women without the assistance of some mutual acquaintance who could "properly" introduce them. And any woman who introduced herself to a man immediately earned a reputation as a brazen hussy! Even ten years ago "nice women" didn't call men and women didn't go out, especially on weekends, unless they had a male escort. Today most people consider it appropriate for women to invite men and for women to go out alone or with a group of female friends.

There are examples all around us of how communication has changed. A few years ago people did not discuss topics like pregnancy and venereal disease, even with their closest friends. Many people felt that the word was the thing, and that you could be corrupted by using bad words. Today, profanity is frequently used, and our media confront us with ordinary talk instead of the euphemistic conversation characteristic of movies and television in the 50's. The euphemisms that were once part of our vocabulary have passed from our speech. Women no longer get "in a family way." Four letter words are commonly used for sexual intercourse and excretion. The best proof of this claim is that most readers will not be shocked to find these topics printed here. The openness of our era encourages us to deal frankly with a range of topics that were once taboo. Intimates are often advised to talk about their sex lives, to tell each other what they like and want as well as what they don't like and don't want. Fifteen years ago discussion of these topics was exceedingly rare even between intimates. What is considered appropriate for communication changes with the times.

Carl G. I just don't know how to help my mom right now. I know she's going through menopause, but she won't talk about it to me. She won't even talk about it to dad and he gets really worried about her health. Sometimes when I'm home for a visit we'll be talking and all of a sudden mom's face will get really flushed and perspiration will break out and she'll stop talking and look faint. If Dad or I ask what's wrong, she says nothing is. I tried talking to Dad about this, but he says it's no use. She won't talk to him about her problems or tell him how he can help or anything. He says whenever he tries to bring up "the change" as he calls it, mom gets all flustered and embarrassed and tells him that's not a fit topic of conversation. So how can we help or even understand if she won't talk about it?

A second way in which time influences communication is in the form and content of talk over the lifetime of relationships. What we say and how we say it varies according to the level of intimacy in a relationship and, in turn, that level varies over time. In initial interactions communication tends to be superficial and rather formal, and its primary purpose is to gain and give information. As individuals become better acquainted their communication becomes increasingly informal and personal; it focuses more on feelings and somewhat delicate topics than it previously did, and it becomes considerably more coordinated since partners have learned how to deal with each other. When established relationships deteriorate, partners tend to return to an awkwardly formal, often guarded, style of communication. We will elaborate changes in communication over the lifetime of a relationship in the next chapter.

Time is an important, pervasive influence on human relationships. The temper of the times in which we live (what the philosophers called the *Zeitgeist*) profoundly affects how we define ourselves and the standards we use to evaluate our relationships. We are further influenced by our personal time-of-life since our self-definitions, and personal goals and standards change as we age and accumulate interpersonal experiences. Time is an important dimension of our relationship life. Though it does not exist as an independent element, it serves as a continuum which enables us to describe and evaluate the evolution of ourselves and our relationships.

So far we've considered four features of human relationships: individuals, social systems, communication and time. These four features combine and interact to shape our social relationships. We can examine our relationships and relationships in general by understanding the influence of each element and the consequences of their interactions with each other.

Yet, these four features do not fully explain one kind of relationship, intimacy. Our intimate relationships have features also found in our social relations, but because they are based on transaction, they have unique qualities about which generalizations cannot be drawn. We need a fifth element to understand the nature of our intimate relationships.

Relational Culture

Relational culture refers to a system of private understandings and identities worked out between partners in an intimate relationship. Sometimes the understandings are explicit and worked out consciously. Sometimes they are tacit agreements. They are transacted by the unique partners in the relationship. When we consider a relational culture we are actually considering an intimate relationship to be a mini-society, in which values, structure and ways of relating are worked out. Relational culture includes a definition of each partner, agreements on ways of making and executing decisions, a means of resolving disputes, a system of ceremonies and events, and a way of facing the world as a unit.

Intimate relationships are not just extensions of interaction. They are qualitatively different. They are designed to accommodate to the *I* of each of the partners. While some conventions from the broader society may be incorporated into a bond, they tend to be less central to the bond than transacted agreements. Relational culture refers to private understandings and codes of conduct beyond those characteristic of the social world at large. It is what intimates negotiate between themselves and for themselves. This private and individualized set of understandings is the basis of intimate relationships because it provides the partners with shared and individually adapted ways of thinking, acting and interpreting.

Relational culture is built by intimates communicating with each other. In intimate relationships, partners share personal thoughts, feelings, hopes, fears and dreams; in short, they reveal themselves to each other. In our interactions we find it necessary to keep a great deal private. In transactions, we reveal whatever is necessary to deal with the important content of the relationship and to understand each other's perspective. Generally, each partner reserves some private space, but the way this is done is also based on agreements between the two. Even communication in families is not as intense or individualized as that between intimate partners. Much of family life is governed by public norms of how mothers, fathers, sons and daughters ought to behave. But it is mother and father who provide, in their private transactions, the temper and tenor of the family. They create *common* understandings that guide specific actions within the private realm. Relational culture is private and unique. There are few generalizations possible about its content.

Merle B.   Our relationship is really something else. It's like we've created this private little world that's all our own and that nobody else can get into and disturb. I guess that's pretty important to both of us because we spend most of our time doing what other people tell us to on their territory. We both work about 20 hours a week in addition to full class-loads. At our jobs we have to take a lot of grief. To them we're just machines, there to produce for them. We have no freedom in our work and no personal recognition for doing our jobs well. That's why we put so much emphasis on the relationship. In it we do what we want and we make sure each other feels important and valuable. When we're together I know who I am and I know that who I am matters. That's a lot more than I know anywhere else.

A relational culture is constructed by individuals, but the reverse is also true. Once created by them, relational culture influences who they are and what they can do. It constrains the partners' range of appropriate behavior and thought. Just as the broad culture of a society guides our social behavior, so does the relational culture of intimacy regulate our private conduct. Relational culture must be dynamic if it is to accommodate to the changes in the partners and the world outside. There are constant features, but how these features are managed differs from relationship to relationship.

One of the hazards in trying to study intimacy is that we are tempted to use the language we use about public relationships to describe private ones. This simply cannot be done. We cannot say how people make decisions in their intimate relationships. All we can say is that every intimate relationship must have a way to make decisions. The same, of course, is true about carrying out and adjudicating decisions. We can count on every private relationship having a way to do it, but each way will be different from every other.

Relational culture has its most profound impact on partners' identities. If our selfhood grows out of our interactions, it must grow even more out of the intense, private transactions that characterize relational culture. Our quest for self-confirmation reaches its height in intimate relationships where our partner's evaluation of us carries immense weight. Disconfirmation by an intimate can be devastating, so the stakes are extremely high.

As we communicate with an intimate or potential intimate, we note which aspects of ourselves are confirmed and rejected and we learn what personal qualities are generally valued by our partner. Typically, if we value that person's esteem, we use these insights to assist our efforts to carve an identity that will be confirmed by the other person, and therefore, contribute to a viable relational culture. A woman who wishes to become intimate with someone who endorses an ethic of naturalism may give up make-up, change her style of dress, read up on organic gardening and become a vegetarian. A man who seeks intimacy with a politically active woman may increase his attention to current news analyses, join activist groups and find himself putting down others who take no interest in political affairs. As each individual tries out different dimensions of identity, the other responds with confirmation or rejection. Those aspects of self that are confirmed become part of the developing relational culture.

Our efforts to carve identity within bonds should not be seen as 'sell-outs' of who we really are. We lose our sense of self only if the quest for confirmation overrides other considerations so that we allow others to define us completely.

Communication with people very important to us can yield new insights into who we are or might become. We see ourselves from the perspective of an intimate and this gives us an altogether novel view. People who never thought of themselves as serious might see this unrecognized aspect of themselves if an intimate emphasizes it. Then they have the option to decide whether to develop that serious side further. If you never thought much about keeping in shape, becoming involved with someone committed to jogging and daily exercise might bring this option into prominence in your own life. Then you can try it out and see whether you wish to make physical fitness part of how you define yourself in the long-term. Communication with significant *others* makes us aware of choices for identity that we might not have recognized on our own. We can experiment with these possibilities to discover which ones we wish to weave into our self-definition and which ones really don't fit into the way we see ourselves.

Each of us has a broad range of real and potential abilities, interests, values and commitments, yet we realize only a small portion of these. We simply cannot develop all of our potentialities; we cannot define ourselves in all of the ways that are possible. So we narrow the range to concentrate on a limited number of potentialities. The responses of the people we regard as most important influence our choices the most. If we make a mistake about who we select as important, we may find ourselves changed in undesirable ways. If we do not find the rewards of our relationships satisfying, we have to consider alternatives such as renegotiating the rules or leaving.

Had you grown up with different friends, parents, and intimates, or had you lived in another country, you would be a much different person than the one you are today. Furthermore, because you never stop growing, who you become will emerge from your current and future choices of social and intimate contact. All of our relationships, especially intimacies, have far-reaching impact on our identities. Who we are and who we become, in turn, influence the evolution of the relational culture that bonds two intimates together.

Intimate involvements clearly increase our options for self-definition, because they make us aware of possibilities in ourselves. In this sense, intimacy expands choice. Yet, as we noted earlier, choice inevitably entails responsibility. Each decision we make forecloses our other choices. If you choose to be a lawyer, you cannot, without great effort, win the awards commonly given to an engineer. If you choose intense commitment to a career, you may have to forego being a parent. If you choose to carry on multiple casual romances, you may never win the rewards that come from an intense commitment. If you have children, you must attend to their growth and welfare and forego other tempting possibilities. Moreover, any choice you make will be constrained by the choices made by your partner in a relational culture. Intimacy implies that partners take each other into account in their choicemaking on virtually every level, including decisions about rights to privacy. In fact, the choice to form such a culture may be the most constraining force of all.

The intimate partners you select affect who you become. As you and a partner create your unique relational culture, you collaboratively define each other and your individual and joint goals. To the extent that you allow an intimate partner to influence how you define yourself, you remain committed to the relational culture. If you discover your partner's influence is unwelcome or is waning, or if you prefer influence from elsewhere, then you begin to disassemble your relational culture. Its rewards become fewer, its costs greater, and less effort will be devoted to preserving it.

Robin P. We'd been going together for two and a half years when we split. All of that time we had a lot in common—similar interests in music, books, even the same major. We were both middle-of-the-road politically and were somewhere between atheist and agnostic as far as religion was concerned. Then Bill started hanging around these people with the Campus Crusade for Christ. At first I kidded him about becoming a Jesus freak and he said, "no way." But the more time he spent with his Christian friends, the more he began to sound like them. He quit drinking and every now and then he'd preach to me that something I was doing wasn't "right," like he had a direct line to what was right. This kept up for several months and eventually I knew that he was really going Christian. At that point I said, "let's split up," and he didn't argue. I think both of us knew that we couldn't have a very solid relationship when we were so different in terms of our religious beliefs. Isn't it strange how well we got along though—I mean before he got involved with his Christian friends?

Relational culture is the hallmark of intimacy. Through intense and extended communication, partners create a shared world within which they feel secure and confirmed. Previously separate perspectives are blended together and supplemented to form common ways of thinking, acting and interpreting events and experiences. Over the lifetime of an intimate relationship, relational culture becomes increasingly central as an influence on individual and joint identities, attitudes, actions, and choices.

Chapter Summary

In this chapter we've explored the nature of human relationships by analyzing the features that comprise them. Four features that characterize social relationships are individuals, social systems, communication and time. As we examined these features it became clear that each one interacts with the others to influence the kinds of relationships we build and the people with whom we choose to build them.

To describe intimacy we added a fifth feature to the picture. Relational culture refers to the private understandings worked out by intimate partners to provide them with a unique perspective on themselves, their relationship and the issues that influence their lives. These five elements and their interrelations yield an organized way of thinking about the dynamics of human relationships. We will illustrate this in the following chapters as we discuss the evolution of intimate relationships.

REFERENCES: CHAPTER 5

L. Breger, *From Instinct to Identity*. Englewood Cliffs, N.J.: Prentice-Hall, 1974.

W. Lederer, *Marital Choices*. New York: W. W. Norton, 1981.

G. H. Mead, *Mind, Self, and Society*. Chicago: University of Chicago Press, 1934.

V. Satir, *Conjoint Family Therapy*. Palo Alto, Calif.: Science and Behavior Books, 1967.

G. Sheehy, *Passages: Predictable Crises of Adult Life*. New York: E. P. Dutton and Co., 1976.

J. Thibault and H. Kelley, *The Social Psychology of Groups*. New York: John Wiley and Sons, 1959.

A. Toffler, *Future Shock*. New York: Random House, 1971.

P. Watzlawick, J. Beavin, and D. Jackson, *Pragmatics of Human Communication*. New York: W. W. Norton, 1967.

V. Wynne-Edwards, "Self Regulating Systems in Populations of Animals," *Science*. 147. 1955.

6

BUILDING AND DEFINING HUMAN RELATIONSHIPS: THE GROWTH STAGES

Reflect on your own relationships for a moment. How did each one come about? How did it get started? What made you decide to continue it beyond the first "hello?" Why did you decide to keep some relationships fairly casual and to invest more heavily in others? What indicated to you that a particular relationship was getting serious? Can you predict which of your current relationships will become more intense, which less intense, which will stay about the same, and which will end altogether?

In this chapter, we will examine some of these issues and present ideas which will help you analyze how your relationships develop and change over time. We will consider how individuals choose how much to invest in their relationships and how communication influences the process of relational growth. To deal with these issues, we'll first introduce you to the notion that relationships evolve through a series of identifiable stages. We trace the progression from individual to commitment through five growth stages typical of many human relationships. Each stage represents progressively increased involvement. The final section of this chapter introduces some of the most common complications that can arise in developing relationships.

We invite you to test the material we present against your own experiences. See if you can identify stages of development through which your own relationships have passed. This may help you understand what is happening in your interpersonal life. The material in these chapters reflects both published research and the interviews we conducted to write this book. Some of these narratives (anonymous and revised) are presented to stimulate reflections on your own relationships. What we tell you may not apply precisely to your experience, but it should be close enough to guide your critical analysis.

Developmental Approaches

Developmental theories start with the assumptions everything changes over time, and that the changes in a later stage of development depend on what happened earlier. Thus, developmental theories deal with dynamic issues such as change, growth, and process. By applying a developmental approach to the study of interpersonal relationships, we will be able to see how people use communication to create and change their interpersonal relationships.

There are a number of theories about how humans change over time. Each of them makes the point that every stage of development is based on the stages that preceded it. Developmental theories are widely used to explain how people learn as well as how they form relationships, groups, societies, and governments. Piaget, for example, describes the development of thinking in the child, from simple to complex. J. D. Bernal discusses how societies become complicated as their technology improves.

The psychoanalysts have contributed a great many important ideas about human development. Alfred Adler explains the growth of the child starts with the perception of a difficulty that must be overcome. Next the child develops the personal courage to deal with it, and finally, the child learns that only by serving the social interest can he or she achieve personal goals. Sigmund Freud was biologically oriented. He described human growth as coming to sexual maturity by passing through oral, anal, phallic and latency stages. Erik Erikson advanced beyond Freud's stages. According to Erikson, individuals pass through eight stages of development: infancy (analogous to Freud's oral stage), early childhood (anal), play age (phallic), school age (latency), adolescence, young adulthood, adulthood, and old age. (Shakespeare offered seven stages for those of a literary mind.)

A more popular version of individual development is offered by Gail Sheehy in her book, *Passages : Predictable Crises of Adult Life*. Her work was based on the studies of Daniel J. Levinson, who pointed out that humans periodically encountered crises in their lives which required them to make major changes. Such important events as graduation, marriage, children, job advancement, menopause, for examples, seriously alter the way people relate to one another. These life changes have individual impact, but their ramifications are also felt in every relationship an individual carries on. Harry Stack Sullivan divided development into stages beginning with dependence on the parents, learning to respond to the requests of others, same sex affiliation, chumming and consensual validation, adolescence and young adulthood. He considered a person fortunate to get through the stages unharmed. Virtually all of the authorities seem to believe that if an individual fails to mature fully in a given stage, the result will be inept or neurotic behavior in the later stages. Our analysis of human relationships leads to the same conclusion. Virtually every troubled relationship is characterized by the inability of the couple to deal satisfactorily with previous stages.

A number of developmental theories focus on human relationships. Reiss describes the wheel of love, consisting of four stages of development in a love relationships: rapport, self-revelation, mutual dependency, and personality need-fulfillment. Davis, a practical sociologist, named his stages descriptively as follows: first encounters or pickups, acquaintanceship, familiarity, intimacy (coupling), work-it-outs, have-it-outs, make-it-works, and breaking-up. The importance of Davis' categories is that they focus on the problems experienced by people as they work to build and maintain relationships. First encounters, for example present people with such issues as, is the individual clear for a contact, or is there some other relationship that might get in the way. By focusing on problems, Davis suggests how communication might be used to work through the various stages.

Researchers in Speech Communication have proposed developmental approaches that illuminate the role of communication in relational growth. Knapp offers a comprehensive set of ten stages that describe both the development and deterioration of relationships. His first five stages describe a couple coming together: (1) initiating a relationship, (2) experimenting, (3) intensifying, (4) integrating, and (5) bonding. The second five stages describe a couple coming apart: (6) differentiating, (7) circumscribing, (8) stagnating, (9) avoiding, and (10) terminating.

Wood traces the process from being an individual to bonding to a return to individual in twelve steps. Individuals and couples are, of course, free to freeze their relationship in any of the stages. It is not inevitable that every relationship will proceed through all of them. We will review these here, and use them, subsequently, as a basis for our analysis of relationship development.

1. *Individual*—the person as she or he exists prior to the onset of a particular relationship.
2. *Invitational Communication*—the individual uses communication to sample relationships with various people to see if they are promising.
3. *Explorational Communication*—a couple forms and talks to see whether or not they are compatible.
4. *Intensifying Communication* (euphoria)—the partners immerse themselves in each other and engage in intense communication about personal issues. Transactions begin.
5. *Revising Communication*—after euphoria wears off, the couple evaluates the relationship and begins to work out the practical details necessary to its continuation.
6. *Bonding Communication*—the couple commits to a future of sustained intimacy.
7. *Navigational Communication*—Partners work to keep their relationship solid as they deal with changes and routines.
8. *Differentiating Communication*—Each member of the couple seeks to individualize.
9. *Disintegrating Communication*—The relationship is in trouble, but the couple tries to avoid dealing with it.
10. *Stagnating Communication*—The members of the pair function as individuals because they can no longer work as a pair, yet their ties are not officially severed.
11. *Termination*—the couple comes apart, peacefully or otherwise.
12. *Individuals*—each member returns to separate existence, changed by participation in the bond.

There are some basic differences between Wood's and Knapp's stages, although some of them are similar. First, Knapp begins with initial encounters while Wood first considers individuals as they exist prior to initiating interaction. This enables us to examine the individual motivations that lead to the decision to seek relationships. Wood also includes two additional stages, revising and navigating. We will use Wood's stages as a basis for our subsequent discussion. We can now consider five premises that are common to all development perspectives.

PREMISE # 1: Human phenomena change qualitatively over time

This is a cornerstone of developmental thought. According to this premise, it is impossible to understand human phenomena by looking at them at only one point in time. We must examine them at different points to appreciate how they change. As we do this we discover that the changes are not merely quantitative, for example, less talk at the beginning than in the middle of a relationship. On the contrary, the more important consideration is that the changes are qualitative. There are alterations in both the nature and function of activities. We will find people doing things in later stages of relationships that they would not have dreamed of doing at the beginning, for example, disclosing private information, or making pledges of affection. To understand human relationships, we must examine them over a span of time.

Dr. Kevin Hanley. I've been studying relationships for twenty years. When we first began to study them, we never asked much about how long the couple had known each other. We just gave out questionnaires and recorded the data. Gradually, we got more sophisticated in research, we discovered that people changed a great deal because of their connection with another person. Sometimes the change is an intensification of the way they behaved as individuals. Sometimes, the change is really drastic. We can even locate patterns of change that seem to apply to all relationships.

PREMISE #2: General patterns of development describe human phenomena

That means, for example, that it is possible to predict with relative accuracy what a person or couple will experience next, if you can identify what is being experienced now. Once people decide to get to know each other better, you can expect them to begin to exchange personal information. In general, an observer can usually find a relatively accurate model to describe change in most human phenomena. The theories only claim to describe *general* patterns to which there will always be exceptions. We assume that most relationships will approximate the general pattern of development proposed by theories. Furthermore, these patterns should be thought of on a continuum, not as a set of discrete, entirely separate steps. We tend to move gradually from one stage to another, and sometimes it is hard to see the transitions. The movement is more like a flow than a series of distinct steps.

Sometimes the process of relational development stabilizes. Where people have the opportunity to make decisions, the process may stop because of unilateral or joint action. In relationships, for instance, we don't always carry through to the final stage of a permanent commitment to intimacy. Many human relationships freeze at a particular level, and if the relationship continues, change may be considered horizontal, that is, the details of activity at that level, change. Thus, if we have a friendship based on participation in a bowling league, we may write a twenty year history of details of bowling matches, without advancing to a more intense stage of relationship. We tend to stabilize most of our relationships at relatively low levels of involvement. When we present the twelve stages of relationship process, then, you should regard them possibilities for all relationships, but likely to happen in only a few. It is likely that you will have only four or five truly intimate relationships in your life. Most of your relationships will stabilize around work, socialization, or common interest. You will meet a steady stream of people, some of whom will remain in your life for a long time and others who will pass through. Check your Christmas or Chanukah card list and how it changes for evidence of this pattern.

If the assumption of generalizable patterns still strikes you as a bit too rigid, you may be confusing form and content. Developmental theorists do *not* claim that the *content* of the stages can be generalized to all people. In fact, most theorists readily admit great variation in the content of stages. In Freud's oral stage of individual development, for example, one infant might fixate on a bottle's nipple, another on mother's breast, a third on a pacifier and a fourth on thumb-sucking. The *act of fixation* marks the stage, not the particular *object* of fixation. Similarly, in early interaction one couple might talk about academic experiences, another couple about hometowns, and a third about athletics. The topic of conversation is not important (or necessarily predictable). The *type* of talk is generalizable; couples in an early stage of acquaintance will talk about some neutral or superficial topic, when they become fully intimate they will have to discuss intensely private matters.

PREMISE #3: The current stage of development reflects prior stages and foreshadows future stages

Stages of development are related. They are integrated, each one connected to those that precede and follow it. This implies that the choices we make at any point in a relationship are influenced by what has gone before, and furthermore, our current choices influence the future nature of our relationships. A married couple trying to figure out what to do when each has had a good job offered to them, but the jobs are 800 miles apart can probably resolve the problem effectively, if earlier in their relationship they had worked out some rules about how they were to go about making major decisions. If they have not worked out a method of making decisions, they may not be able to resolve the issue. The ability to anticipate the kinds of problems that might be encountered, although, perhaps, not the particular content of the problems, is one of the main advantages of learning about developmental stages. If the couple knew that such decisions were likely if their relationship lasted, they might have worked out ways to talk with each other and openly air their feelings and preferences as they consider the job offers. On the other hand, if they had little experience in talking things out, they might find it impossible to deal with the issues that confront them. One respondent in our research provided a clear example of what may happen when partners do not learn how to deal effectively with their differences:

Chris H. The first time we had an argument I think both of us were scared it might mean we had real problems. The issue wasn't that important, at least it didn't seem so at the time, so we sort of swept the whole incident under the rug. We did the same thing with the next argument and the next and the next. None of them were about big issues—they were little things like whose parents to visit over Thanksgiving or what kind of car to buy or what color should the new rug be. Still, I think we made a big mistake in how we handled our disagreements, ignoring them and telling ourselves if we didn't talk about them, they weren't there. Now it's like neither of us is really willing to talk about anything that might lead to disagreement. Neither of us wants to risk another argument we'll have to bury. But, you know, by now that rug's gotten mighty bumpy what with all we've swept under it. Sometimes there are snide remarks like when she says something about the repairs being so high on the car. I know what she *really* means that if we'd bought the car she wanted, we'd be spending less on repairs. It's not just her. I do the same thing. I wish we could turn back the clock to that first argument and find another way of dealing with our differences of opinion.

PREMISE #4: Communication is central to the development of human phenomena

Communication is central to the growth of individuals and relationships. Just as we learn to be human by communicating with other people, we learn how to build and maintain relationships in communication with our partners. By communicating with our partners, we define our identities in relation to them and thus define the nature of our relationship.

In our most intense relationships, communication establishes relational cultures that provide a shared, private world of values, self-definitions and expectations for individual and joint behavior. Communication regulates our movement through stages of relational development creating the quality of our relationships with other individuals. The study of human relationships, depends on concerted attention to communication as a primary means of defining and regulating interpersonal conduct.

PREMISE #5: Individuals are not necessarily aware of stages or patterns of interaction in which they engage

The stages and patterns identified by developmental theorists are efforts to describe order in human processes. We, as individuals, are not necessarily aware of the stages when we are in them. We nonetheless tend to conform to identified patterns.

Sam K. Graduate Student. We studied the protocol reports from all of the students enrolled at a small state college in Pennsylvania. There were 1,778 reports. The first question asked them to name a good friend and describe how they got to be friends. In every case, the report included some description of a first meeting, of some tentative attempts to get together after that, of an important moment when they got very excited about knowing each other, of a period when they seemed to be working out details of how they would remain together. It didn't matter whether they were same sex friendships or intimate relationships with the opposite sex. Although the respondents didn't use our jargon, they did describe stages; they even seemed to be describing the same stages.

The Growth Stages in Human Relationships

Human relationships do not spring to life full-blown. "Love at first sight" is more myth than fact. There are, in fact, a number of myths that create problems for people exploring relationship possibilities. There is, for example, the myth of the "vibe," the notion that there is some mystic force that will signal when just the right person comes along. You can be strongly attracted, intensely interested, deeply committed to making a relationship, but a relationship takes two people to build, and there are an incredible number of details that must be managed before two people are really bound together.

Another myth is "spontanaeity," the idea that "things" just happen in relationships and what is important is "being yourself" and "letting it all hang out." Premature disclosure of personal information is often very dangerous. It doesn't really help relationships either. A pair of people must pass through developmental stages before they really can be called friends or lovers. Pushing too hard for commitment before taking full advantage of the possibilities of each stage often gets people committed before they have any substance on which to commit. Relationships are not acts of passion (although they may include passionate acts).

Sexual quality as the crux of relationships is another myth. Some people consider sex to be the *sole* basis for an intimate relationship. People have the option to indulge in recreational sex, but they must avoid the error of thinking they can build an enduring relationship on that alone. In fact, the idea that it is possible to maintain a sexual relationship with no strings attached has been the downfall of many sincere people. Being together involves some binding. If one member of a couple whose relationship is primarily sexual has made a greater commitment to the relationship than the other, the possibilities for injury are very great.

The notion that a truly loving couple affords each person total freedom to "do their own thing" is another myth. Intimate relationships are reciprocal systems. Whatever one member does affects the other. Therefore, most of what goes on must be a matter of consensual judgment. One doesn't make a commitment to an intimate relationship unless she or he is prepared to surrender a degree of personal autonomy.

The process of building a strong and fulfilling bonded relationship is very orderly. The use of the word "bonded" is also important. It refers to the intensity of the linkages an intimate couple has with one another. In each stage of relationship, the connection grows stronger. If one of the stages is omitted or passed over lightly, the relationship is proportionally weakened. In the following pages, we will use a six-step model to describe how relationships develop and grow. We will start with individuals looking for connections, and we will end with a "bonded" relationship, either an intense friendship or a marriage (or similar arrangement). It is our contention that the best intimate relationships have progressed satisfactorily through these stages using them to build a firm foundation for the future.

These stages represent a comprehensive sequence of escalation of relationships. They are major junctures that can be identified in virtually all relationships. Sometimes individual stages proceed very rapidly, sometimes very slowly, and many relationships freeze at early stages. But every intimate relationship we examined went through all six of these stages. In some there were even rites of passage, memorials and anniversaries to mark the importance of transitions.

Keep in mind that the stages are merely points on a continuum. As you examine your own relationships, you will find that while most clearly fit within one of the stages, some will be in transition from one stage to another.

Stage 1: Individuals alone and receptive

Prior to forming relationships, individuals are looking around. Murray Davis says that the most important preliminary to a relationship is being clear. People who are deeply committed to relationships are not available to form new ones. When they meet new people, their interaction is usually pleasant and casual, but there is little or no effort to extend the contact. Relationships are initiated by an individual who is looking for a relationship and has the time and energy to form one. If he or she finds another person in the same state then there is the potential for forming a relationship.

People do not appear to have formal criteria to guide their quest for friends and intimates. One authority commented that they seem to take more care in selecting a used car than in choosing a companion. Most connections are made at random, in public places, in which people interact according to social norms.

Most connections are made between people who are similar in important ways. Surveys of friend-making covering more than 2,000 people indicated that people tend to pick friends of a similar age and socio-economic level, and of the same race. National origin and religion were not quite as important, although there are growing segments of the population for whom religious compatibility is a very important criterion. It appears that "birds of a feather do flock together."

The decision to make a relationship grows out of a lifetime of interactions. Individuals develop standards of expectations for relationships (CL) based on their self image, from which definitions of appropriate partners emerge. The CL_{alt} also operates. Every social contact offers some possibilities. Even the person who is most secure in a relationship will cast an eye about from time to time; if it appears that there are better options, even the most committed person may seek new associations. There are four basic questions that individuals must answer when meeting new people:

1. Am I interested in forming new relationships now?
2. If so, what am I seeking? (Casual friends, supporters, romantic liaisons?)
3. What kind of self-confirmation am I seeking?
4. What kinds of people might be able to provide that support?

These questions seem to guide people's responses to those they meet. Depending on the answers, a person can actively extend invitations for future contact, accept the overtures of others, defer them for later consideration, or reject future contact with new people.

Stage 2: Invitational communication (Auditioning)

This is the initial stage of interaction. It begins with the decision to approach a particular person and consists of opening comments and responses to them. What happens at this point in relational development depends on how receptive two people are to each other. Our contact with others is greatly influenced by the social systems in which we operate. Our possibilities are, therefore, limited. If you are seeking a contact not represented in your social circles, you must work your way into other groupings in order to hold your auditions. We have already advised you that you are likely to find yourself in contact with people very much like yourself in socio-economic level and background. If you come from a "good family" it is not likely that you will meet many "disadvantaged people," and if you went to a "top school," you are not likely to meet people who attend state universities. Differences in social status tend to limit whom we meet and, thus, whom we have a chance to get to know. The past several decades have produced some healthy breakdowns in class segregation; however, class considerations still pose serious constraints on our choice of associates.

There is a second limitation imposed by social systems, more obvious and more powerful than the first. We can only meet people whose paths cross our own. Even with the recent trend in "singles" advertising in major magazines, the overwhelming number of the people we meet are nearby: the people with whom we work, our neighbors, those who choose the same entertainments or hobbies, and our classmates.

If you take stock, you will probably find that the majority of your friends and dates are people who live near you or did when the relationships began, or whom you repeatedly met in situations such as classes, soccer matches or choral practice. It seems that there is some basis for the old myth about marrying the boy or girl next door.

Our social systems also constrain our choices by providing us with the criteria by which we evaluate the people we meet. Our ideas of who is attractive, both physically and in personality, heavily reflect the acculturation we have had in our family and in our communities. The reference groups to which we belong equip us with information about desirable background, values, and beliefs, and we learn to judge actions by the experiences we have had with the people around us. When we meet people from an unfamiliar social group, we are occasionally completely captivated, but most of the time, we merely pass them by because we cannot understand their mores.

Our criteria for judging are usually modified by the kind of relationship we are seeking. Physical attractiveness may be more important in a romantic partner than in a tennis companion. Our criteria are also affected by our transferences. If we need additional contact with a parent or other important figure, or if we have a need to reject someone from our past, we may seek a relationship with a person whose appearance or personality helps us meet that need.

We usually have very superficial data by which to judge others initially. We tend to infer from what we can see. Physical appearance, conversation style, dress, and possessions are all influential in making an initial decision for contact. In fact, adolescents often do not go beyond "neat looking," "good dancer," "big bust," or "dynamite car." Young adults may also take into account clique membership in initiating contact. After a while, we develop some sophistication in our seeking, but we are still restricted by the values of our social groups.

Ron M. When I go to a mixer I grab a beer and then stand off to the side. I look over everyone there for a while to figure out which women interest me. It's not really how pretty they are that I look at. I try to figure out which women there I could have a decent conversation with—which ones have minds. I tend to like women who are serious types. You'd be surprised how well I can judge that from outward appearances. Take hair, for instance. I never approach women with elaborate hair-styles because I figure anyone who'd give all that time and attention to her hair probably wouldn't make time to read the daily paper.

We often make errors in our initial judgments. Since we have no logical basis on which to make choices, we tend to respond to superficial matters like physical appearance, style of clothing, animation, tone of voice, and similar features. Preliminary efforts to study the association between physical appearance and personality have turned up very little that we can rely on.

Interpersonal communication begins with a comment from one person to another. People exchange greetings, make phatic communion and make a decision about whether they want to say more. Both must want to continue. At this stage of contact, it is easy for one person to break off. If both people decide they wish to have contact, they try to identify themselves to each other. Each person chooses how he or she wishes to appear and makes some statement to indicate that decision. Each then waits for confirmation of the declared identity. If either interprets a response as undesirable, the contact may end then and there.

The situation is very much like an audition. We conduct try-outs for a person with whom we wish to spend some time. Time is our first investment. We must devote time to the discovery of qualities and qualifications in the other person. Depending on the situation, the person, and the type of relationship for which we're auditioning, we may want to be seen as the life of the party, a serious, no-nonsense business person, a smooth character, or a person of warmth and compassion. We select "opening lines" (sometimes prepared in advance) that we think will convince the other person to see us as we wish to be seen. We try to figure out how they wish to be seen, and we respond accordingly. If neither party makes errors, the contact can continue.

There is no formula for initial contact; however, a recent study indicates that people prefer to be addressed directly, "I'd like to meet you," or innocently, "it's a nice party, isn't it," rather than with cute lines like "you remind me of someone I'd like to date," or with cliches like, "what's a nice person like you doing in a place like this." We each have our criteria for what constitutes rejection. In most cases, we also know how to fend off contact we do not want. Sometimes a person bores us relentlessly and we cannot put an end to it, but most of the time we can slide out of the conversation quickly, by refilling our drink, getting some food, or seeing an old friend "over there." If we feel rejected, we may have a back-up plan; if the new person seems terribly important to us, we may want to try again. Sometimes we get a qualified response, one that requires a bit of negotiation. Throughout all of this interchange, each individual speculates on what the situation might be as a pair. What are the possibilities? What could we do for each other? How could we hurt each other? What could we do together, for how long, when and where, and with what result? All of this information is processed against our current goals. If both parties pass the audition, the contact can continue.

Karen R. Sometimes I feel really schizoid! I come across as totally different people in different situations. The Phi Mus are the campus "cool Joes" so at their parties I dress to the hilt and put a lot of effort into being with it about new records and stuff. The Chi Psi's are another story. They're the top academic house on campus so when I'm over there I talk about more serious things like politics or classes. Then there are the Delta Sig's. Now they're into athletics in a big way, really active in all the intramural contests. With them I talk about my jogging and aerobic workouts and instead of dancing we're likely to get up a game of softball or soccer. I have to dress differently for each house, too. One of my suite-mates said she thought I must be pretty artificial to be so different at the different houses. I don't think that's true though. All of those are parts of me. I do like to dance, but I also care about staying in shape, and I stay up on political issues. It's not so much a matter of being artificial as it is a matter of deciding which part of me to go with in each situation.

The second function of communication during the invitational stage is to get enough information to decide whether you want further contact. Conversation is characterized by topics like hometowns, majors, people we know in common and what we do for fun. It is very much like giving your name, rank, and serial number. An important feature of this talk is to establish clearance. During this stage questions can be asked about available time and entanglements. If an individual has a mate, or a schedule that will not permit socialization, it should be revealed at this stage and the other person should respond accordingly. Otherwise, the idea is to establish whether or not there is common ground. It is all part of negotiating identity. If both parties want the contact to continue, they need to present themselves as available and potentially compatible.

Many relationships never go beyond this stage. One or both individuals decide there is no potential for a serious relationship and it would be better, for the moment, to stay uncommitted. Relationships stabilized at this point become acquaintanceships. The individuals will greet each other and exchange small talk if they happen to meet in the future, but they will not seek to expand the relationship beyond this superficial level. We all need to fit in with the people around us, so it is important to have acquaintances.

If, however, individuals are sufficiently intrigued with each other's self-presentation, they may choose to develop the relationship a little further. They may, in fact, wish to get together at another time and place. Murray Davis describes this "dating" phase as an important step in a relationship. By agreeing to get together at another time, both parties show good faith. Such extensions of contact may take place in both same sex and opposite sex relationships.

Auditioning may last only a few minutes or continue through several separate meetings. It depends on how quickly the individuals make up their minds about the potential for a relationship. Sometimes the decision to press on with a relationship may arise because of changes in our social systems. If one of our friends has moved away, or if we break up with a dating partner, there may be sudden interest in escalating a long-standing casual relationship. The change in our social condition changes the way we see our acquaintances.

Throughout this stage of interaction, communication adheres closely to prevailing norms for social interaction. The individuals do not yet know each other well enough to venture beyond relatively safe topics or to develop dual perspective in order to adapt talk to each other's private needs. Skill at meeting and auditioning depends on your ability to keep conversation going and to make effective declarations of your identity. While you're talking you're likely to be evaluating these important issues that come up during the early stages of getting together:

1. With what people do I feel socially safe?
2. Of those around me, which seem attractive as potential friends, colleagues, dates, etc.?
3. What identity do I seek to declare with these people and what response do I want in return?
4. What declarations do the people I contact make and how can I respond to their declarations?
5. Does our initial contact provide a basis for future contact?
6. What goals do I want to set, now that I have some idea of the qualities of the other person? Stabilize the relationship as an acquaintanceship, intensify it further, or end it now?

Stage 3: Explorational communication (Shall we go on?)

If each person is sufficiently impressed by the other's "audition" to judge that it warrants further investment in interaction, a tryout takes place. Sometimes auditioning goes very rapidly, and a relationship jumps quickly into this third stage; at other times we take a long time with the audition because we are not sure about the other person or our own goals.

As the title of this stage suggests, the focus is on exploring the possibilities for a relationship. It is a transitional point between initial screening and commitment. At this stage, people may decide to maintain a relationship that is characterized by limited sharing of interests. A decision to lunch once a week or join a bowling team can come out of this stage. Most of us, in fact, do not pass beyond this stage with very many people.

Gustav K. Sure, I can classify my friends. Joe and Stash, we go to the ball game. I drink with Lou after work on Wednesday. His old lady works at the Red Cross and my mother-in-law comes on Wednesday, so I'm in no hurry to get home. Caz helps me out on the job, and I do some work around the house for him. Ed and Marty, I'm very close to. We been together since high school and we, you know, are like brothers. I see more of Ed and Marty than I see of my brother and sister. If my wife told me my brother couldn't come to the house no more, it wouldn't bother me, but she's got to be friends with Ed and Marty and their wives. The other guys, she can tell me whether or not to bring them into the house.

Auditioning concentrates on surface communication. In explorational communication we progress to personal values and information. We need more insight, now, about the personality of the other person. It is here that we make our real assessment of compatibility, and decisions to go on made at this stage involve considerable emotion. At this point we risk stepping out of our safe social roles like college student or neighbor and we try to expose a bit of our private selves. Our initial moves are usually quite tentative, and we look for confirmation in the form of reciprocal revelation from the other person. Some people are very clever about getting admissions from others which they subsequently use against them, so there is considerable risk in personal exposure. Most of us do not do it unless we feel a strong emotional disposition to move on. The beliefs and values we discuss during this stage help form a basis for an intense relationship.

Nancy D. I knew after that first talk that we were going to be friends for life. After we met each other we talked for four hours and killed three packs of cigarettes. What can I say? It was not exactly your typical first conversation. Boy, did we cover a lot of territory, telling each other about our backgrounds and what we were doing now and what we thought we'd do in our careers down the road. We talked about our academic work and our families and our boyfriends. Like I said, we covered a lot of ground in that talk. It was like finding another part of myself when I met Brenda. We decided right then and there to be friends. I know part of the reason was that we just plain really got into each other as people, but later we also found out that each of us was a little lonely at the time so it was a good point to form a new friendship.

Explorational communication may be brief or quite extended, depending on individuals' interaction styles, their current interest in forming relationships and their speed in discovering what, if anything, they have in common. Sometimes we realize after only one or two encounters that there is no possibility of anything serious; on the other hand, we sometimes decide just as quickly that we could really get involved.

A variety of decisions may follow explorational communication. First, one or both people may conclude there is no basis for serious interaction, so the relationship should be stabilized at the current level. A second option is to decide the relationship should be continued but restricted to specific kinds of interaction. If individuals discover a shared interest in backpacking or tennis, they might agree to get together for hikes or regular tennis matches. Similarly, people sometimes find they have a limited basis for sustaining a complementary relationship useful to both of them. Ellen will teach Jim about organic gardening in exchange for his providing transportation weekly to Sierra Club meetings. A mutually satisfactory exchange is worked out on a limited basis. A third possibility is to escalate interaction into transaction because the individuals think they may be able to build something more than a casual relationship. *Whatever happens, it must be a mutual decision.*

During the explorational stage, communication will expand progressively in breadth and depth. Communication also tends to become increasingly personal as individuals probe each others' attitudes and personalities. Social norms for interaction still influence conduct, but they no longer control it totally. Individuals are likely to step outside of strict conventions for public talk as they try to find out more about each other. During this phase, each person considers questions like the following.

1. What is this person like once I get beyond the public roles?
2. How do I or could I fit with this person and vice versa?
3. Do we share important values, beliefs, goals, and interests that might sustain serious interaction?

Work teams represent relationships stabilized at the exploration level.

4. What am I currently willing to invest in a relationship based on what I now know about this person?
5. What can I infer from interaction about this person's willingness to make investments in me comparable to those I make in him or her?

Stage 4: Intensifying communication (Euphoria)

Moving into this stage is a major step, because it represents a tentative commitment to intimacy. Intensification is really a rehearsal of a permanent commitment. Previous interaction has provided enough information for each person to consider the other attractive.

They enjoy being together. What they do not know is whether there is a basis for an enduring bond, whether they can combine to form a private community satisfying to both of them. These are the issues of Stage Four.

The outstanding characteristic of communication during this stage is its intensity, hence the title for the stage. Communication is much more intense in both quality and quantity than in the previous stage. Partners talk more often, for longer periods of time, and about more subjects. It is not unusual for intensifying partners to spend nearly all of their time together and feel that they cannot get enough of each other. After spending an entire day together, partners may call each other several times to say "good night" and find an excuse to continue contact. Other people and activities are temporarily set aside so that partners can devote total attention to each other. They invest heavily in the relationship to find out whether it might become permanent

---

Lewis R. From the start I guess we both knew there were real possibilities. After we'd dated for about three or four weeks, things really took off! We decided not to see other people and we started talking about what a good relationship we had, how comfortable we felt in it and all. It seems like when we're together the time just evaporates. We plan to go out to dinner and then back to our own rooms to study, but it never works out that way. We start talking and we just don't ever run out of things to say. I want to know all about her, every little thing, and she feels the same way about me. It's like we're trying to absorb each other. We're all that we think of. All the time I feel like I'm just floating, like I'm in another dimension and the normal world seems irrelevant to me. We'd better get out of this soon or we're both going to flunk out of school.

Same sex partners, particularly men, rarely reach this point of commitment. During your entire lifetime, you may have one or two people of the same sex with whom you intensify. The important point here, however, is that intensification is not necessarily sexual, even in male-female relationships. Sexuality may assume a role in a developing relationship, but it is clear that people can have sexual contacts, some very pleasant, without making very much commitment at all. It is equally clear that deep commitment can come prior to or without sexual expression. If sexual contact is part of the intensification stage, it becomes part of the "learning-about" process, and assumes important symbolic importance.

Partners progressively abandon their public roles and lines during intensification. They lower their masks to learn about each other's private self. Philip Slater regards this stage as extremely important, since intimacy is the most important gift one human can give another. It is here that our weaknesses are exposed. The person who seems so confident in public may be insecure underneath. The highly threatening competitive person whom you feared, may appear warm and tender once the combat gear is removed. You learn how one person fears his brother, another yearns for more contact with her father. You learn about guilt and shame and embarrassing times. You also learn personal quirks and habits. She likes lemon in her coke and he reads the comic pages even before looking at the headlines; he buys a bag of catfood every time he goes to the grocery store in order to donate it to the ASPCA in memory of the cat that he couldn't keep in his dorm room; she doesn't write home but sends her parents a cassette every week. Personal information like this is hard to share, for it is all too easy to use it as the basis for ridicule. But sharing it helps us understand each other as unique people, and it provides us with a basis for transaction by giving us a private view of our potential partner.

A second function of intensifying communication is to develop dual perspective. As our communication becomes increasingly personal we begin to get a real sense of the other's perspective on events, experiences, situations, people, values, and other things. We emphasize again that this rarely happens. We normally have a very limited sense of how most of our associates view things, so our interactions with them are based on public norms. This, of course, is good enough to keep most interaction running smoothly. However, our intimate transactions require a specific, in-depth appreciation of an intimate partner's perspective; our communication must take this into account, and we expect the same in return. We want our intimate partners to take into account our personal perspective as they deal with us.

Intensification marks a critical point in relational development. The deep understanding we acquire of the other person makes us realize how much impact we can have on each other. We must take considerable responsibility for the choices we now make. In intimate relationships it is difficult to plead ignorance, claiming you did not intend to hurt, offend or ridicule. Because you have so much information about your partner's feelings and views, you must use that knowledge to avoid doing harm. There is little excuse for careless communication between intimates; in general, they are able to anticipate most of each other's interpretations and expectations.

Once you really understand another's perspective, you incorporate it into your own outlook. Just as a young child incorporates society's general views into *ME*, we must incorporate what we know of our intimate partner, and accord it the very highest status in our decision-making. We come to know our partners so thoroughly that we cannot avoid taking their perspectives. They become part of us and we part of them.

Bennie P. The other day I was sitting around and shooting the bull with some friends and we got on the subject of the environment. I said some things about how important it is for us to think about future generations and to preserve some wilderness for them. Then I mentioned one of the bills that's up before the Senate right now, and it's really important for environmental issues. Then Jane interrupted and said I sounded just like Tom. He's my best friend and room-mate. When I thought about what she said, I realized Jane was right. I never used to talk this way. I wasn't into issues like environment. But that's Tom's big thing and I guess I've come to see the issues like he does just from talking about them so much with him. It's not that I'm just mouthing his ideas or saying things I don't believe in. I've really come to care about what happens to our natural resources in this country.

After a while, it becomes difficult to know exactly where you stop and your partner begins. Your partner has become so completely a part of you, that you cannot avoid being influenced by his or her ideas in all your thinking. Dual perspective is the foundation of intimacy. It is the basis for a joint way to view the world as a relational culture and for each partner's taking the other into account in transactions.

The final function of intensification is to establish a pair-identity

Euphoria at work!

in the minds of the partners and the world-at-large. Obviously, people do not surrender all of their identity when they form intimate bonds. Each retains personal interests and some privacy, but the great change is that the partners are now seen as a unit both by themselves and the people around them. Their pair-identity communicates the importance of their relationship. They say "we" and "us" instead of "I" and "me." They find "our song," their favorite restaurant; they may coin nicknames and pet names and develop a private vocabulary that cannot be understood by anyone else. They begin to get invitations addressed to *them* as a couple.

Intensification is an exciting and consuming stage of relationship development. It can also lead to resentment if the partners feel they are sacrificing too much individuality to sustain the new relationship. Such negative feelings tend to be blocked out by the idealization that characterizes this stage. Partners see each other through "rose colored glasses," minimizing weaknesses and exaggerating strengths. Little tiffs and disagreements are brushed aside. In male-female relationships, there is considerable physical contact which blocks out possible disagreements. It is for this reason that the term *euphoria* is associated with this stage. Critical analysis of the relationship at this stage should include these questions:

1. As I discover more about my partner, how do I define him or her?
2. As I reveal more of myself, does my partner confirm me?
3. How do we fit in relation to each other?
4. What values and beliefs has my partner revealed to me that he or she does not reveal publicly?
5. What quirks and preferences have I learned about my partner?
6. Does my partner take my perspective into account?
7. How much have we incorporated each other's ways of thinking?
8. How have we defined ourselves as a pair?
9. Am I able to recognize my partner's weaknesses as well as his or her strengths?

Stage 5: Revising communication

The excitement and idealization of intensification cannot last forever. Eventually, the partners come down out of the clouds to take a hard look at their relationship and to make decisions about where to go from there. They rethink the value of the relationship, take note of its problems, and reconsider their willingness to continue. As a result of this review, partners often make decisions about the future. They may abandon the relationship, scale it down, or commit to an extended future together. The relationship cannot stay where it is, because euphoria cannot be maintained indefinitely. That is why this stage is called "revising communication," and its emphasis is on the question: "will this relationship work over the long term?"

The euphoria stage permits partners to sample intimacy under the most positive circumstances. They have experienced the best and they have a store of pleasant memories to sustain them through the more mundane bargaining that characterizes the fifth stage. Several decisions are possible here. The most common is to let the relationship coast, continue on a physical level for a while, perhaps live together, and then drift apart. They decide that they can find enjoyment with no strings attached. This is sometimes dangerous because one partner may invest more heavily than the other.

A second option is to call it quits because there is no hope for the relationship on a long-term basis. It is possible to love people with whom we could not live permanently, and infatuations are sometimes enjoyable if they do not become regularized. Furthermore, after the first rush of excitement, it is possible for both partners to cool off very quickly. Particularly if there was heavy emphasis on sexual contact, it is possible for the partners to lose interest once they discover they really have nothing else in common. There is no moral or legal reason to continue a relationship just because it has become intense, although coming apart at this stage is often emotionally draining to both parties.

Inevitably both partners evaluate the relationship using the CL and CL$_{alt}$ previously discussed. Each examines the relationship to see if it meets the standards they have set for relationships. Each examines the alternatives to see what they must give up if they continue the relationship. Once beyond euphoria, partners can return to examination of the problems they overlooked previously.

This stage centers on a cost-benefit analysis of a relationship. Costs include how the relationship might restrict personal behavior, consume important time, interfere with goals, and irritate the emotions. The greatest potential loss is disconfirmation of self. Sometimes during the revising stage, one partner discovers that the other has designs to make him or her over to fit their image of an ideal partner. Men often have a "Pygmalion" urge to "improve" the women with whom they are intimate. Women often nurture the illusion that they have the power to "reform" a man who has a major flaw. (The media offer drinking and gambling as possible flaws.) Sometimes the changes demanded are easy to make and sometimes they are flagrant interferences in the other person's growth. The analysis also includes examining benefits: companionship, shared status, mutual assistance, the fun of joint activities, and the possibilities of continued self-confirmation.

Few people conduct this cost-benefit analysis consciously. The process goes on without full awareness that it is happening. All people know is that they are asking questions about their partner. Sometimes tests are conducted to check commitment. Eventually, either or both partners may decide, "I'm just not getting enough out of this" or "I guess we have enough going for us." The CL$_{alt}$ cannot be ignored in this analysis. It is much harder for us to make a permanent relationship if our social systems contains many desirable people. Conversely, commitments made out of lack of alternatives often come apart when alternatives appear. Individuals who attempt to achieve an intimate relationship simply because they want a relationship often find themselves trying to work out a relational culture with a person with whom they are incompatible.

Ginny V. Mom keeps asking me why I don't settle down with some nice young man. I think she's really worried that I'll be an old maid since I'm 29 now and have no plans for a trip to the altar. It's really weird to go home and see my old friends from high school. Almost all of them are married and have several kids. I just can't see myself in that scene. Maybe if I'd stayed in Roxville, I'd have done the same thing, I mean, how much is there to do in Roxville? But I went to a big university and then landed the job in Atlanta and I meet a lot of interesting people. I do a lot of traveling. I just can't get psyched on the idea of marriage. In this city there are plenty of men and I go out a lot. A couple of times I've gotten pretty involved with one person, but then I'd see some new man and get curious . . . poor Mom!

Options to a relationship include more than other relationships. It is a legitimate alternative not to enter into serious interpersonal attachments. For example, life commitments can be made to jobs. In this case, it is important to be aware of possible consequences.

Carolyn C. Anyone who knows me will tell you I've always been a serious person. In college, I'd rather read or study than party. Sure, I went out sometimes and I still do occasionally, but it's never been an important part of who I am. Then, after college, I attended law school (my grades were good enough to get me into the top school, too). Again, my major interest was my studies. Law fascinated me from the start and I got more pleasure from reading cases than from going out drinking and dancing. I've been practicing five years now, and I'm completely wrapped up in my work. And before you start thinking how sad that is, let me assure you this is my preference. I have no trouble attracting men, but I simply choose not to spend my time on them. They take too much energy and time away from my profession and that's what's really important in my life.

Fred W. Tom T. Hall used to sing about all the wine and lonely girls in this best of all possible worlds. Women's Lib was the best thing that ever happened to me. I travel the world, North Sea, Arabia, work on oil rigs, repair them, plenty of money in it. I get to spend time in London, Paris, New York, you name it. I like stewardesses, secretaries, executive women, I don't care, I can show them a good time, they can return the favor. I don't want any alliances. When I'm fifty and get a paunch, then it's time for alliances, and then I want a woman of the same age, who's been around the barn a time or two so we can settle down and get to know one another. Sex is one thing, a hobby, you know. Work is work. Marrying is when neither of the other two satisfy any more.

Your social systems have impact on these options. Up to a few years ago, people who did not marry and raise families were considered abnormal. In some communities this is still true. Women, for example, were judged on whether they could "catch a husband." Men were evaluated as workers. Now the options have expanded materially. There are so many choices that the CLs and CL$_{alt}$ represent a way to get ideas crystallized. There certainly is no reason why we should spend more time choosing a car or picking a job than we spend on choosing a permanent mate. It is important to your future fulfillment to base your decisions about permanent relationships on something more substantial than a few good times or an emotional or physical response to someone.

Each person privately judges the relationship. One may want to talk with the other, but the decision to commit is personal. If both partners agree to continue, then they must discuss how they will advance together. Once partners accept this third alternative, they can begin to work out the details of the bond. From this point on, transactions take place with an eye toward a permanent future.

Before a relationship is permanently viable, a great many details must be worked out.

1. How will the decisions be made? Who is in charge? Are we to be equals or will one party have primary control?
2. Who will carry out the decisions? Who will be responsible for obtaining funds, spending them, arranging living space, and so on? Who will do the cooking and cleaning, and who will take charge of child care, if there are children?
3. How will we resolve our disputes?
4. Are we to be intellectual companions, lovers, social partners, taskmates, or some combination?
5. What support do we expect from each other for our personal goals?
6. What independent activities will be available to each of us and what will we do together?
7. What are the future plans? Where will we live? Will there be children?

8. How will we present ourselves to others? How will we relate to parents and other friends?

Discussion of these issues will help the partners develop roles and rules unique to the relationship. The more partners agree on in advance, the less trouble they will have later. There are some traditional assumptions still made in segments of our society about the woman's role and the man's role in a marriage. If one partner rejects these assumptions without the approval of the other, the relationship has rough times. In addition, problems do not disappear in intense relationships; in fact, the closeness of the pair underlines the seriousness of the problems. Couples that stay together and have happy marriages or permanent relationships are characterized by their understanding of how to solve their problems and manage their arguments. Because the stages in a relationship are so closely connected, unresolved issues at one point can result in severe problems at a later point.

Larry T. I figured we had things pretty well worked out by now, but I'm not so sure any more. It seems that I've learned a lot since Susan and I decided to get married. I knew she was pretty independent, and that's one of the things I liked about her. But you can carry a good thing too far. The other day we got into one of those "ten years down the road" conversations. We were talking about what our lives would be like. I talked about how much I hoped by then we would own our own home and have ample room for a couple of kids and dog. She went into shock. Susan says she doesn't see kids in the picture. She admits she might feel differently later, but she says I have to understand that right now she has no intention of ever being a mother. She's gung-ho on her career in public relations. It's not like we hadn't discussed these issues before or anything, but I always figured she was sort of over-stating her feelings about kids, just to make sure I respected her independence. Now I'm not so sure. I love Susan, but I really want to be a father, some day. I guess the decision to get married just forces you to deal with a lot of issues that didn't matter when you were just going together.

Another important issue to resolve is the rules of conduct for both partners. Relationships seem to be most satisfying when each partner understands what the other expects, and what is out of bounds. Such issues as the following must be considered:

1. How much time is to be spent together and how much alone?
2. How much time is permitted with old friends outside the relationship?
3. Do we talk at meal-times or can we have TV or stereo on?

4. How do we manage money? What kinds of bank accounts do we have? Personal or joint?
5. Must we account to each other for our expenditures?
6. Will we have a regular daily schedule?

These issues are subsidiary to the larger ones, but they must be dealt with. It is not enough to agree generally. Like roles, rules for relationships can be negotiated explicitly or implicitly. Generally, it is more effective to work them out so there is less chance of misunderstanding or incompatible expectations.

Murray Davis describes this stage as a "probationary period" because each person can still get out if agreements cannot be reached. That is why this stage is so important. It is the final chance to revise or quit before making the big commitment. Revision should not be viewed as a sort of combat between the partners. Good communication should encourage systematic problem-solving toward the mutual goal of designing a solid relational culture for the bond.

Bill T. At first I was wary about bringing up some of the things that were bothering me about our relationship. I guess I figured they will work out in time. But this Bible-study group we belong to emphasizes honesty and openness in relationships. So we agreed to give it a try by telling each other some of the things we were unhappy with. I told Laurie I don't like the way she plans every move on our weekends and expects me to go along with it and I don't like it when she mothers me. There was some tension for a while and some hurt feelings, but you wouldn't believe what a productive discussion we wound up having. It turned out that Laurie was really bothered by some things I do too, and I had no idea they irritated her so much. Now that we both know how the other feels, we can work the problems out. We couldn't before because we didn't talk about them.

Dr. Spencer, Marriage Counselor. Be careful about communicating. Just because you talk about a "problem" doesn't mean you've solved it. It's not enough to bring something up. You have to decide to do something about it. The popular myths say just talk about it. But once the issue is on the table, it must be resolved.

The revising stage is an opportunity for the partners to work together in designing the relational culture. It is a breathing stage between euphoria and enduring commitment. During this stage, import decisions are made about sex, security, sharing of secrets, other relationships, how to make adjustments, and whether there is a better future outside the relationship. During this stage partners individually and jointly address these questions:

1. What's good about my partner and this relationship?
2. What are the weaknesses of my partner and the relationship?
3. What are the alternatives to this relationship and how do they stack up in comparison to it?
4. What's the overall balance when I summarize the rewards I gain from the relationship against the costs I incur?
5. What changes do I/we want before I/we are ready to make an extended commitment?
6. Who do I see myself to be in relation to my partner and does my partner agree on my role in the relationship?
7. Who do I expect my partner to be in relation to me and is she or he in agreement with this role?
8. What are our current rules (patterns) and what rules do I/we want for our future as a pair?
9. Do I see evidence that my partner and I are willing to discuss disagreements about the relationship and to try to work them out by making reasonable adjustments in order to improve our bond?

Stage 6: Bonding communication (Blood brothers/sisters, or let's take the big step!)

Unlike the previous stages, bonding does not extend over time. It is a specific event that occurs at a particular moment. Bonding is a voluntary commitment to an extended future of intimacy. Voluntary means personal choice, not a coincidence of events or birthright. You can choose to commit intimately to family members and friends or you can moderate your commitment. However, when you bond into an intimate partnership, you commit yourself to being together for the future. There are few ways to do this in a limited way (Some very bad marriages work out techniques: George and Martha in *Who's Afraid of Virginia Woolf?* demonstrate how people can stay bonded despite heart-wrenching arguments and terrible betrayals.) For the most part, however, you are either bonded or you are not.

Romantic bonding usually takes place through a wedding, but sometimes couples make commitments in private and choose not to institutionalize their agreements. Sometimes bonding takes place in intense friendships. The Indians had the ceremony of becoming blood brothers. There is no similar ceremony in our culture, but commitments can be made. Friendships like these can be as important and enduring as romantic relationships.

Once a bond is made, the future of the relationship is as important as the present. Every decision one person makes affects both partners and the future of their relationship. The ultimate commitment is that each person is willing to accept and deal with the other "for better and for worse; for richer, for poorer; and in sickness and in health."

Bonding is just the beginning of enduring intimacy.

Rose N. I thought Mike and I were as ready as any two people could be, but when we started talking "marriage" I realized what a new involvement this was. It's not like, "gee, let's get more serious," it's a totally different kind of involvement. Nothing is the same once you discover you have to consider somebody else in everything you plan to do. He can't apply for jobs unless there is some opportunity for me. That means he may have to turn down some good money jobs, or jobs that require a lot of travel. I had to withdraw my application from M.I.T. which was the best program in my area, because I had to be ready to fit his plans, too. Sometimes I think it takes too many accommodations, just to stay together, but most often I think it's worth the effort to work things out.

Bonding means a joint identity. Even if people keep their own names, once they are identified as a permanent couple, a great deal of independence must be sacrificed. However, the commitment also means some stability. Uncertainty about personal value and fit is reduced. The emotional jolt of discovering each other's shortcomings is over. The fear of being alone is over. If it works, it can be for life and it can be very good.

A Final Look at the Growth Stages

We have examined six stages in relationships. As we promised, we have described how intimate relationships start and evolve from first meeting to permanent commitment. Each stage builds naturally on those that preceded it. The growth stages are characterized by the way communication is used to develop a relational culture. There is no magic in relating. It happens because people talk with each other and work out agreements. However, we don't always work things out as well as we might wish. Complications often arise.

Complications

A number of complications plague the growth stages of intimate relationships. We'll examine four of the most common.

Unrequited love

For centuries poets and romantic writers have catalogued the trials and tribulations of one-sided love. There are few experiences as painful as loving someone who does not return our love in full measure. Caring deeply for another person is one of the most intense human emotions, and one which places our self-esteem on the line. When we care, we invest ourselves in another, commit to that person's goals, and sacrifice part of ourselves. When we do not get anything in return, we are hurt, we feel pain, frustration, and sometimes resentment. We may also feel personally inadequate.

Dr. Spencer, Marriage Counselor. There is no such thing as a happy divorce. We may be relieved to get out of a mess, but there is no doubt that every divorced person feels inadequate. There is no way out. Divorce is failure and we know it inside, even if we won't admit it outside. Even when a close friendship fails, we know the sense of failure. And there is no such thing as a relationship with "no strings." There are always strings, sometimes ropes, and every time they are cut we feel pain like we had been cut.

The following pages should not be construed as a "Dear Abby" column. We merely wish to raise some issues worthy of consideration by people involved in an uneven love relationship. Examining the CL and CL$_{alt}$ is a useful way to keep your head on straight, but sometimes it is hard to keep cool when you are feeling pain. If there is only a little unevenness in affection, it is no great problem. Gaps can be filled. But the question is, how much of your dignity and self-respect must you sacrifice to stay in a relationship in which you are undervalued? How does it affect your goal-seeking? Is it worth the pain to stay in it? Can you handle the short-term pain involved in getting out? If your partner is exploiting your affection, it may be wise to move on.

Arthur Hechbauer, M.D. Psychiatrist. There is no advantage in being used and abused in a relationship. Women particularly let themselves get beaten physically and psychologically, sometimes until they are completely destroyed. In my experience, the most frequent cause of depression and hysteria is a terrible love affair. If you can't get a kind word from the person who is most important to you, then you can't grow as a person. Getting out is sometimes like surgery: it hurts like hell for a while, but you might survive because you did it.

Unrealistic expectations: prince charming really is a frog

An important complication can set in immediately after euphoria ends. During the period of intensification, feelings were high and visions were idealistic. When you begin seeing flaws in a partner, you feel a real let-down. The relationship begins to bump a little. You discover it isn't perfect after all.

The problem is not the realizations—they must happen, otherwise you can never get the relationship on a realistic permanent basis. The real problem is the over-reaction to the imperfections. If one partner decides that because the other is less-than-perfect, the relationship must end, then a potentially good relationship can go down the drain, and one or both partners can be hurt badly.

We are victims of the cultural myth of "happily ever after." We've been misled by this since childhood. But when Cinderella got to the palace and settled permanently she discovered not only that it was drafty but there was no indoor plumbing. The best of relationships are like that. Getting yourself set to accept human frailties is a practical necessity for sustaining a relationship that might be very important to you. Recognizing that long-term relationships will be characterized by the emergence of defects and problems is also helpful. You can use your assessment of potential problems to tell yourself how much you want to commit. It isn't the problems that should deter you; only if you can't figure out a way to solve them should you be deterred.

Premature commitment: it seemed like a good idea at the time

Sometimes people pledge themselves to others before the other is ready to receive a pledge. You have only yourself to blame if you commit to someone before you are sure that someone will take responsibility for your commitment. Rushing into marriage during the euphoria stage is an example of such commitment. You need the time to discover how the other person really sees you before taking the plunge.

Rushing ahead without confirmation presents two serious problems. First, if you pushed the commitment and then found it unpleasant, you can feel very guilty because you pressured the other person into it. If the other person has really become committed, it will be very hard for you to find a respectable way out. Second, if you rush a person into commitment, he or she may feel trapped. That person may not want to admit that rushing into the relationship was a mistake, but their resentment will build and the person who rushed them will feel it one way or another.

Carole E. I liked Jennifer from the first time I met her. I was brand new in New York and she was the first person I met. I was unsure of myself and Jennifer was settled in the city. She was popular, she knew her way around, and really had her act together. The more I saw of her the better I liked her. I looked forward to visiting with her, and I found myself inviting her to go to lunch or coming to dinner frequently. I found that I was paying the checks but I really didn't notice that til it was too late. I told her she was my best friend and the best friend I ever had. I guess I should have noticed that she didn't respond at all.

I just kept inviting her to do things. The other day I dropped in on her and she was packing. She was being transferred and she was thrilled because it was a big promotion. She had known for two weeks and she hadn't said a word. All she had to say about our friendship was, "too bad, we won't be seeing each other any more," sort of what you might say to the mailman when you move. I guess I looked pretty dumb to her, always waiting around hoping she'd honor me with her presence. Looking back, I guess I was pretty dumb, too. It cost me, money for a lot of dinners and a lot of esteem as well.

Once we have said the words, it is hard to take them back. People who move to intimacy too quickly sometimes do things that they regret later. They feel ashamed, embarrassed or disgusted with themselves. They wind up feeling like a sucker and it gets in the way of the next relationship. The same thing is true of premature anger and hostility. If you blow your top about some small thing, you have very little room when something important happens. Early in this book, we advised you about the difference between expressive and rhetorical speech. The idea is to stay rhetorical. If you choose to express affection or hostility, be sure it is a reasonable response based on a careful assessment of the situation.

Retribution

Most of us refuse to admit the possibility that someone, especially a former intimate could want to do us harm. The people we have been close to have access to a great deal of private information that can be turned against us. Unfortunately, they sometimes choose to exploit this power. There isn't a great deal you can do about someone who chooses to abuse your confidences. Perhaps the most legitimate course of action is simply to concentrate on not lowering yourself to the same level. In that way you exercise control over how you will regard yourself in the long run.

Dr. Hechbauer. Divorces can sometimes be exceptionally bitter. Former partners can attempt all sorts of legal action against their ex-mates. When children are involved, the possibility of child-stealing must be considered. Ex-mates who violate court decisions and literally abduct children from their legitimate guardians have been defined as criminals. If someone is extraordinarily hostile to you and attempts this kind of physical harm, you must not delay in seeking legal and whatever other professional help is necessary to defend yourself. You have reason to expect hostility, but you needn't compromise with tangible harm.

Chapter Summary

We began this chapter by introducing developmental theories about the process nature of human phenomena, and we applied them to relationships. We described the role of communication in six growth stages in relationships: the seeking individual, invitational communication (auditioning), explorational communication, intensifying communication (euphoria), revising communication, and bonding communication. Finally we introduced the idea of relationship problems that frequently arise during the growth stages.

In the next chapter, we will talk about how permanent, intimate relationships are regulated and how complications and problems can be handled through expert interpersonal communication.

REFERENCES FOR CHAPTER 6

I. Altman and D. Taylor, *Social Penetration: The Development of Interpersonal Relationships.* New York: Holt, Rinehart and Winston, 1973.

E. Berscheid and E. Walster, *Interpersonal Attraction.* Reading, Mass.: Addison-Wesley, 1969.

M. Davis, *Intimate Relations.* New York: The Free Press, 1973.

S. Duck, *Personal Relationships and Personal Constructs: A Study of Friendship Formation.* London: John Wiley, 1973.

M. Knapp, *Social Intercourse: From Greeting to Goodbye.* Boston: Allyn and Bacon, 1978.

T. Newcomb, *The Acquaintance Process.* New York: Holt, Rinehart and Winston, 1961.

I. Reiss, "Toward a Sociology of the Heterosexual Love Relationship," *Marriage and Family Living.* 22. May, 1960. Pp. 139–45.

G. Sheehy, *Passages: Predictable Crises of Adult Life.* New York: E. P. Dutton & Co., 1976.

J. T. Wood, "Communication and Relational Culture: Bases for the Study of Human Relationships," *Communication Quarterly.* 30, 2. May, 1982.

7

THE NAVIGATING STAGE: CONTINUITY AND CHANGE IN INTIMACY

It is relatively easy to plunge into a new friendship, to form an alliance with a colleague, or to fall in love with an engaging man or woman. In fact, launching a new relationship is fun and exciting. It is far more difficult to maintain those relationships once the initial intoxication fades. Rising divorce rates testify that a great many people cannot sustain long-term relationships. Compounding the problem is the fact that experts offer little guidance about how to prevent break-ups or what to do once relationships are shattered.

Consider this evidence from the *1980 Information Please Almanac* (New York: Simon and Schuster, 1979):

The number of divorces has tripled since 1959. Over a million divorces were granted each of the past five years. There are approximately 1.2 million children left with one parent as a result of divorces last year. The median length of terminated marriages was 6.8 years. The West has the largest divorce rate, 6.6 per 1,000 population. There were however, more divorces in the South (439,000) than in the East (177,000), the North Central Area (293,000), or the West (272,000). We have no figures on the number of "live-together" and close friendship relationships that came apart during the same time period.

There are a great many books on how to start and how to end relationships. Subjects such as no-fault divorces, how to make sure a divorce settlement is fair, and handling palimony are all covered in recent books. But the handling of problems by two people who wish to stay together is rarely addressed. Moreover, there is virtually no information on how to keep a relationship healthy over many years. This chapter deals with issues pertinent to sustaining relationships. While our discussion will focus on marriage, we do not rule out long-standing relationships of couples who have agreed to be together as mates or friends. We will explain how communication may be used to deal with the problems and pitfalls that threaten relationships, and how communication may be used to enhance the joys of enduring bonds.

The word "navigate" refers to the process of maintaining relationships or keeping them on a course satisfying to the partners. Most people do not expect to spend their lives in a state of euphoria. If they do, they are doomed to disappointment. People yearn for relationships that they can count on. But we have already pointed out that nothing stays the same in relationships. To keep a bonded relationship stable partners must use communication to maintain an even keel just as a ship's navigator uses a gyroscope to maintain the ship on course, despite the currents, tides, and waves. To explain the role of communication in long-term relationships we will deal with four main issues: (1) the structure of long-term relationships, (2) the changes that such relationships commonly undergo, (3) strategies that can be used for managing and initiating necessary changes, and finally, (4) some of the complications that may arise during this stage.

Relational Structure

When two people formalize a bond, they must develop a structure for governing their relationship. We have previously identified decision-making, administration, adjudication, and the formation of policy for internal and external affairs as the main features of a relationship structure; these issues define how the parts (individuals, values, roles and rules) fit together and operate in the relationship as a unit. Bonding confirms the rules, roles and communication styles that developed during the growth stages, but only at the beginning of the relationship. What the partners agree on during the revision stage emerges from their personal and social needs as individuals in a partnership. When two people commit to a permanent relationship, they ratify the patterns of transaction for their relationship; thus they mutually accept each other's identities. That is why the revision stage of relationship is so important. It enables partners to put some substance into their roles and rules before making a commitment. Commitment before some of this substantive work is done usually means early failure; without substantial agreements on structure, relationships are vulnerable to the first difficulties that may arise. Since the bonding is a confirmation and ratification, it is often more difficult to change the rules after the bond is formed than before.

Intimate relationships tend to fall into three basic structures: (1) complementary, (2) symmetrical, and (3) parallel. Each of these suggest how the partners fit together overall; in most relationships there are aspects of more than one of these structures. There is no *best* or *right* structure. Consideration of the structural alternatives may help you to understand some of your current relationships and to make informed choices about future ones. These structures also provide a way to classify and evaluate information that was gained from observation of relationships.

Complementary structures

When we say one thing complements another, we mean the two go together so that each works better in combination than alone. Complementary relations consist of partners who have found a way to relate so that neither is as effective independently as in combination with the other. In this kind of structure, *differences between the partners are emphasized*. Each partner has distinct roles, status, rights, and obligations and there is minimum overlap between them. The partners are interdependent, since differences are stressed and each partner counts on the other to obtain needed services and sentiments. Examples of such relationships would be student/teacher and doctor/patient relationships. These types of relationships work because each partner needs something from the other.

Power is the main difference between complementary partners. One partner in such a relationship has more power than the other. Interdependence in such relationships is characterized by unequal dependence. Thus, students have less power than teachers, but teachers cannot teach without students. Doctors have more power than patients, but doctors cannot practice unless people seek medical help. Power in relationships is often conferred by position. In the complementary marriage, the husband is typically regarded as the more powerful partner.

Complementarity is the traditional basis of American marriages. The husband's career provides the money to maintain the family. The family is identified by the breadwinner's career. The wife is the home-maker and is associated with the husband; she provides emotional support, cares for the home, and rears the children. In the traditional complementary relationship, the husband controls the money, decides where the family lives, and takes charge of most major matters. He assigns tasks and grants responsibilities to the wife. The wife supports her mate's decisions, depends on the husband for financial support, and lets him depend on her to tend his nest and raise the children.

Complementary relationships are notably *stable*. Because the partners are interdependent, it is hard for them to separate. Even when they do not get along well, so long as each provides what the other needs, the relationship has a basis on which to sustain itself. Stability, then, is an outstanding virtue of complementary relationships.

Jimmie and Blanche N. BLANCHE: I haven't worked since we've been married. That's the way we wanted it to be. I thought that as a mother I had to be with our three children when they were young. That's where a mother belongs. Now that our youngest has left, I spend most of my time working in the garden or improving the house. I've repaired the furniture and I make all our clothes. I was supposed to do those things, and I wanted to. I never worry about the money one bit; that's Jimmie's job. My middle daughter says she wouldn't have a marriage like ours, calls me old-fashioned. Well, I told her, it has worked for us for over 30 years. She should try to match that with her ideas about marriage! JIMMIE: Our marriage is a good one. Right from the start we got straight on how we were going to run it. My part was to earn an income for the family and I always provided well for all of us. Blanche's job was to take care of the house and the kids, and I have no complaints about her at all. She raised all of them to be responsible and gave them good values they wouldn't have gotten in one of those day care places. When I got home at night I could count on a good dinner and a clean house and a woman who cared about what happened. I told her about my day and she told me about hers. That was our bargain and it has worked all these years.

One of the drawbacks of a complementary relationship is that it reduces each partner's ability to function alone. Because each relies on the other, neither is really able to manage alone. Wives, for example, may be expert at managing home and children, but may lack the financial knowledge they need to survive on their own. Husbands may be able to handle earning an income, but they are unable to take care of even the simplest details of running a home such as cooking, cleaning, shopping, or handling children.

Steve L. Maybe staying home full-time and having two children in three years was too much for Anne. Whatever the reason, she's gone now. She got someone else and walked out on me, leaving the kids. Good riddance to her. I wouldn't take her back. But I sure wish I'd learned a little more from her, like how to shop for the boys' clothes and how to cook the kinds of food they need. If they were old enough to eat real food we'd be at the hamburger stand every night. The house seems to stay dirty even though I try to keep it up and even have someone come in once a week. How the hell do you get the stains from baby carrots off a white shirt?

Fred B. When Irma got the good job offer, I said, I can get a job anywhere so I'll go along. We arrived, set up house, she had the baby and went to work, and I took over on the kid, and tried to look for a job between feedings and changings. It's been a year now, and I know the plot of every soap opera, I cook meals on a tight budget, I've enjoyed seeing the kid grow. But the lady neighbors are suspicious of me, and the mailman thinks I'm a bum. And I suspect Irma thinks that taking care of the house is all I'm good for. I didn't expect this kind of marriage, and I wish I could do something about it. I wonder what she'll do, If I ever get employed.

A complementary marriage can be long-lasting and strong, but the fallout from long-term interdependence is reduced ability to function alone. If the relationship should end suddenly, this disability is often crippling.

Helen M. I thought we had a good marriage for twenty-six years. He was a manager at the plant here, and I stayed home with the kids. Both of us felt this was how a relationship between a man and woman should be. I had no desire to go to work. I loved my home and kids, making the house a good place to live. I did community work and had lots of friends. I counted on Ed to take care of us. We had some tight times, but somehow he would provide, and the rest of us didn't have to worry about money. Then Ed died last year, unexpectedly. That's when I started thinking we hadn't been so smart about the way we set up our marriage. I found out Ed only had $15,000 in insurance. That doesn't go very far once you pay for the funeral and settle the debts. It certainly didn't last long taking care of the household expenses. I had to sell the house but what with the second mortgage on it, there wasn't a lot of extra cash from the sale. I found out Ed had no pension at the company because he had elected to take full pay while he worked. He never discussed that with me. I can't help the kids with college, and I can't even take care of myself. And who will hire a woman of 46 with no education and no skills? The marriage worked fine for both of us, but now there's just one . . .

The complementary relationship emphasizes differences, particularly in power. The relationship is reciprocal, and its strength is that the partners need each other, which tends to enhance cohesion and satisfaction. Ironically, the very stability that may be good for the bond is the worst hazard for each individual since it impairs their ability to function independently should they ever wish or need to.

Symmetrical structure

The word "symmetry" means "balance." That is the defining feature of the second type of relationship structure. In symmetrical structures, partners define themselves as balanced, or matched and equal in most ways. Their stipulated goal—often not attained—is to be equal in all activities of the relationship.

Symmetrical relationships are counterparts of complementary ones. Complementary relationships emphasize differences between the partners, symmetrical ones emphasize similarities. Symmetrical partners define themselves as similar in roles, rights, status, and obligations. Consequently, they feel quite independent of each other. Each has exactly the same rights although, by agreement, they may have different responsibilities. A doubles tennis team may qualify as an example of a symmetrical relationship; however, the concept may be more of a guiding ideal than a tangible reality. Two colleagues of equal rank are symmetrically related since they are defined as equal by a supervising authority. The advantage of such a relationship is that power can be exchanged, sometimes very rapidly, so that each partner has roughly equal control in the overall relationship.

Balanced power is the goal of symmetrical relationships. Each partner claims an equal say in any decision that affects both. Furthermore, each partner reserves the right to make unilateral decisions on personal matters without necessarily informing the other. For example, husband and wife need not disclose their salaries, and they may keep independent bank accounts and make separate investments. Decisions about their shared living space are made only when both agree. Each may claim a private domain both inside and outside the relationship.

The independence characteristic of symmetry not only affects transactions between the partners, but also their conduct outside of the bond. Individuality is encouraged, so each partner tends to have a number of interests which exclude the other. They may have some separate friends and neither feels obligated to relate to people selected by the other, even for political purposes. Friends shared in common are agreed on. In essence, they have separate or only partly-shared social worlds.

Friendships and collegial relations are almost always symmetrical. Two people of equal professional and social status build their friendships out of important similarities. Within their relationship, each has an equal right to influence what the two will do together, and each has the right to pursue private interests without the other. A number of people who have complementary marriages have satisfying symmetrical relationships with others. Symmetrical relationships can provide exchanged assistance (I'll cover your shift if you cover mine) or collaboration (let's write a book).

A number of contemporary men and women view symmetry as an appropriate structure for their marriages. In such marriages, both have careers which provide income as well as status and recognition outside the home. The partners try to set up their relationship so that each has equal power and responsibilities. They both cherish their freedom and privacy. There is usually a good deal of negotiation about how to divide up unpleasant chores like cooking, cleaning, shopping, yard work, and repairs. Child care often requires very complicated arrangements to ensure that the children are well-attended without interfering with the professional interests of either parent. It is not unusual in such relationships for each partner to put an equal sum of money into the marriage and to do what each wishes with the remainder. In one such relationship, when the husband failed to do his share of the house-cleaning, the wife hired a maid and billed him for it.

Martha W. and Jack K. MARTHA: I wanted my freedom. That's Number One with me. I told Jack when we first started getting serious that I wouldn't be in a marriage that in any way infringed on my individuality and my right to do what I want with my life. We've worked things out so that we pool our resources and share responsibilities, but each person's life is their own business. The greatest thing about our marriage is that we don't stay together because we have to. Each of us could walk out any time and do just fine. It's a choice to be together. I like knowing that. JACK: I didn't exactly marry a girl like Mom. In fact, until I met Martha, I figured I wasn't the type for marriage. I just wouldn't have hooked-up with most of the women I met in college. I don't want to be tied down to someone who depends on me for so much. I am willing to contribute my half, but I expect Martha to pull her share, too. Besides I just can't see myself married to some female whose life revolves around diapers and dust.

Couples with symmetrical marriages often express pride in their arrangement and in the personal freedom it affords them. Symmetrical partners claim that this structure preserves the individuality which they feel would be sacrificed in a traditional marriage. But freedom and individuality can work against the durability of unions. Partners so committed to independence do not count heavily on each other. There is less emphasis on the relationship and more on each individual than in a complementary marriage. Partners who can go their separate ways do not feel any necessity to stay together when the going gets rough. Many marriage counselors believe that symmetry in marriage contributes heavily to the current divorce statistics.

Ruth J. Rick and I had been married three years when we split up. Actually, the marriage was pretty good in a lot of ways. We got along really well, had a good income and respected each other's space. Everything was going along nicely. Then I was offered a big promotion that would mean moving half way across the country, exactly what I'd been working my tail off for two years to get. I hoped Rick would be willing to move, but he wasn't. He didn't want to start all over from scratch. I understood that because I would have felt the same way. So I took the promotion and he stayed there. It's been a year and a half now. Both of us are so busy with our careers so we don't have time to visit much, and we're growing farther and farther apart. I suppose we'll end up divorced. We certainly aren't keeping up the marriage any more. I doubt that either of us even thinks about it any more. It's strange that I haven't found it very difficult to live without Rick. I still care about him, and if I hadn't moved I bet our marriage would still be fine, but I found that I can get along well without him too. I guess a relationship can't be that big a part of your life when you're trying to get ahead professionally.

Symmetrical partners have the option to alter their arrangement to meet changing circumstances. Sometimes, for example, it may be necessary to change to a complementary relationship if the couple wants children. Couples who must change the nature of their relationship for purposes of child care generally leave an "escape clause," to ensure the return to symmetry when the child no longer needs total care. Symmetrical relationships, while less secure than complementary ones, may be especially well-suited to relationships in which both partners are professionally committed.

Ariadne B., Ph.D. Marriage Counselor. I am very concerned about couples who follow the idea of symmetry in their marriages. The concept was invented by Dr. Watzlawick, who used it as a criterion for evaluation of the marriage process. It was a research concept, not an advisory concept about how to be married. What I am concerned about is the notion of "for better or for worse." It is not too hard to divorce when each partner is young and vital, but as people grow older, they acquire needs, and part of the purpose of marriage is mutual care. If a couple has the idea that they can split any time one is discontented, there will be little protection for either as they approach old age. We are already beginning to see some of the despair in people over forty, whose partners deserted them in a time of need.

Parallel structures

For purposes of classification, the complementary/symmetry dichotomy works fairly well. However, in the practical world there is a middle ground that combines the features of both kinds of relationships. In a parallel relationship, partners are symmetrical in dimensions of their life where independence is important but they develop systematic complementarity in those aspects of their life on which their relationship depends. The partners are committed to a common direction but they recognize that their contributions might vary and that each person requires independence in some areas.

Therefore, partners can agree that one will keep the budget and pay the taxes, while the other does the shopping and yard work. The decision is based on the qualifications of the individual. Exchanges need not be in kind. It might be very valuable to a person in a tense occupation to have a partner able to maintain a light atmosphere around the house. The exchange rate for that kind of contribution could be very high.

The exchange of trust between the partners in a parallel relationship involves considerably more commitment to the relationship itself than in a symmetrical one. He may trust her with the money; she may trust him to supervise the child care. The point is that there are aspects of the relationship in which one party is superordinate to the other *by agreement*. Some complementarity is highly practical in the assignment of roles if competency is viewed without reference to social stereotypes. The main strength of the parallel relationship is its flexibility to take advantage of the best features of the other two relational structures. In parallel bonds high premiums are placed on both the relationship and the individual partners. This is the greatest value of parallel structure. Its drawback is the amount of effort and commitment required to maintain the delicate balance between interdependence and autonomy.

Doug R. and Bev H. We spent a lot of time talking about what marriage should be *before* we took the leap. It seems not many people really think it through ahead of time. Neither of us wanted the kind of marriages our parents had where the man was the "lord and master," and the woman a slave. But we didn't want a relationship like a lot of our friends had either where you can't count on anything. Honestly, some of the couples we know are so hepped on independence that they aren't really couples. What they have is more like a merger than a marriage. We felt that if we really wanted to marry, then the relationship should be a really important part of our lives. Yet we also felt each person should grow and have interests beyond the marriage. So that's what we're working for. We split responsibilities, but we usually trade off after a few months. That way nobody gets stuck too long with anything. We have a lot in shared interests like music and sailing, but I'm interested in local politics and Doug likes to spend a lot of time in his shop working with wood. We have different personal friends, too, and a number of friends we share in common. We're 100% committed to this relationship and we're willing to sacrifice for it, but it's not the only thing in our lives.

Navigation is not a brief point in relationship development so the structure that characterizes a new relationship is not necessarily permanent. It may have to be revised to meet changing circumstances. If the wife gets pregnant or the husband disabled, major changes may be necessary. The changes may be temporary or permanent. The couple must be alert constantly to make the changes when needed, for if necessary accommodation is delayed too long, it is hard to keep the relationship together. The newly-married woman may find her job very important and she may insist on a symmetrical relationship. When children come it may be important to her to be able to devote full time to their care, and some form of complementarity or parallelism may be necessary. When the children are grown and the woman is ready to go back to work, it may be appropriate to return to symmetry. Similarly, most parent-child relationships are complementary for years and are redefined as parallel when the child reaches adulthood. Therefore, the structure of relationships responds not only to the personal preferences of the relating parties, but to the demands of the social world as well.

Relational Change

The word "relationship" implies process. It is naive to assume that a relationship will remain as it was at the time of bonding. Over the life of a relationship there will be numerous changes arising from changes in individuals and social systems. When individuals change, they must change the system in which they reside. When the system changes, the individuals must adjust accordingly.

Changes in individuals

Humans constantly undergo major and minor changes in physiology, social life, outlook and economic capability, among other things. What happens to us in the world outside a relationship affects our values, our personal decisions and our intimate relationships. The closer our relationship is with a changing person, the more important it is that we learn to adapt.

For example, young people who marry while in college confront major changes as they switch from student to worker. Entry into a career is challenging, tension-laden and time-consuming. Time is scheduled and controlled; partners need to make drastic changes in the way they deal with each other to meet the regularities of the new schedules. If partners work different shifts, life is even more complicated.

Outlooks are also affected by economics. Promises made during the student years are sometimes hard to keep when the chips are down. It is not uncommon for couples to divorce shortly after the male's graduation because the husband would not keep his promise to send the wife to school after the wife had worked for three or four years to support the husband's education.

Eric P. When we both landed jobs in Dallas, we thought we had it made. Fate was on our side. We could stay together. So, a month after graduation we got married and moved here and got going. After training, I got moved into personnel, and Sharon became an assistant marketing director in her company. She really moved ahead fast, two raises and a promotion in the past six months. I'm still doing what I did at the beginning. It annoys me a little, too. Sharon brings home more money than I do, and the thing that really grates on me is that she doesn't have time for *us*. Sharon knows I'm happy about her success and she's been great about supporting my ego and not making a big thing about her promotions. Still, there are times when I want to go to the beach for a weekend and she wants to stay in town and work on a new account. It's funny the way things turn out. I always saw me being the go-getter in the two-career marriage, and maybe even doing so well that we could step over to a traditional marriage. I never dreamed it would be Sharon that was the career dynamo, and I'd be the one pleading for more time.

In a perfect world, both partners in a marriage change at the same rate and concur about how to handle the changes, but this is not always the case. As one partner advances ahead of the other, the partner who stays behind is likely to become uneasy, competitive, or jealous. Simple aging also takes its toll. The most obvious effects of aging are physical. Bodies change. They are not quite as willing and able at fifty as they were at thirty. Appearances change. It is a little harder to be a sex symbol or a stud as you near forty, and sometimes it doesn't seem worth the effort. Needs for sleep change. Sexual incompatibilities can arise because of physiological changes. People acquire "disorders," like high blood pressure or diabetes, that physically affect the way they act. To accommodate to these physical changes partners should continue to offer assurances of worth to each other.

Cordelia C. I'm glad I didn't marry Will for his looks, because if I had, we'd be on the rocks now! Don't get me wrong; Will still looks good to me, but boy, he's changed. When we were going together his glasses were for the movies only. Now they are a permanent feature on his face. And his partners convinced him to shave off his beard. I miss that beard. Now I have to look at that undershot jaw. And to top it all off, he's going bald. He has almost no hair left on the top of his head. Brace yourself for the shocker: he's only 29 years old! This has all happened in the six years we've been married. I admit I kid Will about falling apart, but, what the hell, he's still the same man I fell for. In fact, it's kind of interesting to watch the changes. I can't help wondering what he'll be like in six more years. But, then again, he doesn't say anything about the wrinkles on my face.

As we grow older we experience important changes in the way we view our own powers. The younger we are, the more we think we can do. Along about age thirty, we begin to specialize, although many of us still keep trying to do it all. By age forty, we must face the fact that our powers are limited. We try to operate so that our weaknesses are minimized. We restrict our activities to those we can do well. Such changes have concrete effects on relationships. Some of the things that were fun and served to cement the relationship ten years before, must now be abandoned, and it is sometimes hard to find substitutes.

Most authorities feel that it is not the physiological changes themselves that cause the problem; it is our failure to adjust our goals and our activities to these changes. People may get bored with work and they may also find work harder to do. In either case, changes are necessary. When people become anxious about finances, problems arise. Aches and pains may require medical attention. Each of these changes presents the relationship with a problem to be solved. A great many marriages suffer real problems at this stage. Women's sexual abilities increase as they approach the middle years, men's decline. Each may blame the other for what is a natural process that requires change in both.

Age also has a way of altering our view of what's important in social and political spheres. Students are bored by tax legislation and social security laws. They have limited income and seldom think about growing old. By middle age, however, people may become intensely interested in these issues, since they have good incomes and they are growing old. They tend to become conservative, to believe less in liberal causes. Idealism is overcome by an urgency to conserve what you have earned. If one member of a couple takes on different political values, this can stimulate some real rows in the home. Religious commitments can change as well; however, in this case, it is likely that people become disillusioned and bored with religion as often as they become intensely committed to it. Either way, problems arise if the change is not mutual.

One of the most profound changes that can take place in a bonded relationship is when the partners assume the role of parents. With the birth of a child, partners are no longer defined exclusively by each other; they are also defined by their offspring. The pair has become a family, and the former partners must take on new roles to harmonize with the addition to the family. The infant makes it difficult for the partners to coordinate their lives. Caring for the infant inconveniences them. They may lose sleep. They find it hard to find time alone together. Since the infant will not adjust to the family itself, parents must either change or clash. Sometimes simple frustration over the accumulation of little changes caused by the child makes the relationship perilous.

George I. We both wanted a baby. We planned the pregnancy together and attended natural childbirth classes. We read everything we could get our hands on so we'd know what to expect. But one thing I hadn't counted on was how much of Kathy's time Joey would take. We agreed to split the chores but let's face it, I'm not equipped for breast feeding. Sometimes she spends a half hour nursing Joey and they are so wrapped up in each other, I guess I feel left out and a little jealous. I've told Kathy about my feelings and I think she understands, but we don't yet know how to work it out. Sometimes she nurses in bed and the three of us can be together. Maybe there are some other things we can do to make me more a part of it.

Personal changes require serious commitment and effort on the part of the partners in a relationship. It is hard enough to meet major changes in friendships where there is no bond. When friendships do not work, they can be terminated without legal confusion. Furthermore, casual friends are relatively easy to replace. Even then, the pain of conflict and separation can be very intense. For couples, uncompensated change may mean a painful end to what had been, up to that time, a thoroughly satisfying relationship. Throughout

Navigating involves staying in touch with each other's interests.

the life of their relationship, partners face the challenge of navigating through changes in individuals.

Changes in social systems

Many external changes in social systems can affect bonded partners. Economic conditions can trigger layoffs at work. Changes in social norms must be considered. As career possibilities open up for women, a great many aspire to be "superwomen"—loving partners, good mothers, and successful professionals. Inability to attain this impossible goal may spell failure for them. Similarly, some men, confronted with a successful wife, seem unable to maintain their own emotional stability. One of the most striking features of the last decade has been the increase of emotional illness, largely a result of people unable to handle the new possibilities in relationships available to them. Even today, the landscape is dotted with new circumstances that mean changes in possibilities. The singles bar, the single person household, the swinging singles condominium, the public sale of sexual materials and sex aids, and changes in the kinds of issues the film and media deal with are all part of the new scene.

The economy also forces changes in relationships. Increasing inflation has confronted Americans with the realization that a good standard of living often cannot not be maintained without two people in the household working. A great many complementary marriages turned symmetrical as once-contented housewives took their place in the economy.

Fiscal strains restrict possibilities for choice. When couples work, they feel that they ought to have something to show for their money. But money does not go far. It is virtually impossible for the average wage-earner to buy a house. Prices are skyrocketing and so are interest rates. Most new families will have to be content with rented housing. Unemployment and strikes take their toll as well. The traditional image of the male as breadwinner still prevails. As unemployment goes up, the self-esteem of the unemployed goes down, generating pressures that can tear couples apart. Financial pressures often require major changes in the goals of a relationship; this, in turn, requires that new roles be assumed by both partners.

It is one thing to accept the challenge of "keeping up with the Joneses." This is always a possibility if there is no drastic economic difference between the Joneses and you. But keeping pace with your own standards of what constitutes the good life is something else again when prices are outstripping income by a considerable figure. When a couple actually finds itself moving backward economically, there is a tendency to blame each other and to engage in some rash decision-making.

There is also constant pressure to measure up to social norms. The media tell us what love and marriage should be like. The popular magazines tell us how to evaluate our sex lives. Experts of all sorts have formulas for bringing up the children. In addition, the norms of fashion must be observed, weight must be kept down, muscles well-toned, and the proper soaps and deodorants used. Many people find themselves trapped into trying to keep up with what they think their society demands of them.

Clearly one of the serious problems confronting relationships is the lack of standards by which to judge success. A few decades ago it was easy enough to measure the success of a marriage by home, car and other possessions, job, physical attractiveness and children's accomplishments. Couples who try to measure up to media standards risk IFD disease because the idealistic goals promoted by media encourage frustration and demoralization. It is easy to get demoralized when you can never win.

The emotional state of one member of a relationship materially affects the mood and behavior of the other. When one partner is depressed and pessimistic, it can have a depressing effect on the other. Sometimes psychological pressures and stresses on the job temporarily cripple one partner. Partners who are able and willing to provide support help each other overcome their psychological stresses.

Temptation from others in our social circle can also challenge a relationship. Our CL and CL_{alt} are constantly signalling us about possibilities. It is easy to shift goals, particularly in circumstances drastically different from those when the relationship was formed. Couples who marry early find that experiences in their careers expand their possibilities by exposing them to new personal and professional choices. Furthermore, we continually meet new people, any of whom may cause us to reconsider our choice of a partner. Involvement outside a bonded relationship, sexual or otherwise, may impose serious stress on the primary relationship.

Ross D. I liked Emily when my wife, Molly, introduced me to her. Emily and Molly worked together and I was glad Molly had found someone she liked to work with. That is, at first I was glad. Then, instead of just being colleagues, they became friends, really close friends. Now they are writing a book together. The two of them stay out late working. They grab dinner and then stay at the office to work. Lately it seems that Molly spends more time with Emily than she does with me. The other night Molly said the two of them were thinking of taking a working vacation together to finish their book. I had looked forward to the vacation Molly and I had planned. I resent this a lot, but it's not like she's having an affair or being unfaithful. Emily is her friend. Maybe I need to find some friends of my own instead of counting so much on Molly.

When either member of a couple is confronted with tempting possibilities outside, it may foreshadow major changes in the way the couple operates. A previously complementary marriage can turn symmetrical, if the weaker member discovers ways and means to independence. The partner must adjust or the conflict could become insurmountable.

The most frequent change couples are called on to make is management of talk. They need to develop ways of talking constructively about their relationship. Otherwise they may talk themselves into trouble. The simple possibility of divorce as a topic of conversation is threatening. If partners spend too much time discussing such possibilities, they may pressure themselves into the possibilities generated by the talk. If this sounds circular, it was meant to be. The idea that a divorce is the answer to problems is sometimes very tempting to a couple in trouble. It may appear an easy way out once divorce has become a topic of discussion. What is intriguing is the popular observation of marriage counselors that divorces tend to become epidemic in some social circles. When the first couple in a group of couples divorces, the possibility becomes very real for all the rest, and it sometimes sets off a syndrome where each couple elects immediate divorce as the remedy for whatever ails them.

When one partner in a bond is threatened from the outside, each member must make some individual choices. Threat tends to individualize the partners, to split them apart regardless of their relationship structure. The decision of how to change rules or roles must be made jointly and carefully by committed individuals. There is nothing quite so pathetic as one member of a relationship trying to live as though nothing has happened when major changes have come about in the other partner.

Agnes D. It was just like a soap opera. It started with working late at the office. Then my friends started telling me about this woman they saw Ben with in various places. He talked about her a lot, the new junior exec at the company. I waved it off. He had a right to work with whomever he wanted. It was no business of mine. I could not accept the possibility that Ben was finding more in her than he did in me. I did not examine my behavior to see if I was driving him out. That might not have been right, but it would have been action at least. I never blamed him. I just put up with and waited for Ben to become what he had been, right up to the moment when I came home from an afternoon with a friend to find Ben's possessions moved out of the house and a note on the table telling me that I would hear from his lawyer. I was a damn fool. I didn't look at my alternatives. I didn't protect myself. Now I have to pick up the pieces the best I can.

Communication Strategies for Managing Change

By now it should be clear that changes include not only adaptation to major stresses and crises but also day to day fluctuations of human beings living their normal lives. Change is neither good nor bad. Whether change helps or harms our relationship depends on the nature of the change as well as how we plan for and manage it. The effectiveness of change must be measured against the problem it aims to solve. If couples cannot specify their problems, no amount of change will solve them. As the saying goes, if you don't know where you're going, any road will do.

The least productive response to pressure is refusal to recognize it. This ostrich approach solves nothing, but sadly, it is the approach many people take to stresses on the relationship. Many people feel that, if catastrophe is inevitable, there is nothing they can do to ward it off. People are naturally wary of changes they see in the people around them. Change is unsettling for it disrupts established patterns. But one sign of mental illness is the maintenance of inappropriate behaviors long after conditions warranted change. The demand to change often throws us into a freeze state. But, in order to deal with problems, one must take flight or fight back. Doing nothing rarely works.

Committed partners can do a great deal to manage change in constructive ways. We will now consider some of the ways communication helps us deal with changes. We cannot control everything that happens to us in our lives, but we can control our communication. Therefore, controlling communication is a productive basis for making sensible adaptive change in intimate relationships.

Baseline communication strategies

If you wait until changes are on top of you before trying to figure out how to react to them, you are already operating at a deficit. Sensible couples talk about how to make changes early after bonding. Even if they do nothing more than review their successful modifications and note how they came about, they will be better-prepared than if they ignore the issue entirely. Furthermore they can anticipate some changes easily. Changes in the economy, pregnancy, and temptations from other people can be planned for. Policies can be established. In fact, instead of settling into a phatic routine, this kind of planning gives couples something important to talk about that helps cement them together.

Monitoring, the process of observing and regulating behavior, assists efforts to make constructive changes. If you are sensitive to your partner and to events around you, you will be able to spot potential irritants before they become intense and you will be able to call them to the attention of your partner.

An ongoing evaluation of the relationship can be characterized by a discussion of potential changes. Key lines like, "they are considering me for a promotion but it will require moving to Billings," "I find Ken really attractive," "housing costs have taken another jump, maybe we ought to consider making the move now," or "I am feeling some urgencies about becoming pregnant," will alert the partner to the need for planning. Monitoring and sharing perceptions help partners maintain control over their transactional patterns.

Celeste B. It's hard to pinpoint when my room-mate, Betsy, and I stopped having those conversations that had made us best friends. When we first got our apartment we used to have marathon talks through dinner and into the evening. Then Betsy's folks gave us the TV and somehow it just started being on when we fixed dinner. Then we had Dan Rather join us for dinner and the TV just sort of stayed on. Neither of us meant to give up our talks, but they just ended. And, when the talks ended, so did our relationship.

The inaccurate perception in Celeste's narrative was that the television just started being on. Televisions do not turn themselves on. Somewhere there was a decision by one of the partners to turn the set on. It's a simple choice, but only if you realize there's a choice to be made. When we fail to notice what we are doing, we can thoughtlessly interfere with something important. That is the reason why monitoring and regular reports are so important.

Rarely do we have to respond to dramatic crises. Our lives are not as compressed as soap operas. Sometimes serious health problems can hit unexpectedly, but there are few disasters that have no forewarnings. Most often, changes creep up on us. It is, for example, an axiom in mental health that people don't just go crazy. They don't suddenly begin behaving peculiarly. Mental illness proceeds by accretion, by small increments, and for the most part, so does trouble in relationships. At what point does weekend drinking turn into a few drinks during the week, to a mandatory highball before dinner each night, then to two, and then to . . . ? When does the late night at the office become so routine that a night at home is exceptional? When does a regular exercise program drift into a once-a-week workout and then into no exercise at all? At what point do a few cigarettes turn into a pack a day? How do intimate conversations between partners deteriorate into logistical conferences about errands to be run and schedules to be coordinated? When do daily compliments and words of affection turn into grunts? When do loving partners begin to dispense with the normal courtesies granted to any stranger?

Monitoring will help you spot these changes and address them *before* they become so habitual that they are very difficult to alter. Few couples come apart in a traumatic way. Most drift apart and the gigantic fight at the end is a ceremonial dance that provides an excuse for officially ending what had already ended.

Communication Climate refers to the atmosphere people in a relationship create for talking with each other. It is important to maintain an inviting climate where partners feel free to talk about themselves and the relationship. Partners who feel that talk is annoying or unnecessary cannot engage in productive problem-solving when they need to. Some couples agree to discuss important things for a while before going to bed each night. They must be constantly willing to listen to each other. If this courtesy is not granted, the relationship is already on the rocks.

It is not so easy to keep the door open for conversation. Most of us have all too many days when we lumber home from the office and want nothing more than to sulk in sullen silence or collapse into a comatose state in front of the TV. Such habits require a dose of "sulk" vaccine, loving and considerate conversation from a partner who cares enough about the relationship to motivate us into caring again.

An activity as complicated as human communication cannot sustain itself. People must commit to talking. When talking becomes an effort, it is a signal that an effort must be made to talk about talking. It is risky to believe that once a commitment is formalized the relationship will be self-sustaining. By monitoring changes as they begin to happen and by maintaining an open atmosphere for talk, couples can minimize perils that otherwise might put them in a lawyer's office.

Strategies to Control and Create Change

Maintaining an atmosphere conducive to talk does not actually address specific problems. In addition to monitoring and maintaining an affirming communication climate, couples will need to develop some specific methods to deal with issues that affect their relationship.

Intimate communication

Extended and concentrated talk called "intimate communication," brought the couple together in the first place and allowed them to build an initial relational culture. Ironically, intimate communication is one of the first casualties of intimacy.

People seem to think that once they have taken the step of declaring their intimacy, they no longer have to act intimately. Sometimes partners feel they know all there is to know about each other. But we never learn everything, and since we are constantly changing, we can never keep up with everything. A second interference with intimate communication is each partner's assumption that the other knows she or he cares, so there doesn't have to be regular confirmation. That's what the bonding was about, after all. Finally, there is no norm in society that encouarges sustaining intimate communication after bonding. Whatever the reason intimates stop talking intensely, it is the clearest indication of a drift from intimacy.

We have described a problem. The solution lies in reviving the kind of communication that created and characterized the relationship at its most exciting moments. It requires at least one partner to motivate involvement. If one (or both) partner(s) keeps prodding for regular talk about important topics, the habit of intimate communication can be made a part of the relationship. Topics like each partner's career, goals, perceptions of problems, fears and dreams are important to discuss. What partners do in their time alone, and new people they have met are all legitimate topics of conversation. Does one partner see some important changes ahead? Does one partner have some new opinions and want confirmation, or at least interest, from the other? These represent the basis for intimate communication.

It is also important that partners talk about how they see each other. A kind of "good and welfare" talk for the good of the order that characterized the old fraternity/sorority system, is useful in relationships. If partners have legitimized inquiry into perceived changes in each other, then it is relatively easy to communicate information that might affect the relationship. This does not mean you have to spend a great deal of time picking each other apart. It does mean that it is valuable to set aside time for intimate talk frequently and regularly and to treat this as important. Each couple, of course, must decide how much time is wanted. In the last chapter of this book we will provide you with a number of formats you can use to regularize your talk about your relationship, if you care to use them.

There are two major benefits that accrue from maintaining intimate communication. One is understanding between the partners. By talking about each person, the nature of the bond itself, and perceptions of each other, partners stay up-to-date in their understanding of what is going on in each other's head. This facilitates the crucial process of maintaining accurate dual perspective in transactions. Even if you think you know your partner as well as possible, there is nothing that can be lost by making sure that you stay current. Most likely you will pick up something important that you did not know and which will enable you to respond more perceptively to your partner's concerns and priorities.

Laura and Willie W. LAURA: There wasn't any problem or anything really wrong in our marriage, but it just seemed we were finding less and less time to talk like we used to when we were going together. When we dated we were always drifting into these really fabulous talks, but it didn't seem to be happening any more. So I suggested to Willie that we start "dating" again, once a week. I know it sounds a little kinky, but after all, why should a couple stop dating just because they're married? We decided to have a regular Saturday night date night, because that's always when you want to be with your most important date. I think Willie went along just to humor me at first, but now he looks forward to Saturday night as much as I do, and he won't let anything interfere. WILLIE: Laura's right about why I went along in the first place. To be honest, I thought the idea was pretty silly, but I thought, "why not?" It will get us out of the house. At first it was kind of strange. Neither of us knew what to do on our first date. I think that's when I realized it wasn't silly at all. I mean, it's a bad commentary on a marriage when two people forget how to talk to each other. So we went and parked on the hill and necked a little and we talked plenty. I found out a lot about Laura since then, how close she was to her

Communication is the life blood of navigation.

grand-parents when she was a kid, and how messy the politics are in her office. And she knows some of my hopes about expanding the business next year. The main thing is that we're on top of what's happening again, and we look forward to learning something new each week or just being together intimately.

Maintaining intimate communication protects your relationship from the possibility of gradual erosion. It is an insurance policy against failing to understand changes in each other. It has the additional benefit of affirming both the self-hood of the partners and the integrity of the relationship. Simply devoting time to serious talk proves that each partner wants to invest in the relationship. Talk breathes life into relational culture.

Intimate relationships should be at least as important as planning a vacation or organizing household chores, yet couples usually talk a great deal more about trivia than important relationship issues. Intimacy will not flourish on conversational drivel. The amount of communication exchanged is not enough. It must be intimate in quality; it must focus on intimate content. There must be concern for the other, intimate and private topics, and emotion exchanged. Laughing, crying, reminisicing, and planning together provide great adhesive for any bond.

Revitalizing communication

This is a conscious effort to make the talk in the relationship meet new needs as they arise. It is often desirable to redefine aspects of relational culture so they keep pace with changes in the partners' values, self-definitions and goals. Relationships, like institutions, have a tendency to settle into patterns, but patterns don't always serve a useful purpose. Inertia sustains patterns inertia and the feeling that problems will not arise if you keep your eyes closed.

Revitalizing communication can revise aspects of a relational culture or it can add new dimensions. Even the best relationships can benefit from a bit of innovation. Behaviors and activities once novel and interesting can easily become routine. Keeping communication vital and challenging affects all aspects of a relationship. For example, the decision that once a month the couple should do something absolutely new has value. Go to that first hockey game. It is *not* unusual to bring home a new puzzle to work on together, to decide spontaneously to eat out in an interesting new restaurant, or to plunge into a new activity that provides you with a wealth of topics to talk about with your partner. Unexpected and unrequired thoughtful acts are important revitalizers. Bringing home flowers or a new fishing fly can generate excitement, particularly if she brings him the flowers and he brings her the fishing fly.

It is important to maintain revitalization rituals. Societies and religions maintain a regular routine of holidays in order to keep people interested in the prevailing ideas and to celebrate important commitments. The same can be done for relationships. Anniversaries and birthdays are, of course, almost mandatory celebrations. Establishment of major events to accord with holidays like Christmas, Thanksgiving, and Passover, or Super Bowl Sunday, and the opening of trout season can provide partners with something to look forward to and to work together to plan for.

Once a year celebrations are important, but they are not enough to sustain intense commitment. Small gestures, acts of consideration and concern, surprises, and expected demonstrations of caring keep intimacy vital. A little novelty added to transaction can help both parties remember how special they are to each other. On the practical level, revitalization also helps to keep intimacy alive. A special dinner, soft lights, and a bit of awkward dancing, just like old times, can set off some truly intense talk capable of putting real vigor back into the relationship.

Nell Z. If I ever doubted that Jeff loved me or if I ever thought maybe he'd become bored after 9 years of marriage, I don't after my last trip. I was attending a week long medical convention while Jeff stayed home with his work. When I got registered at the hotel, I went to my room and started unpacking my suitcase. Right on top of all my clothes was a note from Jeff saying he'd miss me. As I unpacked I found three more little messages tucked among my clothes. But the best surprise came the day I was heading home. After I'd packed everything, I got out my return ticket to verify my flight time. Taped to the ticket was a note saying he'd pick me up at the airport and we'd go out to dinner to celebrate my return. Whoever said romance has to go out of marriage?

Revitalization can also tackle some major issues such as goals and new directions. One couple reserves their entire anniversary day each year for a kind of retreat to conduct an intense review of their marriage. They even have a check list of important points to consider. They discuss all of the things that brought them together in the first place, and they check off how each of them still figures in the relationship. Their "annual check-up" as they call it, is designed to trouble-shoot problems that may have arisen during the year. They spend the first part of the day isolating problems. Then they focus on solutions and changes they want to make during the year. As the evening wears on, it becomes a brainstorming session, with each party generating ideas for invigorating their life. The day usually comes to an end with a rather amorous engagement.

Ideas like the annual check-up are important. We have annual physical check-ups, twice yearly visits to the dentist, and periodic tune-ups for our cars. Maintaining your most important relationships is at least as important as saving a molar or having an oil change.

The strategies we've suggested for regulating intimacy are not startling. Nonetheless, they suggest important priorities for maintaining intimacy. To an extent, they are almost cliché-like. All these strategies are based on communication. It is really up to each couple to decide how to sustain intimacy, but the one thing that is for sure is that they will have to communicate about it. There is no escape from changes, problems and threats, and tough decisions to be made. Bonded relationships will change over time and through the efforts of the individuals in them. When intimate partners do not change or do not manage changes as required, their relationship tends to become strained and sometimes terminates. Intimate partners have choices about whether and how they will change, and if they learn to change together, the prognosis for permanence will be good. The phase of relationships where the couple navigates through problems and changes is the most challenging of all, because it is the phase of longest duration and greatest diversity. Up to this point novelty sustained interest and promoted intimacy. During navigation, commitment is what sustains interest and promotes intimacy. Communication, therefore, demonstrates the commitment necessary to maintain a rewarding relationship.

Complications

Three complications frequently arise during the navigating phase of relationships.

Unequal effort (it takes two to tango)

A recurrent problem in intimate relationships is that one partner seems to invest more than the other to keep the relationship going. This can occur for a number of reasons. One partner may have more time to give or the relationship may mean more to one partner than to the other. Regardless of the reason, the recognition of imbalance in a relationship can create serious tension between the partners. The heaviest investor can feel used, the other can feel guilty.

To deal with this problem you must determine how serious the imbalance is. If the differential is because one partner is temporarily distracted and involved with other issues, the couple can work out ways to support him or her during the stress period. If, however,

the problem is because one partner is losing interest in the relationship or does not understand how to invest, then it may be necessary to explore some of the core elements of the bond, the basic roles and rules of the relational culture. It may be that the disparity can be worked out by mutual decision. It may be that one person feels he or she is not getting enough from the relationship and changes can be made accordingly. Other alternatives may be tempting one party out of the relationship. Disparity in investments is an important diagnostic for it helps to reveal serious problems. A person may elect to stay in a relationship even though it doesn't measure up to the ideal, but if this is his choice it should be an informed choice.

Incompatibility

This sometimes occurs because partners have changed the behaviors and attitudes that brought them together. It is hard to keep track of changes, and sometimes they happen so gradually that partners become incompatible and do not even recognize it until much later. Incompatibility is not an infallible sign that the relationship is over. It is, rather, an indication of the need for revitalization and redefinition. Love and concern can overpower incompatibility, provided the partners know what they are doing and are willing to devote energy to resolving the problem.

The problem is considerably more sticky when one partner thinks the relationship is over and the other does not. There are no pat solutions to this. If one partner wants out there is little the other can do besides wheedle, bribe and threaten, and such activities seldom produce a healthy outcome. Certainly it is important to inquire whether there is any reason to hope to save the relationship. For example, if the marriage is threatened because a retired housewife is now working and the husband feels aggrieved because his needs are not being met, there is some reason for hope. Situations like that can be talked out and ground rules revised.

The partner who cares least about the relationship has the most power in such a situation. When there is a disparity, however, it is good to find out about it early enough to make a constructive exit, if that is your choice. It helps to understand that a relationship must end when partners do not get enough out of it to warrant their input. Talking through these perceptions can lead you to a sensible exit. We will deal with this issue in detail in the following chapter.

Benign neglect (if only we could find the time)

Sometimes partners just stop making an effort. They are not aware that they are not making an effort, but they are aware that good things are not happening like they used to. Lack of time, preoccupation with the job, the kids, or personal health are the most frequent causes of neglect in the relationship. It is easy to get caught up in personal concerns. Illness, for example, is all-consuming. The healthy partner can never really understand how fearful a serious illness can be, and how much it can cause a partner to change. If the sick partner is too embarrassed to talk about his or her fears, the healthy partner can lead the discussion and guide the partner back to the relationship. Guilt about real or imagined violations also leads to personal preoccupation. When individuals retreat inside themselves for any reason, they neglect their partner. These are the kinds of problems that intimate talk and revitalization can best ameliorate. By finding a way for partners to express their deep and distracting worries and fears, healthy changes can be made; this will strengthen the relationship so that it can handle the worst that can be thrown at it. If dissolution is an undesirable alternative, then individual concern, preventive maintenance and sustaining intimacy will help keep you together.

Chapter Summary

An intimate relationship is a full-time responsibility for both partners must constantly revise themselves and their relationship to meet important changes as they come. Throughout the navigation stage there will be pressures to change that are imposed from inside and outside the relationship. Our world is in a state of constant flux, and so are we as individuals. This means that in order to remain vital and viable, our relationships must also keep changing.

An enduring bond is one that is constantly in process. Because it is dynamic, individual efforts are required to keep it strong. Partners should work out ways to communicate with each other to solve personal and joint problems without sacrificing romance and excitement. Divorce is a legitimate alternative, of course, but it may not be a desirable alternative.

Thus, it is important to keep investing and communicating to keep your bond truly intimate. Choice and responsibility are the key issues here. You have the right not to make the time to invest in your bonded relationship, but you incur the responsibility for that choice and the consequences it entails. The material covered in this chapter should make you realize how easy it is for partners to drift apart and for bonds to falter through a series of changes and oversights that are individually so minor that they go unnoticed until they are collectively so overwhelming they cannot be reversed. This is the potential consequence of the choice to neglect an intimate bond. If you are willing to accept that responsibility then both your goals and actions should be informed. It is more usual that partners do not recognize choices or foresee consequences until there is damage, that is sometimes irreparable.

However, the situation is far from hopeless. Most intimate relationships not only can be maintained but also continually enriched, if partners take the trouble to learn how to trouble-shoot in advance and communicate constructively about key issues. This is the challenge of the navigating stage and the rewards of meeting the challenge are a satisfying bond that continues to grow as you do.

REFERENCES FOR CHAPTER 7

P. Berger and H. Kellner, "Marriage and the Construction of Reality," in D. Birrset and C. Edgely (Eds.), *Life as Theatre*. Chicago: Aldine Press, 1975. Pp. 219–233.

C. Bird, *The Two-Paycheck Marriage*. New York: Rawson-Wade Publishers, 1979.

M. Davis, *Intimate Relations*. New York: The Free Press, 1973.

M. Fitzpatrick and P. Best, "Dyadic Adjustment in Relational Types," *Communication Monographs*. 46, August, 1979. Pp. 167–178.

W. Lederer and D. Jackson, *Mirages of Marriage*, New York: W. W. Norton, 1968.

W. Lederer, *Marital Choices*. New York: W. W. Norton, 1981.

N. Lobenz, "Marriage Talk," *Woman's Day*. April, 1970. P. 18 *ff*.

W. Nolan, "What You Should Know about Male Menopause," *McCall's*. June, 1980. P. 84 *ff*.

J. T. Wood, "Communication and Relational Culture: Bases for the Study of Human Relationships," *Communication Quarterly*, 30, 2. May, 1982.

8

ENDING HUMAN RELATIONSHIPS: THE STAGES OF DETERIORATION

You've probably been involved in a number of relationships that no longer exist. Some you ended, some the other partner terminated, and some were dissolved by mutual agreement. Some probably ended very abruptly, perhaps when a more attractive potential partner entered the scene. Others decayed gradually, perhaps due to the growing realization that there was no future or perhaps just becoming a little less important each day until eventually they were non-relationships. The demise of some relationships probably produced pain for you, while in other cases you felt mainly relief. Just by thinking over your own graveyard of relationships, you can probably identify examples of most of these types of termination.

Now that you're thinking about relationships that have ended, focus on a few questions. Were you aware of different stages in the deterioration? Were you aware that you had choices about whether a relationship should end and *how* it should end? Are you satisfied with your personal actions in the latter stages of your past relationships? Have you learned anything about yourself from what happened in your previous relationships that ended? From your past bonds have you derived any insights about what kind of partners are appropriate for you and what kind of relational cultures you want to try to achieve in the future?

In this chapter we will focus on deterioration, the third and final part of relational evolution. Not all relationships end, and not all endings are bad. Some people build relationships so strong they outlast all hazards. In other cases everyone involved benefits by ending a bond. When a relationship shows signs of serious trouble, the partners have to decide whether to repair or dissolve it. It's important that partners know how to decide which is the more constructive option.

Like most human activities, terminating relationships can be done well or poorly. To repair ailing bonds, or if appropriate, to sever them effectively, you must understand what choices individuals have as relationships de-escalate. This chapter is organized into four major sections in order to provide you with information about your options. (1) First, we'll examine major reasons for relational deterioration and point out which reasons preserve the possibility of revitalizing a bond and which almost inevitably lead to termination. (2) Next, we'll present a typical sequence of relational decay. (3) Then we'll take a final look at the stages of deterioration to identify major choices and responsibilities for managing the process so that it is as civil and constructive as possible. We'll emphasize the value of analyzing a failing bond so that you learn from what has happened. (4) We'll conclude the chapter with a look at some of the frequent complications that plague relationships on a downhill course.

Reasons for Relational Deterioration

Why do intimate relationships deteriorate? How does it happen that two people who voluntarily interwove their lives decide to break up their common world? The reasons fall into three broad categories: (1) individual expectations, (2) factors intrinsic to a bond, and (3) factors extrinsic to a bond. One or any combination of these three factors may jeopardize a bonded relationship.

Individual expectations

Perhaps the greatest single cause of relationship deterioration is our individual expectations, the beliefs about relationships we carry with us when we make our bonds. Marriage counselors point out that marriages don't create troubles. We create our own problems and bring them into marriage, like doweries. Our expectations about what we can expect of a partner and of the relationship may constrain our satisfaction.

Each of us forms expectations of how a relationship should operate. When we agree to form a relationship, we do so because we believe it will provide something for us. Our anticipation is that we will gain more than we will lose. This presents no problem, so long as our expectations are reasonable. If any of our major expectations are not met, however, we become discontented and may seek to get what we expected or find a way out.

Unrealistic expectations seem the most frequent source of difficulty in romantic relationships. We have already pointed out the perils of believing that once love is declared we will live happily ever after without problems. While most people claim they don't believe this, deep down we all want to believe the myth that our romances will remain forever sunny. This notion is encouraged by the romantic lore of slick magazines, soap operas and films. Romance is the adult fairy tale.

Bruno Bettleheim believes that as children, we learn to take the fantasies that we read about seriously. Children compare their lives at home with what they read in their school books. The happy families in the stories represent a contrast to the typical family with its reasonable share of disagreements and disruptions. Children may decide that there is something wrong with their families or with themselves if there is no correspondence between what they read and what they see at home.

Children's textbooks are generally devoid of stressful and anxiety-evoking themes. According to Bettleheim, you cannot help stimulating some unpleasant feelings if you represent life accurately. But children need to know that they will encounter difficult situations, and more important, that they can manage them. Children who grow to adulthood without learning this are poor relationship risks, for they expect their partner to conform to the fairy tale they have made part of their lives. Suppose one did a story about divorce; wouldn't it seem threatening to children?

One of the most telling signs of our addiction to romantic fantasies is the incredible popularity of romance novels which follow the old fairy tale formula: exciting man (knight in shining armor or Prince Charming) meets beautiful woman (damsel in distress or princess). They fall madly in love. An obstacle intervenes (a dragon, a wicked stepmother, or a decadent debaucher). The exciting man courageously overcomes the obstacle (slays the dragon, takes lovely lady away from wicked stepmother, or brings decadent debaucher to justice). Man and woman embrace and walk away (ride off into the sunset) to a life of wedded bliss. They live happily ever after. The end. Books based on this fairy-tale formula are selling in record numbers. The public, it seems, wants to believe in perfect love, unblemished romance, and happily-ever-after endings.

As long as we accept such stories as fantasies, they are harmless and pleasant diversions from the problems of everyday living. However, trouble's in the making if we start to regard them as descriptions of how relationships actually work. Fairy tales and romance novels do not depict real relationships. Their counterparts, soap operas, claim to present reality, but they make tragedy so appealing and noble that viewers learn nothing useful about managing their own lives.

Lydia C. I do not use the word 'friend' lightly. I've known enough people to realize that most people are not worthy as friends. In fact, I've been consistently disappointed even in those rare people whom I invited to be my friends. In my mind, when you say, "I'm your friend," what you're saying is that you care deeply about me, you'll be there any time I need you, you'll support me when I need your help, and you'll celebrate in my victories. You're also saying you'll always make time for talking between us, because we are that important in your life. And you're saying that I come before other people you know. That's what a friend is. I wish people would realize how wrong it is to say "I'll be your friend" when they aren't willing to live up to their words. It just hurts too much when they let me down after I counted on them to be there, to care, and to always have the time.

Since we have all been exposed to fairy tales, all of us can expect to have some unrealistic expectations. But its one thing to have idealistic expectations and quite another to cling to them inflexibly. Actually, ideals can be quite useful because they give us something to shoot for. They motivate us to work on our real relationships and to improve them.

Idealistic expectations are dangerous only if we refuse to bend them enough to apply to real relationships between real people. There must be enough leeway in expectations to allow for human imperfections. Standards by which to evaluate relationships must be built out of human experience not from literary imaginations.

Expectations can cause trouble when they are incongruent between partners. A relationship can work only if partners develop common, or at least compatible expectations about it. If there is no congruence on basic assumptions and general goals, it is impossible to define roles and develop rules to guide the relationship. Congruity should develop during the revising stage and continue as part of navigation. Partners must expect to change their expectations and to adjust to their partner's changes.

A clear example of expectations that grow to be incompatible is found in the impact of the Human Potential Movement that swept our society in the late 1960's and into the 1970's. Many long-established relationships ended when one or both partners sought the ideal of self-actualization. Self-actualization, of course, is not inherently evil. The problem was that too many who sought self-actualization failed to recognize it as an ideal and an extremely abstract one at that. They didn't know what they were after, and therefore, they were often unproductive in their mystical quest for self-improvement.

We referred earlier in this book to IFD Disease (Idealization, Frustration, Demoralization). One hazard of self-help methods is everything is phrased generally to allow potential customers to interpret as they see fit. However, since nothing specific is offered, no one can set clear goals. The result of most such methods has been very frustrating. There is very little evidence that they produce tangible permanent improvement in many relationships. However, there is considerable risk of emotional problems stemming from the pressures of seeking a goal which can never be specified.

Katie B. Our relationship had been good from the start. We were able to solve our problems and got along really well for three years. Mind you, I say that *now* with good old twenty/twenty hindsight. But the relationship ended nearly two years ago and I'm still not really sure why. Some of my friends introduced me to books on reaching your personal potential—one by Maslow. So I read the books and we all talked about them. The more we talked, the more I came to believe that I wanted more in a relationship than what Roger and I had. More what, you might ask. Well, I didn't know—then or now. I couldn't define what I wanted; I just felt there had to be more than a good, solid relationship. In all fairness I have to admit that Roger was pretty patient for a long time. He tried to understand. He asked what I wanted that he wasn't giving, what was missing in our relationship, what problems about us bothered me. I'm sure if I could have told him, he'd have done something about it. But, I didn't have any answers for him. I couldn't think of anything concrete I wanted from Roger that he wasn't already giving. I couldn't point to any specific problems we had. I just felt that there had to be more. To make a long story shorter, Roger gave up after several months of this routine and he moved on. And now, two years later, I still don't know what I was after then. I do know, though, that I haven't found another relationship that can even come close to the one I threw away. At least now maybe I can define what I'm after—the kind of relationship I demolished!

Expectations of a partner

Each member in a relationship has some expectations about what a partner should be and do. Often, individuals will focus so intensely on their own goals they forget the principle of reciprocity. To expect more than a partner can give and to fail to reward the partner by meeting his or her expectations can demolish a relationship. People often expect their partners to compensate for their own weaknesses. We all need a little help now and again and we all have faults. To expect a partner to meet all your needs and not have any faults is dangerously naive. After the bond is established, partners find themselves ill-at-ease as they begin to learn things about their partners that they did not expect. It's unrealistic, not to mention unfair, to expect a relationship or another person to cure your weaknesses or to compensate for qualities you do not have. One of the most damaging assumptions you can make is that your partner will, somehow, make you what you want to be. Nor will you be able to repair major flaws in your partner. Many a person has married an alcoholic, believing that the relationship would cure the disease. One of our respondents provided this account:

Harriet W. Ed drank. I knew it. I saw him drink, all the time. He would drink himself into a stupor. Every Saturday, he would tell me how tough the week was and how he had to let down. But he was so tender and loving. I knew that what he needed was me. Then, on the honeymoon, he stayed smashed for four days. When we got home, I discovered that he drank every morning to get himself to work. He wouldn't go to a shrink and he wouldn't go to A.A. and instead of helping him, I made matters worse, and he finally went on a toot and landed in jail, and I packed up and went home. I'll tell you this—I got trained as a bookkeeper, not an alcohol abuse counselor and there was nothing I could do about Ed's drinking except ruin my life! I should have known better.

Your intimates affect how you see yourself and they can support your personal growth, but *you* must do the growing. That is your responsibility. No partner can do it for you. No relationship can make it happen. Your partner cannot make you smarter or more confident or stronger or whatever you want to be. This expectation is an almost guaranteed method of sabotaging a relationship, because you can never be satisfied and your partner will continually feel frustrated about being unable to satisfy you.

It's wise to be wary of what others expect of you, as well as what you expect of them, before committing. Unrealistic expectations do not suddenly develop after bonding. Clues exist throughout the growth process. Once the euphoria has evaporated and you begin to make revisions, you should discuss mutual expectations. If your partner wants to make you over, or if you feel that you must make your partner over, the relationship has a shaky foundation. A bond based on faulty expectations contains the seeds of destruction. It may take time before the bond actually caves in but the potential is there from the beginning. Far better to get expectations on the table and to revise them as necessary *before* deciding on a full commitment.

Factors Intrinsic to a Bond

A second major cause of relational deterioration is problems within a relationship. The trouble does not lie in either partner, but in the choices they've made together. Occasionally people who alone are decent, civilized, sane and reasonable can become mean, petty, exploitative, even vengeful in relation to each other. Furthermore, partners may change over the course of the relationship so they no longer fit well together. What was once a workable combination becomes a forced fit. Whether this lack of fit is chronic or a temporary response to external changes, it materially changes the nature and course of the relationship, and, if not repaired, may spell the eventual end.

Changes into incompatible states may come from failure to maintain the relational culture, from some fatal shock to the relational culture, or from response to the changing identity of a partner. Sometimes these issues can be remedied by talk. Sometimes they are signs that termination would be constructive.

Failure to maintain a satisfactory relational culture

When partners gradually lose sight of the meaning of their bond, they lose direction in the relationship. Each can be discontented and blame it on the other. Without a shared belief in the value of the bond, there can be no intimacy. When partners do not engage in revitalizing communication, there can be a steady drift apart. If partners do not adapt to changes in each other, their original relational culture may become unacceptable. If time is not taken to rebuild the relational culture, the partners may become incompatible.

Marc T. So I said, "Rose, we don't have a relationship; we have shared housing. We aren't lovers, we're roommates!" She acted like she didn't understand, but I know she did. She just didn't want to get into the hassle of discussing it. I guess we're both to blame. I'm doing my residency so my hours at the hospital are long and erratic. Rose is doing field work for her M.A., so she's gone a lot collecting data or working late in the library. We live together, sure, but we don't ever see each other. I have no idea what stage she's at with her research. She doesn't even know I've moved to a new rotation in the intensive care ward. I haven't had a chance to tell her I'm thinking about taking a speciality in cardiovascular diseases. And I have no idea where her head is now about Ph.D. work. I could go on and on about what we don't know about each other's lives these days. At the moment our relationship boils down to nothing more than an agreement to share the rent.

If partners share few common values, they may be able to share space without forming a relational culture. When each partner begins living an independent life and talk is confined to paying the bills or filling the refrigerator, the relational culture becomes an historical artifact. There may be no hostility at all in such cases of benign neglect.

There is a lot that you can do to keep the relational culture from disintegrating, but you must take action before the trouble starts. Careful thought and taking time for talk during the navigating stage are the best ways to prevent the onset of deterioration. Sometimes deterioration is caused by simple drift. People often forget to attend to matters that are very important. Sometimes affection leads us to take people for granted. On the other hand, drift may also result from an unwillingness of partners to confront the fact that they are no longer compatible. By letting the relationship slide, it is easier to make an exit. Disintegration does not happen overnight. It takes considerable and prolonged inattention to dissolve a union.

Fatal ruptures of relational cultures

A collapse of the relational culture may happen as a single, sudden rupture. This can occur when one partner violates a critically important aspect of the shared relational culture. Of course, none of us obey all the rules for our intimate relationships. Most bonds can survive numerous minor transgressions, bending rules, even breaking rules not central to the bond. In every relationship, however, there are some values, rules or expectations which are considered non-negotiable. They are fundamental and inviolable. Failure to adhere to these may move a bond below the CL necessary to its continuance. A partner who chooses to disrespect a basic requirement of the relational culture can expect no forgiveness or absolution, no return to grace. Even if a second chance is granted, the bond will probably never again reach the level of trust and solidity that it had prior to the violation.

What is considered absolutely fundamental, of course, varies from relationship to relationship. Some issues frequently seen as "the bottom line" in marriages are fidelity, shared faith, sobriety, and financial responsibility. Friendships may hinge on key issues such as confidentiality, availability and reciprocal support. Yet we cannot generalize. The bedrock of one relationship may be marginal in another. We know of one marriage that split up when the husband renounced religion, yet we know of another in which the identical act produced only a minor ripple. We've watched several of our acquaintances walk out on spouses or long-term partners when sexual infidelity occurred, yet we also know couples who weathered that breach and even some couples who decided sex outside of the bond would enrich their relationship. Many women say they would walk out on any man who was physically abusive even on one occasion, yet thousands of women remain in marriages where they are chronically beaten. While we cannot generalize about "bottom lines" in bonds, partners know the rules of their own relationships. When a fundamental violation takes place, it is not an accident and the consequences can be anticipated.

Dennis P. I knew going to bed with Sally would end my marriage. I knew it and I could not help myself. I was a virgin when I got married. I had to know if it was different, and if you could have seen Sally, my God, what a woman. Helen was, you know, kind of straight up and down, a great kid, but quiet. She'd never get excited when we had sex, and I had to know whether I was any good. Well, I did it with Sally, and I had to tell Helen about it. It wasn't any good. I'd never do it again, but it was too late. It's high price to pay to find out that you really aren't a stud.

Evoked negative identity

How you define yourself is influenced by your interactions and transactions. Association with different people evokes different dimensions of our own identities. Communication with some people may bring out your humorous self while other people evoke your serious side. In some relationships you may be cooperative, while in others you feel more competitive; you may feel supportive toward some people, and toward others, critical. You may assert yourself in some relationships, be submissive in others. Any relationship activates only some of our personality potentials.

As long as we like who we are in relation to another person, all goes well. The trouble comes if we dislike who we are or who we have become in relation to a partner.

Linda P. I can be many different persons. What I choose depends a lot on who I am with. A good friend makes me kind and considerate, a bad one, sharp and unpleasant. For example: Alice and I were close during our wretched teens. Both unsuccessful with boys, insecure and awkward, we formed a smart-aleck team to make fun of more fortunate contemporaries. We could devastate an inarticulate cheerleader or an easygoing athlete. Years later, after we had both married, we wound up in the same town and picked up where we left off. Alice was as abrasive as ever and still had a curiously destructive effect on me. Once again at parties we would gang on some inoffensive male, bewildering him with our motiveless malice. When we were alone together, our conversation inevitably turned to character assassination. After a few such experiences I made a firm decision: "I didn't want to be the person I became with Alice; the friendship had run its course." (Adapted from: M. Lear, "The Real Reasons Behind Marriage Failure," *Woman's Day*. June, 1973.)

We may be dissatisfied with ourselves because of the way we act with a particular person. If someone consistently changes our self-image so that we are discontented or unahppy with it, we begin to lose confidence in the person and in the relationship we share. If we dislike who we are in a relationship, self-confirmation goes on the rocks and the relationship is a source of pain.

An evoked negative identity may arise because one partner has changed in such a way that jealousy is evoked. Bitterness because of a change in the other may cause the other to be hostile or bitter, and partners may begin to work unpleasantly on each other. If one partner assumes a parental role and continually admonishes the other, it may result in the other partner acting like a truculent child. Once partners begin to act unpleasantly when they are together, or tend to evoke the worst in each other, both can become dissatisfied with the entire relationship.

Peter B. My wife started the day after we married and it has continued ten years now. She expects me to take care of everything financial. She is like Blondie at a Tudbury's Department Store Sale all her life. I must tell her how much to spend, how much to save, what to buy, what to spend for it. She has made me into her father and I don't like it, because she sometimes acts like a brat and makes me want to punish her. The other day I wanted to tell her to stand in the corner, she was such a child. I don't like it. I see a lot of competent women. My wife will either shape up or she will ship out and have to deal with her finances all alone. I want to be a husband to a real woman. It's getting so bad, I sometimes regard her as one of my kids. I feel incestuous when I go to bed with her.

Our intimates have a profound effect on our self-images. Individuals must protect themselves in their intimate relations by keeping alert to the identity they are forming in the relationship. If you can pick up small changes in yourself, you can prevent yourself from slipping into the kind of person whom you cannot admire. You also need to keep tabs on who you are inviting your partner to be. If you find that you or your partner are more acceptable outside of your intimate relationship than in it, you may have to make some decisions about whether to continue and, if so, how to revise your transactional rules and roles.

Factors Extrinsic to a Bond

Relational demise may stem from factors extrinsic to a bond and the individuals comprising it. Social systems can exert intolerable pressure on a relationship that is floundering, thereby pushing it over the edge. On the other hand, social systems may provide attractive alternatives to a bond, pulling one or both partners out of it. We will consider both kinds of external pressures.

We have already pointed out that social systems have a concrete effect on intimate relationships. It is not possible to make an intimate relationship into an exclusive relationship. There are always messages coming from outside, and there is always responsibility to respond to outside pressures. Even the strongest bonds are vulnerable to pressures from outside the relationship.

Our social and professional relationships influence how we view our intimate partners. Our perception of them may differ in different systems, like a diamond looks beautiful on black velvet, but dull on glass. A partner attractive in college where sociability is important may seem less desirable in a professional context that stresses discipline, responsibility and ambition. Someone who appeared to be a suitable partner in a small town may be judged unacceptably unrefined and unsophisticated in a cosmopolitan city.

Tom B. A guy's status depends a lot on the woman he's with. It may not be very cool to say so, but it's true. One of the reasons I liked dating Sherry was that I knew she impressed the hell out of all the other guys. She is one terrific-looking woman, so everyone figured I must have a lot on the ball to interest her. When I graduated Sherry moved here to live with me awhile to see if we wanted to get married. Am I glad we waited. The training program I'm in has a lot of socializing to build team spirit among employees. So all of the new people get together for dinners and parties, and everyone brings a spouse or date. I couldn't wait for the first get-together, because I knew when I walked in with Sherry I'd increase my status one hundred per cent right fast. Well, she was the best-looking woman there all right, but nobody seemed to notice much. Then I heard people at work talking about the party and they were saying things like how interesting Joe's wife is or what a dynamo Frank's date must be to have started her own business or how intelligent Ben's fiance is since she's just made Law Review. I guess around here the high marks go for brains, not looks. That sure lets Sherry out, so I've asked her to go home.

Tom's view of Sherry may have been cynical, but Sherry was probably better off. If Tom was that responsive to the evaluations of his peers, she would have found herself in a position where she was intolerably pressured to change in directions that might have been impossible for her. When a partner becomes excessively concerned about how outsiders see his or her mate, there is very little hope for the relationship, since it is virtually impossible for an individual to measure up to invidious comparisons.

Even more powerful forces are exerted by major forces and values in the society. Our currently-troubled economy exerts severe pressure on intimate relationships. Marriages that might prosper or at least survive in a thriving economy may crumble under the pressures of poverty. It is hard to remain optimistic and charming if you're compelled to work extra shifts, live in cramped housing, eat dull food, drive an old car and forego vacations. When economic pressures force cutbacks or put the wage earner out of work, there is a tendency for the partners to use each other as scapegoats. Since there is no way to attack the economy, the partners assault each other. Furthermore, widespread inability to afford housing is sure to have a serious effect on couples who cannot obtain sufficient privacy in living space to work out their relational problems.

Probably the most serious impact of culture on private relationships is the manner in which it defines relationships. American values until the 1950's emphasized family cohesion and discouraged divorce. Cultural norms urged couples to work through marital discord, particularly when there were children to consider. Divorced people were looked on with pity and suspicion, and people whose marriages had dissolved felt considerable guilt.

Current cultural values are much less supportive of marriage and more permissive about divorce. Divorce is, in fact, regarded as a legitimate solution to marriage problems that most people, thirty years ago, wouldn't have dreamed of using as a basis for breaking-up a marriage. Most states have liberalized divorce laws. We suspect that many relationships that have ended in the past twenty years would have survived in the 1930's. Conversely, it is likely that many marriages which managed problems and survived in the 1930's would not do so today. We are not evaluating these two very different ethics. We are demonstrating how major trends in society influence our CL_{alt}s and, therefore, the choices we make. Whether society is responsive to the urgencies of couples to separate, or whether couples are motivated to separate because it is easier to do so than to revise the relationship, the net effect is the same.

There are many subtle social factors which threaten our private relationships. Even a healthy bond can be pushed into extinction by environments hostile to intimacy. For example, it is very difficult to resist attractive alternatives to current relationships. Any of the new people we meet may seem more desirable than an established friend or mate. The new person can provide novelty and excitement as an alternative to a relationship which may have grown mundane or stale because of the pressure of day-to-day survival. Romance may enter once more; an intensification stage may provide a kind of thrill, a euphoria that is lacking with our current partner. The new person may seem to meet our needs more effectively. Sometimes impulse will pull us out of a satisfactory relationship because we are captivated with the possibilities of a new relationship and we do not consider the consequences of such a choice. The CL_{alt} may clamor for attention to the point where we lose sight of our basic long-term values.

Edwin Hellerstein, Marriage Counselor. Romance is an inadequate criterion for ending a relationship or beginning one. People are sometimes very irrational about the way they deal with new people. Middle aged males, particularly, bored with their jobs and worried about their potency, seem to need a lift. Their wives may be getting more effective, more competitive, and so they turn to a "fluffy" young woman, one they can impress. The wide eyes and total adulation turn the men into satyrs. They cannot resist. They develop a surreptitious relationship and discover that they are able to do some things they forgot how to do. On a basis of one good sexual encounter, many men end their marriages. But they don't realize how temporary it all is. So many of them marry the young girls and then discover that young girls grow into women and they have the same problems they had before only it is even more difficult to keep up with the younger partner. It is hard to get men over this hurdle. It is not difficult with women since society does not encourage encounters between older women and younger men. It may sound like discrimination, but it is to the advantage of the women. They, at least, don't have to carry a burden of both guilt *and* stupidity.

We've reviewed three basic reasons for relational deterioration. Bonds may gradually decay or they may snap because of basic violations, problems inside the relationship, or pressure from outside. Often, there is more than one force pulling a relationship apart. The three forces tend to push partners into reevaluation. Comparison to the CL or CL$_{alt}$ may indicate that it is no longer possible to continue to value the relationship. If a discontented partner does not clearly see how the relationship can be improved, the choice to leave may seem appropriate. If the discovery that the relationship no longer measures up is not enough, once better options appear, the end is likely.

The Deterioration Stages in Human Relationships

Few relationships end abruptly. Most decay through stages that seem to parallel the stages that led to the bond. There are four intermediate steps on a couple's return to being separate individuals: (1) differentiating communication, (2) disintegrating communication, (3) stagnating communication, and (4) terminating communication. The content of deterioration varies from relationship to relationship exactly as each relationship develops uniquely. Still, there are general issues and forms of communication common to each stage representing progressively decreased involvement.

Differentiating communication

To differentiate is to make different, to distinguish, or to separate one thing from another. Differentiation is the first step in relational deterioration. Through word and deed, partners begin to separate their lives and values. This stage reverses the explorational phase in which individuals sought to find similarities. Now they deemphasize similarities, and highlight differences.

There are some very clear symptoms of differentiation. The primary clue is one or both partners' increased involvement with people and activities outside the relationship and a correspondingly decreased involvement with the bond partner. There is a change in whatever levels have been standard for particular partners. This condition may be accompanied by one or both partners demanding more individual consideration from the other, a tendency to think less about the relationship as a unit and more about individual goals. Partners may reduce attention to each other's needs and concerns. These symptoms, collectively, serve to reduce the partner's sense of being attached.

There is not only less talk between the partners, but what talk occurs centers on individual experiences, usually outside the relationship. There may be talk about details of housekeeping or trivia. Talk about relationship goals or shared experiences gradually dissipates. Previous focus on "we" changes to "you" or "I."

Differentiation may be unilateral and far along before the partners recognize it. The drift is gradual; outside attractions do not usually pull people traumatically out of their relationships. Increased involvement with work or other people may take a long time to reach a point where it is noticeable. If partners do not have a regular way of discussing what is happening to them, benign neglect may have them apart, sometimes against their will, before they realize what's happening. Differentiation need not be malicious. But it can progress to the point where even if there is no ill will, there is insufficient interest to save the bond.

However, the realization that the relationship has deteriorated may come suddenly. Sometimes partners wake up to the fact that they are no longer intimate at a point where there is virtually nothing they can do about it. This is why maintenance of regular talk about the nature of the relationship during navigation is so important. Effective navigational communication reduces the likelihood that partners will allow themselves to reach a point where they have grown apart without intent.

Edna Garrett, Ph.D., Marriage Counselor. When the couples drift apart, the prognosis for counseling is fairly good. There usually is little malice in relationships that come apart because the partners are distracted and stop paying attention to each other. In fact, it is sometimes fun to come back together. I urge the couples to start courting again. We work out regular romantic schedules. We try to recapture the feelings they had when they first discovered each other. The idea is to get them to make a comparison between what they had, what they have, and what they could get if they permitted the drift to continue. This kind of comparison usually convinces them that it is worthwhile to try to rejuvenate their relationship. If they haven't drifted too far to remember how it was, and if neither of them has an attractive potential new partner on the hook, we can usually get them back together.

Deliberate differentiation occurs when one or both partners intentionally emphasize separate identities by increasingly demonstrating their individuality and independence of the bond. Sometimes this is a temporary period in which one partner needs private time to work out some personal problem or is preoccupied in a struggle to establish an identity at work. Periodic withdrawals are normal in most relationships: so, in themselves, they do not signal trouble. The best strategy for transient deterioration may be patience while it runs its course. However, it is useful if the person who seeks temporary distance offers assurances to the partner that the withdrawal does not threaten the bond. This is another value of regular communication.

Finally, there are cases in which differentiation is intentional and enduring. Either or both partners may feel that the bond is constraining their autonomy. They may feel little satisfaction from identifying with the relationship and inadequate pleasure from associating with each other. This kind of change is frequently unilateral. One partner wants out, the other is startled and tries to save the relationship. Often guilt leads to an attenuation of termination. The partner who wants out feels some obligation to the former partner and tries to make a "friendly" exit.

Through intimate communication and renegotiation of roles and rules, partners may resolve the issues that give rise to differentiation, and return their relationship to the navigation stage. If, instead, partners choose not to communicate about their growing separateness, they pave the way for further deterioration. There are six basic questions partners should consider once they discover they are differentiating.

1. Do our actions and communication indicate we are leading increasingly separate lives?
2. Are we drifting apart by design or benign neglect?
3. Is the drift unilateral or mutual?
4. Is the distance between us a temporary withdrawal or a chronic condition?
5. Do we want to do something about our differentiation?
6. Will communication help us solve our problems?

Stacy H., Homemaker and Mother. At first I didn't object to Randy's traveling, but he started being gone more and more of the time, leaving me to take care of two pre-schoolers and run the house and take care of all the family business and finances. Finally, I said to Randy, "you can take this as a statement of fact or as a warning, whichever you please, but more and more it's becoming just as easy for us to get along when you're not here as when you are." I didn't say that to hurt him, but the fact is I've had to learn how to run the whole show on my own because I can never count on him to be here when I need him. I've learned not to need him, not to depend on him for anything. Well, Randy's response was that he is part of this family and it wouldn't be a family without him. So I asked Randy, "if you take your fist out of a bucket of water, how much of a hole do you leave?" I think he got the message then.

Disintegrating communication

When something disintegrates it falls apart due to the breakdown of whatever substance formerly held it together. In intimate bonds the binding substance is relational culture. So a bond enters the disintegrating stage when its relational culture begins to erode or break down. The focus on individual partners that started during differentiation now progresses to a siege on the culture of the relationship itself. Entry into disintegration is a substantial step in deterioration, one that indicates greatly increased risk to the bond's continuity. This move sets the stage for terminating the relationship by breaking down the common world that has unified two individuals.

There are some definite symptoms of the onset of disintegration. There will be even further reduction in the quantity and quality of communication. Partners tend to avoid intimate communication and, in fact, communication of any kind. They will not acknowledge the importance of the relationship and avoid demonstrating the value of the bond to others. If they talk about their relationship at all, it tends to be in negative terms, usually divorce talk like "We sure seem to have a lot of problems," or "Sometimes I wonder why we stay together." Finally, the most telling symptom is partners' decreased adherence to rules and roles of the relational culture. Infractions now become frequent and often flagrant, and they are seldom followed by apologies. By violating agreed-upon roles and rules each partner says, in effect, "I deny our bond. I do not accept the guidelines we've worked out for shared life, because I no longer embrace the idea of a shared life with you."

As you might expect, these symptoms tend to create tension and conflict. Partners may feel awkward and defensive around the other, because they are not accustomed to dealing with each other as nonintimates, yet that's essentially what they've become. Even well intentioned efforts to discuss problems openly may result in aggression and resentment if one or both partners no longer admits accountability to each other for attitudes and conduct. Tension and conflict are exacerbated by the breakdown of rules that previously coordinated transactions. Partners can no longer count on what each other will be and do. Thus, unpredictability and insecurity invade their transactions, further complicating any efforts to resolve differences.

The symptoms we've identified are the surface indicators of an intricate process through which partners disassemble the shared perceptions and visions that had bound them into a unit. Piece by piece, thread by thread, they pull apart their relational culture until they no longer perceive a common, unifying sphere of existence. A critical test of whether a relational culture had been destroyed is partners' views of themselves in six months or a year. When partners can no longer see their futures linked, the relational culture has ruptured.

A primary symptom of deterioration is reduced communication.

Lloyd B. If I had to pinpoint the moment when I knew it was all over with Mary, it would be the first day of my training program. To help acquaint us new employees the director of training told each of us to make a list of things we hoped to be doing in 5 years and then we'd discuss our lists to get some insights into each other. My ideas came quickly—completion of my M.B.A., more hiking in mountain areas, assuming a position in upper-level management, more time for reading, owning a Jaguar (I figured I might as well dream big!), and so on. When I looked over my whole list, I realized that not a single item referred to or included Mary. That's when I knew that she wasn't part of my future.

It is exceptionally difficult to reverse the process once the relational culture has been dismantled. The bond itself has been thoroughly ravaged and its nucleus removed. Repairs and remedial treatment tend to be insufficient at this point. Thus, if partners decide they want to make a go of their relationship after this stage has run its course, they must rebuild a relational culture again, almost from scratch. If they succeed they are likely to construct a relational culture far different from the original, sometimes better. Generally, they will not succeed without some outside help. It is this kind of situation in which marriage counselors most often find themselves, and they testify to the difficulty of repairing this kind of relationship. In the first place, antagonism interferes with discussion of the situation. Even if the partners care for each other very much, they have usually habituated hostility patterns sufficient to overcome kind words and efforts to cooperate. Furthermore, each needs to declare personal identity as an individual in front of the partner as well as the counselor. To check the severity of disintegration counselors look for symptoms, such as decline in quantity of talk, lack of confirmation of each other and the bond, violations of rules, taking on new roles antagonistic to the partner, attempts to have the final word in exchanges, declarations of separate identity to society-at-large, looking around for new partners, and general unwillingness to work on saving the relationship. At this point, without major and mutual commitment, there is almost no reason to believe such relationships can be saved. During disintegration partners should ask these questions:

1. Do we still perceive ourselves as couple?
2. Do we communicate at all about our bond?
3. Do we violate rules we've worked out for our relationship?
4. Do either of us see the other in our future?
5. Do we wish to invest the effort necessary to rebuild this relationship?

Stagnating communication

Sometimes it is inconvenient to terminate the relationship despite the fact that both partners know it is over. Relationships which do not move from disintegration to termination will stagnate. The partners will adopt a holding pattern in which they do nothing to improve their relationship, yet make no move to end it formally. They are simply marking time in an undesirable bond until it is convenient to end it completely.

Some relationships entirely bypass this stage and move directly to termination. The more direct exit is chosen in relationships where both partners can see alternatives, or where partners are so hostile continued co-presence would be intolerable. Stagnation is sometimes the result of partners feeling guilty about abandoning the other. Sometimes they stay around in the hope of rejuvenating the relationship, sometimes because it is too painful to end it completely.

There are instances in which partners feel unable to leave a relationship because they feel trapped by children, economic pressures, or religious convictions that prohibit divorce. Sometimes people even stay in relationships out of habit and convenience. If there are no alternatives on the horizon, it may be easier to hang around than to face the problem of moving, dividing property, notifying friends and relatives, and having to tend to one's own needs. It may even be that a partner's career would be hurt by a divorce. At this point, a compromise can be made to stay together by simply agreeing on some rules of individuation. Partners work out routines to leave each other alone. They may also work out a technique of facing the world so that others continue to see them as a couple. In some cases, they may even agree to discrete contacts outside relationships.

Stagnation can be very destructive for individuals. Lingering in this stage tends to increase apathy and hostility between partners. Further the habits of the relationship and the attention that must be given to putting a face on it for the world might interfere with the ability to find new associates. Then, too, a stagnant relationship puts each partner's life on "hold." Each needs to find constructive alternatives to the dying bond, but neither can because of the commitment to the unhealthy relationship. Living in a situation in which one's value is not affirmed can materially reduce self-esteem and effectiveness in the outside world.

Intimates may sometimes enter a stagnation phase because they are not certain they want to break up in which case it may provide constructive time for reflection. But living in a state of perpetual uncertainty is hazardous to mental health. It is important to consider the damage done by lingering in a stagnation stage, since the logical progression is often to psychic depression. It is usually healthier to make a clean, decisive break so that both partners can pursue new directions in their lives. When partners feel no desire to rebuild their bond and discover that it is costing them more to stay together than to be without any relationship at all, termination is the obvious alternative. Individuals who are in a stagnant relationship should ask these basic questions.

1. What am I gaining by staying in this relationship?
2. What is it costing me in self-esteem?
3. What opportunities for new relationships am I sacrificing?
4. What is it costing my partner and what is he or she gaining?
5. Do I want to revive the bond? Is it possible?
6. Is remaining in this stage in any way constructive for either of us?

Terminating communication

Termination is the final stage of communication between partners. Sometimes it is an oddly cooperative stage. Once the partners have displayed their hostility and anger and have finally agreed to end their relationship, they are free to cooperate to end it effectively.

The primary function of terminating communication is to tie up loose ends, settle logistical issues including distribution of property, custody of children and pets, and to make financial arrangements such as alimony and child support. Most talk at this stage is likely to be conducted through attorneys, or at least with attorneys present. Recent legal trends make cohabitations similar to marriages in their termination procedures. Terminations involving friends or roommates usually focus on such issues as which records and books belong to which partner and whether each person's half of the rent and phone bill is paid up. The matters may not be exciting, but they can be very important.

A second important purpose of terminating communication is to define the nature of any future relationship between the partners. Will they be friends or enemies? Will they see each other from time to time? If they happen to run into each other, how will they act? If there are emergencies requiring joint decision how should contact be made? If there are children, how will their future be managed? What will they say to others about the breakup? How can they avoid injurious gossip about their situation?

Couples that terminate without settling these questions often face many extended discomforts. Furthermore, it makes life very difficult for friends and relatives if there is no policy. Even if each person is adamant about never seeing the other again, public declarations will guide others in decisions about invitations and future contacts.

Communication in a terminating relationship may also focus on analysis of what happened in the relationship. This is not typical of most endings. However, both partners can learn a great deal from a frank discussion sharing perceptions of reasons for deterioration.

Individuals

We began our discussion of relational evolution with a discussion of individuals. We end it the same way. However, the individuals at this point are not the "same" ones who launched the relationship. Intimate involvement changes people. As a result of thieir participation in the bond, each person will be altered. Their values, definitions of self, and standards for future relationships will have changed materially.

Bernard J. Even though Pat and I don't want to get back together, I still think that our relationship was the best thing that ever happened to me. It taught me a lot I didn't know about myself. In one of our last conversations, Pat said that I was a selfish bastard and that our relationship had failed because I was always so preoccupied I couldn't even make a halfway effort. At the time, in the heat of the moment, I denied it, but I've thought about it a lot since, and I think she was right. I never thought of myself as selfish but I am. I have personal goals, things I must do, places to go, and I won't let anyone or anything interfere. I don't want to change, but I want to approach relationships differently. Before I get serious with anyone again, we either have to agree that the relationship is not a priority for either of us or I have to change my attitude and be willing to put in a lot more effort than I did with Pat. If I'd known this before, maybe I wouldn't have misled Pat.

A period of re-socialization usually follows the end of an intimate relationship. Individuals must figure out how to reschedule and reorganize their lives without their partner. Each develops new interpersonal contacts or reestablishes old ones neglected during the intimacy. Some tax their friends' patience with complaints and requests for consolation. Individuals must relearn how to engage in the small talk characteristic of invitational communication and how to date again. Unmarried men find their friends "fixing them up," while unmarried women may find their married friends fear their husbands will be tempted by a divorcee.

Following a split, it is not unusual for individuals to mourn. Even when ending was a mutual decision, individuals can mourn losing what was once so good or grieve about personal failure. A brief period of mourning can mark official closure, but extended mourning can interfere with making new relationships.

Perhaps the most productive result of a breakup is serious self-reflection. Individuals can analyze what happened and why and identify and accept their responsibility for the deterioration. To forego this process means they learn less than they should from their experience and increase the likelihood of repeating their mistakes. During the aftermath of intimacy individuals may profitably confront questions such as these:

1. How have I changed as a result of being in that relationship?
2. What have I learned about myself as an individual and as an intimate partner?
3. How might I avoid making similar mistakes in the future?
4. How did I contribute to the deterioration of the bond?
5. What have I learned about my desires and expectations of intimacy?
6. What does this imply for future choices of partners?
7. Under what conditions, if any, would I bond with someone else?
8. How can I get on with my life?

A Final Look at the Stages of Deterioration

We've examined five stages in the deterioration of human relationships. They comprise a natural progression. Each stage sets the scene for those that follow. The sequence typifies de-escalation and provides a useful way to view the decline of intimacy. While some relationships may end abruptly, and others may not pass through all these stages, the pattern we have outlined typifies most endings.

Before leaving this analysis, there are two important points that need to be discussed. They relate to attitude and communication of the partners during deterioration.

Self-fulfilling failure

We have referred several times to the idea that deterioration is not inevitable. The fact that a bond has problems, even serious ones, does not necessarily mean that it must terminate. There are many options that may be pursued before throwing in the towel. It is possible for one or both partners to make changes that will permit the bond to continue. Partners also may negotiate revisions in their expectations and behaviors sufficient to improve the situation. The couple can overhaul their relational culture to transform their relationship from complementarity to symmetry or parallelism, or whatever they choose to suit each other's current needs.

Too often partners overlook their options. At the first sign of serious tension or the first realization of flaws in a bond, they assume it's just a matter of time until they part. To themselves, they say, "It's all down-hill from here." Saying this can make it so. Partners often create self-fulfilling prophesies of failure in which negative attitudes end a salvageable bond. People can talk themselves *into* trouble as well as out of it.

Relational problems can be dealt with in many ways. Ease of divorce provides the obvious out. Friends, of course, may separate at will. But serious problems can either be seen as evidence that a relationship cannot work or they may be interpreted as challenges to be met in order to make a relationship work. If you assume that problems mean failure, you are unlikely to work to solve them. If, on the other hand, you assume that problems are natural challenges that you and your partner can meet, then you're likely to make a much more committed attempt to work out differences and overcome troubles. Bear in mind that most relationships that survive over time have survived numerous difficulties along the way. Resolving difficulties becomes part of the history of enduring intimacies, because it testifies to partners' willingness to stand by commitments even when the going gets rough.

We are not advising the people stay with a bond no matter what. Sometimes ending an intimacy is the wisest course of action. However, we are reminding you that this is not the *only* option for a troubled relationship. Attention to repair in the early stages of deterioration could spare each partner considerable pain and might even rescue the bond. If the partners learn how to handle problems characteristic of early stages of relationship, they have the means to deal constructively with problems in later stages. Intimacy is not a state; it is a process requiring constant investment from both partners, if it is to endure.

Communication during deterioration: A time for caution

Relational deterioration tends to generate tension in individual partners and conflict between them. The early stages of de-escalation may be accompanied by ambivalence as partners oscillate between wanting to revive the relationship because of its good points and wanting to lay it to rest because of its weaknesses. If deterioration progresses, feelings are likely to become more negative as partners focus increasingly on the problems in each other and in the bond. Typically, each person experiences a range of unpleasant emotions including anger, disappointment, frustration, self-doubt, guilt, envy and hostility toward the other. In turn, these emotions may influence how partners communicate with one another. There may be an urgency to inflict hurt. Intimates have extraordinary power to wound each other, because they know each other's vulnerabilities so well. Thus, it is no challenge to deliver a devastating verbal blow to a partner; the challenge is to resist the temptation to do so when you are hurt and angry. It may be useful for individuals to admit their anger and pain, and even to decide not to have any further contact with the ex-partner. On the other hand, there is little to be gained from furious argument and lashing out. If combat must occur hire a good attorney. There is no innocent partner in a breakup. Individuals fool themselves if they try to blame it all on the other and do not look at their own culpability. We make this point here because it is terribly important to those who are exiting from relationships to stay in good enough shape to form constructive new relationships. People who leave relationships feeling excessive hostility and anger may find themselves soon locked into a rebound relationship that has all the potential to cause more pain than the relationship they left. Closing out the old bond respectably and with civility will heighten your self-esteem as you move into your new relationships.

Individuals may need some help over the rough stages of exiting. Many turn to friends and family only to find them excessively interested in the details of the breakup and, therefore, of very little help. There are well-qualified counselors available. The American Association of Marriage and Family Therapists has compiled a superior record of helping people through painful relationship experiences.

Jason P. I guess you never really know how mean you can be til you get in a situation that brings out your worst. I found out just how low I can stoop when Jane and I split up. Things hadn't been good for a long time, but each time one of us tried to end it, the other argued, "give it one more chance," you know that routine. Looking back, I wish one of us had had the guts to end it before it got so ugly. The last few weeks we were together Jane and I spent most of our time exchanging insults. Well, in our final talk the insult game got out of hand. It started when I said she was getting fat. (I know how hard she works to stick with her diet, so that always hits home). So she replied it was muscle from playing squash, but that I wouldn't know much about sports seeing as how I didn't make the team this year (that was a pretty direct hit). So then I said some of her size might be muscle, but probably a lot was fat since Italian women tend to get 'blubbery' (a little ethnic dig). So she said that was better than redneck southern 'boys' who got pot-guts from drinking beer while they watched games with athletes *who made the grade.* I'll spare you the details of the rest of our conversation. But by the end we had attacked each other's appearance, intelligence, sexuality, everything. It was total destruction. It got bloody before we were through. I can't forget some of the things she said about me, and I doubt she'll ever get over some of the things I did to hurt her. I'm really ashamed of how I acted and of the things I said to Jane. And I'm disappointed to find I am capable of acting that way.

The point is that little of value results from this kind of warfare. If you deliver a crushing insult, your pleasure is likely to be short-lived; it lasts until your partner's return volley strikes home. Meanwhile, neither one of you has done anything to advance constructive resolution of your situation.

Complications

Deterioration often give rise to serious complications. We will consider three of them.

Rebound relationships (Once is not enough)

We've all known people who bounced from one intense involvement to the next. Before the former relationship was laid to rest, the next one was well underway. A rebound relationship develops rapidly after a terminated bond. It becomes intense because a person who has just experienced a painful termination may be highly emotional. It is easy to release the emotions on a new relationship that can provide some support. It is most unsettling to be alone after a prolonged period in which part of an individual's self-definition depended on a relationship with a partner and was guided by a relation culture the two of them had built. The now-ended bond remains a part of each individual's identity. Without an intimate partner, that aspect of identity is threatened and unfulfilled. It is tempting to recruit someone new to fill the void and restore a pair-identity.

Although it may be tempting to take the plunge into a new relationship, evidence suggests that it is usually unwise. Individuals need time to reflect on what happened in the former bond and to discover the implications for future interpersonal choices. Individuals must rediscover themselves and their assets before trying to coordinate themselves once again with someone else. The new involvement may trap them into making major changes in order to persuade the new partner to accept them, only to discover they have given away too much in order to obtain a relationship.

Unilateral terminations: guilt and self-deprecation

One of the most painful forms of termination takes place when one partner wants "out" and the other wants to sustain the relationship. There is little hope of saving this kind of relationship, although in some cases, the partner who wishes to save it bribes, threatens, coerces, or persuades the other partner to stay around for a while. When this happens, the partner who was induced to stay builds up a resentment that may later materialize in the form of extreme anger and hostility. The exiting partner may then feel relief at making the exit but guilt at the pain that was caused. Another alternative is that the aggrieved partner, martyr-like, makes it easy for the exiting partner. The result is still guilt for the departing individual. And the partner who was "deserted" may feel humiliated, deficient in esteem and competency. Both people can be seriously damaged by this kind of termination.

There is little to be gained for the partner who persuades the other to stay. To remain in a relationship in which one person is held against his or her will does little for the self-esteem of the person who has executed the strategy. In fact, it is punitive to keep a person who desperately wants to leave locked into an unrewarding relationship.

One solution for a person who wishes to terminate but is opposed by the partner is to seek the help of a counselor. A neutral third party can bring the couple together long enough to convince them that termination is much more profitable than remaining in a relationship that could seriously damage both of them. A relationship that endures under duress can often turn violent. There is more risk than just personal insult in trying to intimidate a reluctant partner to remain.

Furthermore, no relationship can be sustained on the effort of one partner. No matter how much the aggrieved partner tries, if the other wants to escape, there is really no hope of rebuilding a mutually rewarding bond.

Ida S. The life went out of our relationship months before I decided I had to get out. We were spending all of our time sniping and complaining, so there was nothing good left. So I told Vernon I was moving out of the apartment. Once he realized I meant it, he went crazy. He promised to change, promised to go back to school, anything I wanted. We'd been through that scene before so I knew better and just kept packing. Finally, he threatened to kill himself if I left him. That took me back a few feet. I was scared. I felt I just couldn't live with myself if I caused someone's death, so I stayed. But a few weeks later he was drunk again and got really abusive, slapping me around and stuff. So I packed up while he was passed out and was gone. He found me and told me to come home or he'd kill himself. By then, I wasn't as scared about his killing himself as maybe his killing me. So I said to him, 'go ahead, baby, but you won't kill me with you. This bird had flown!'

Expressive communication as exemplified by threats like this is not uncommon, but no one has to take responsibility for them. Individuals who receive these kinds of threats will find considerable help from a counselor who can show them how people, in the final analysis, can control only their own choices.

Power and abuse in intimacy

More often than we care to think about, intimate relationships result in physical abuse. For generations, it was widely accepted that husbands had the right to "discipline" their wives. Women could not escape. Courts tolerated behavior from husbands they would have punished severely under other circumstances. Even today, the law favors the male in abuse cases. There are, however, support groups, and legal aid societies that offer help to women seeking to leave relationships in which they are physically harmed. We cannot avoid taking a stand on this issue. It is morally reprehensible for a physically strong person to abuse a weaker person. We urge anyone in a relationship that is characterized by physical abuse to take every possible step to escape, for abusers rarely reform and anyone who waits around until they do faces the possibility of serious, and sometimes fatal damage.

Intimate relationships should be taken seriously. They can elevate humans to levels that they could not achieve alone, or degrade humans by destroying their self-esteem. We believe people honor their intimate commitments through careful and considerate choices implemented by intelligent communication.

Chapter Summary

We're going to follow some of our own advice at this point and terminate this chapter in a quick clean manner. In examining the anatomy of declining relationships we have identified some of the major reasons for deterioration and some of the issues and problems that typically arise during the process. We've also pointed out key symptoms of each stage so that you can diagnose what is happening in your own relationships and make informed choices about when termination is and is not constructive for all concerned. For those instances in which letting go is the wisest course of action, we've offered some guidelines for managing closing communication so that it is constructive and so that both partners retain their personal dignity and learn from the entire experience of intimacy. Nothing can so enrich our lives as healthy human relationships, and nothing can so debase them as unhealthy ones. It is crucial to know the difference and to know how to respond to each.

REFERENCES FOR CHAPTER 8

B. Bettleheim, *The Uses of Enchantment: The Meaning and Importance of Fairy Tales.* New York: Alfred Knopf, 1977.

S. Braudy, *Between Marriage and Divorce.* New York: Morrow, 1975.

M. Davis, *Intimate Relations.* New York: Free Press, 1973.

M. Knapp, *Social Intercourse: From Greeting to Goodbye.* Boston: Allyn and Bacon, 1978.

M. Lear, "The Real Reasons Behind Marriage Failure," *Woman's Day.* June, 1973.

W. Lederer and D. Jackson, *Mirages of Marriage*. New York: W. W. Norton, 1968.

R. Weiss, *Marital Separation*. New York: Basic Books, 1975.

J. Wood, "Communication and Relational Culture: Bases for the Study of Human Relationships," *Communication Quarterly*. 30, 2. April, 1982.

9

THE MEN TESTIFY

The premise of this entire book has been that people have the ability to decide and act in accordance with their own ideas and values. Our theory is that humans are self-aware and able to use symbols to implement personal decisions on how to achieve their goals with the collaboration of other humans. The last two decades have been marked by important changes in economic and social opportunity for women. Progress by women in industry and the professions has brought about an interface of social interests between women and men. While a few recognize that collaboration will bring about a satisfactory outcome for everyone, women are still restricted in many of their choices by entrenched male privilege. There is a potential for serious social and economic consequences in a society that needs the maximum contribution of *all* of its competent people. It is important for both men and women to reassess their attitudes toward each other.

In the next two chapters we will examine attitudes and opinions from men and women about their friendships and intimate relations. Our report is based primarily on the responses to our oral and written interviews (see Appendix A). It is not customary, in a textbook, to editorialize. However, the authors of this book agree that *it is absolutely essential that both men and women modify their attitudes and their behaviors to adapt to new social and economic conditions to provide equity in opportunity for both sexes.* This may mean overcoming stereotypes about what is masculine and what is feminine. It may also mean learning to control some hedonistic urgencies.

Whether physiological make up accounts for a major portion of the differences between men and women is not an issue. Clearly, in our society, there are no discernible differences in intellectual capability between men and women; therefore, there is no basis for assigning either to particular categories of employment or to justify expectation of sex-linked social behaviors. Discernible differences in social behavior between men and women can be ascribed to messages presented early in life by parents and school. Girls learn to be women, boys learn to be men. Thus, both men and women ought to have the privilege of learning what they choose to learn, to seek careers satisfying to their own goals and personality needs, and above all, have the right to compete fairly under a set of rules applicable to both sexes.

With these premises before us, we can turn to the question of how men and women view their social relations. In Chapters 9 and 10 we will review the modal responses our respondents made to our questions. (See Appendix A for a review of the method we used to gather data.) The material quoted is constructed so that respondents cannot be identified. In those rare cases when we quote a real person, the source and/or qualifications will be identified. Any resemblance between the statements quoted in this book and direct quotes is coincidental.

From Boyhood to Manhood

The message society gives to boys is disorganized, but there are some basic themes most boys hear and are expected to follow. They reverberate with physical courage, tenacity, originality, perseverance, discipline and separation from women. They focus on heroic deeds, the "playing fields of Eton and Harrow," Dink Stover at Yale, Tom Swift, Audie Murphy and John Wayne. There is the mischievous Tom Sawyer and courageous gridiron heroes like the Gipper. There is also a touch of motorcycle gangs, Don Juans, and a dollop of Portnoy to round it out. Boys are made of "frogs, and snails, and puppy dogs' tails," and the myths of the media and the legends of our land.

The American view of manhood is deeply etched into young boys by adults, especially parents, by their peers, and by public institutions. Boys are encouraged to group together in "teams." They often form voluntary groups, or gangs. Within tightly-established social units, they act out the social message of manhood. They are supported by countless hours of sports broadcasting and the exploits of the various heroes on TV. They learn to find joy in a "hard-hitting" game; and the harder the hit, the better. Notice also how many male heroes physically hurt people, carry guns, and take advantage of women. There are, no doubt, a great many men who dislike or reject this ethic, but they are judged by it nonetheless.

Bob C. Student. What do I see in the contemporary male? One who still retains prejudices toward females and races, tends to associate in groups and teams, opposes androgyny, and, above all, here at the university the one drive that most males talk about is how much they want to lay such and such a girl, in effect seeing women only as sexual conquests. So I guess I agree with the idea that most males are not changing much, the traditions and socialization are just too strong. *But* not all males are like this. My concern is over being judged like most other males. I reject standard male values and I resent being classified with them. Other men mistrust me because I reject the values they live by, and women are suspicious of my sincerity. There's really very little acceptance for a man today who does not buy into the dominant values and very little encouragement for any change in those values.

While an undetermined number of men would like to move away from traditional definitions of manhood, there is considerable pressure by their peers to live up to society's expectations of them.

In the following pages we will report what our male respondents had to say about these major topics:

- Male attitudes toward friendship and the family.
- Male attitudes towards male/female relationships.
- Male attitudes about manhood in general and what it means to be a man.

Survey of Male Attitudes Toward Friendship and the Family

Best friends

Most male friendships start in high school or earlier. There are a few occupations that seem to encourage formation of close friendships. College professors, lawyers and physicians, for example, seem to abandon their home town associates and form close relationships with people they met in graduate school. Policemen also seem to select their best friends from among their comrades. Managers and executives seem to avoid forming friendships with their associates, although they will form alliances.

Al Kaplan, C.E.O. I tell my people to keep away from the folks they work with. It causes trouble. There is nothing worse than having a couple of people who were once friends and then had a falling out who have to work together. We see each other too much from Monday to Friday. On weekends we ought to leave people alone. That goes for relations between men and women too. I don't discriminate, but I don't like married couples working here, and even worse are couples that have a "relationship." When they break up, the whole company breaks up. Usually one of them has to leave. It costs me too much to break in my technical and supervisory people. I don't want them ruining the company because of their emotions. Friends belong outside. Me? Do I have friends? Yeah, back home. Some people at the lake where I fish in the summer. I don't have time for them here.

College students form relationships, usually temporary, with dorm-mates or roommates, although most maintain home town connections. There was some evidence of growing strength of college fraternities. Those who claimed fraternity affiliation verbalized fraternity values of "brotherhood."

Best friends appear more important in memory than in reality. Respondents reminisced a good deal about their best friends and about the good times they used to have together. Most actively employed males reported active socializations with contacts usually selected because of business interests, and sometimes because of common political and social concerns. Those who were married tended to socialize with people selected by their wives, and most preferred to have their wives take the initiative in making social connections. Single employed males seemed acutely uncomfortable in matters of friendship. Most seemed to gravitate toward places where they could meet women, and very few were able to describe regular on-going relationships with their own sex.

Bert Heffernan, Engineer. The summer after we graduated from college, and before we got jobs, Craig and I hitch-hiked from Finley, North Dakota to Vancouver, B.C. We rode over the Rockies in a heavy rig, and I think we damn near walked the whole hundred and some miles of the Lewis and Clark Trail along the Kamiah River in Idaho, and we slept out next to the river, and pulled in fish when we were hungry. It was like it used to be when the country was young. He and I were young and we needed to talk a lot about civil liberties, and masturbation, our parents, and how to get women to go to bed with us, and football, and what it would be like to be a stockbroker. Craig majored in agricultural chemistry and he is an executive of a fertilizer plant. I'm a broker and I'm bored stiff. I'll be forty-five years old on my next birthday and I have never had as many connected days of peace and pleasure as I had walking along that river with Craig.

Successfully employed men seemed to be somewhat suspicious of one another. The competition of the business arena led them to look for allies and supporters rather than social friends. Taciturnity seemed to be the norm. They exchanged little personal information on the job. Important events like a child's graduation or a wedding anniversary were mentioned, but problems at home were concealed. There is a good deal of neutral professional gossip about who had been fired or promoted, who got a new job, or griping about company rules and routines. There was also conversation about experiences with women, alleged liaisons in the office community and arguments about sports. Men swapped jokes, sometimes sexual, racist or cruel. Joking seems to be a technique of maintaining neutral relationships and expressing hostility which is not socially acceptable in other forms.

David R., Student.   After reading the chapter on comtemporary men's views I found myself having to stop and really think. I couldn't be like those men, there's no way! But it is true and I am glad somebody wrote about it so I don't feel so weird. I want to share my feelings and emotions with other men, but would that be queer or gay? I thought I was just shy, but I really don't think that's the problem any more. I feel like I must be reserved and sometimes find it hard to express what's on my mind, especially to other guys. So I find myself acting 'cool' or joking about my fears. I can joke with the other guys and none of us has to admit how much something bothers us.

Both the protocols and the interviews gave the impression that men had a hard time talking with each other about their values and their fears. Those who needed a confidante selected a male of lower rank or confided in their secretaries. Younger men just avoided topics that made them uneasy. A great deal of socialization was done over drinks both in the adult and the college samples. By focusing attention on manly activities (drinking, sports, group socialization, swapping jokes), they could avoid considering ideas that bothered them.

College students spent a good deal of time talking with each other seeking consensual validation. They talked about things they feared like "I don't know what kind of work I want to do," "my parents feel I am not doing well enough," "I am not making it with women," "I think I may be a homosexual," or "I am not tough enough." What most of them learn is that others fear the same things and there is little that can be done. Eventually, conversations get boring and beer-drinking begins.

Lionel Tiger wrote about how men form hunting packs. It is obvious that men tend to group together. They feel uneasy going places alone or in casual socialization with women present. As men get older, their pack behavior becomes more subtle. They join organizations that separate them from women. (The Junior Chamber of Commerce of the United States, as of October, 1981, confirmed a resolution not to admit women, and furthermore, provided for automatic expulsion for chapters that violated the rule.) Exclusive male contact points appear very important. When women enter on one of their sanctums, the men cleave together and though it is not premeditated, they seem to act in ways designed to make women feel uncomfortable. Women also set off competitions among the men for the women's attention and thus, distract men from their normal interaction patterns.

Stanley, Age 6. Billy and me and Joe and Eddie got a club. We got a club and I'm the vice president and Joe is the president and Billy is the secretary and Eddie is the guy with the money, what's he called—the treasurer. And what we got the club for is to keep Mollie out!

When the conversation returns to best friends, the reminiscences start again. There is considerable talk about the good old days. Several of the respondents over forty reported they had tried to return to their old home and check out the friendships. Here is the author's experience with his return to the "good old days."

Jerry Phillips, co-author. We had sort of a club. It was modeled after college fraternities, but we really didn't know much about fraternities. We saw them in movies, Peter Lawford and June Allison and all that. We had jackets with our fraternity letters on them, and we had meetings where we did business, though no one was ever clear on what the business was—mostly planning parties and talking about how we could get dates. We talked about girls a lot, gossiped much of the time, but sometimes a member had an experience, and with great embellishment, like an ancient minstrel, he sang of his glories, what it was like to get his hand inside her blouse. It was a simpler era. We knew that if we had intercourse before marriage, our equipment would fall off and we would be rendered "morphs" (our word for hermaphrodite, our worst fear).

Exclusion of women defines male domain.

I went to the reunion, the professor returning to the scene of the crime. I was the only professor there. The other one, the literary critic, stayed home, unwilling to face the boredom. There were three medical doctors. Two were obviously important. Everyone tried to sit near one of them. They ignored the third doctor because he had married out of his faith. I sat with the rejected doctor. I didn't fit either. They all wore leisure suits and talked about country clubs, and remodeling their houses and the weddings they were going to have and their investments. Nothing fit. I talked awkwardly with the rejected doctor, but he was suspicious of anyone who was not an M.D., so that didn't work out. Odd, he was the guy I spent the most time with when I was in the club. He didn't want me to talk about what we did back then because his wife was around.

I went later on to visit the other college professor, a very close friend in high school. We talked shop for a while. Then we tried to talk about our kids but we really didn't care since we didn't know each other's kids and we didn't want to play "Can You

Top This?'' There was no point to reminiscing; we discovered that we remembered things differently and embarrassed each other. We tried really hard. We even got together a year later and it still didn't work. Fake reminiscing wasn't fun any more.

In the light of these data, the comment that you will probably not have very many close friends in your life-time makes a great deal of sense. Men seem to hang together. Some form intimate bonds with women and between their wife and their work, they have little time left over. The rest mostly see little reason for friendship. The seniors in the college sample seemed about to reach that point. They were urgent to get out of school. Some even commented that they probably would not miss their college friends.

A definition of friendship

Attempts by men to define friendship seemed to emphasize allies and team members. They mostly wrote of mutual favors and being on the same side of arguments.

Art Grant, Sales Representative. I've known Eddie for 28 years. I see him every time I get to Houston. We talk about our early days in the company. Eddie wasn't a go-getter. I never felt he was after my job. When he hit the top it was because of his invention. I clawed my way up and hurt a lot of people doing it, so it's always good to see Eddie because I never feel guilty about anything I did to him. That's the test of a friend, you know. If they last. Friends come and go, they say, but enemies accumulate over the years.

Some of the college respondents wrote a kind of communal notion about friendships. "I can make it with anybody. The whole world is my friend." "Jesus Christ my Lord and Savior, my only true friend, who is there when I need Him and with whom I can always talk, for he hears me and he hears my prayers," said one respondent, and nearly ten per cent made some allusion to Jesus being their best friend. Most college students defined their best friend as the one person with whom they shared the most secrets and experiences. Many confined their best friend to the high school crowd, specifying that they hadn't been at college long enough to find a best friend there. Older respondents were cautious about discussing best friends. Most reported that pressure of work prevented them from forming friendships.

Men tend to socialize with people very much like themselves. Most reported that when women were present at social gatherings men tended to group in one corner and women in another.

Men who traveled talked of their distress when away from home and how they socialized with others like themselves at bars, exchanging stories (much like the drummers who met Harold Hill on the train through Iowa in *Music Man*). They console each other, talk of great sales and great lays, and go back to their rooms; the "shots" are sometimes enough to get them to sleep. The more intrepid may find a lonely woman or pay the price for a professional hooker. There is no social disapproval for this behavior and many apparently can conceive of no alternative.

The *stud nouveau* may be a new breed. There is an emerging male type who socializes almost exclusively with women, tending to avoid male companionship since it interferes with the "pickup." They try to live the *Playboy* philosophy, and if they can't live it, they talk as if they do. They seek sexual contact constantly or talk about it if they don't find it. Some, when challenged, admit that many of their stories are not true. They argue that anything is okay between consenting adults so long as there are no strings attached and no one gets hurt. While this sample numbered less than five per cent of the respondents, the appearance of this type is important. They were all of college age or slightly older; they appeared antagonistic to women, and seemed to be devoted to the ideal of exploiting them.

Nelson Borgesi, Sociologist. I know you don't go to horror movies. There is an interesting phenomenon in them. The women that are killed and maimed are all "liberated." It is the cute little stay-at-home, the fluffy and empty-headed one looking for a man that is spared. It is important for us to be aware that there is a vigorous minority of men who really dislike women and who resent any economic or political advances they make. The stud you talk about is one, and I guess the people who make the horror movies could be included. Who watches those things and what effect do they have?

Looking for friends

Most men reported they did not look for friends, they dealt with whoever happened to come along. They felt it was important to impress people and to deal with impressive people. Men seem more aware than women of social and economic differences and were particularly sensitive to power and status of potential associates. While few respondents admitted prejudice, it was clear that most rejected association with minority group members, people in lower status occupations, and people who appeared different (too fat, or sloppy dressers). This was a surprising finding, since the social myth is that women are more snobbish than men.

Grant Hackman, Advertising. I don't understand these engineers. I don't understand how they can sit all day at a drawing board making lines and punching numbers into those calculators. I suppose somebody has to do that kind of thing, but I don't know, I can't seem to find anything to talk about with those guys. I had to sit next to one at a banquet once and I mentioned the Redskins and he seemed to think I was talking about some Indian tribe and he said he wasn't interested. I think it's important to be with the people who understand you, you know, your own kind of people, who do what you do, so you have something to talk to them about.

When we asked some of the interview subjects what they would do if they were on a new job all alone in a new town where they knew no one, and how they would go about meeting people, the unanimous reply was, "in the office or go to a bar—there's always somebody."

The mentor relationship

A great many of the older respondents indicated that they had close relationships with a younger man in the company, in the same profession or on the job whom they were training, breaking in, getting ready, or some other phrase that indicates assumption of almost a parental responsibility. Daniel Levinson identified this as the "mentor relationship," and explained that it was the traditional way that younger men were initiated into the secrets of the tribe in which they sought membership. The relationship was useful to the older man because it gave him a feeling of security and power to be sought by a younger and more vigorous man. The younger men received advice based on years of experience about how to compete and were pushed by their mentors to advancement. Women in careers suffer greatly because it is difficult for them to find mentors. Relationships between older men and younger women quickly become topics of gossip (see the Mary Cunningham case). Younger men seemed to be suspicious of the mentor process and, in fact, a great many of the reports from the college undergraduates expressed hostility toward older men, whom they felt were incompetent and held onto positions solely to keep the younger men out.

Alliances

Most men believe they have to protect themselves and they are not able to do so alone. On the job, they attempt to exchange favors, to make themselves useful to people in power, and to support some of the people around them. It is very much like the exchange characteristic of friend-making, though it usually does not include disclosure of private information. Those who held responsible positions seemed more alert to the possibilities of making alliances; they were more "political." There seemed to be long-term loyalties among allies as well, something like battlefield camaraderie. Most such relationships did not go beyond the office and did not last if one partner left the company.

College men seemed hostile to the notion of alliances. They were concerned about being manipulated and used by older men. Several

Allies.

wrote about how older men monopolized the best women. It might be jealousy; the "old guys control the pie," said one respondent.

One exceptional interviewee commented that he "welcomed women into the executive suite." "Women," he said, "were hungry for competition, and once they learned how, they made splendid allies." He referred to three women he was moving "through the ranks." But most women figure marginally in alliance relationships. Women who are new to the organization are either ignored or "hit on." They are left to protect themselves. The trend toward the formation of female networks is well-advised, though it will take a long time for women to gain enough power to compete with the male network.

The "old boy network" is no myth! If you have control over who works near you, you can feel secure that you will not be attacked. By depending on your allies and those with common values to supply you with personnel, you protect your flanks against your competitor who is doing the same thing. Every woman who is hired takes away a potential old boy position and is thus resented. Most men have not yet recognized women as potential allies.

The nature of competition

It is very difficult for men to cooperate. Their work together must be carefully coordinated and controlled both by an agenda and by a strong leader. Men see each other as potential competitors and they tend to base their self-esteem on the people they can beat.

Chris McKechnie, Design Engineer. I love it when these young kids tell me they don't believe in competition and they only want to try to improve themselves. That means I've got them. If I'm competing and they are not, I win. But, I really don't believe them. Their protests of goodwill and love and that business are so much———. I sometimes think of myself as a Western gunfighter and when one of those kids calls me to a shoot-out, I draw first and shoot straight. Everyone is a competitor. When you know it you can work things out and at least get some rules that protect both of you. When you don't know you are competing then you can't be trusted. So I will continue to knock these kids down until they are able to stand on their feet and tough it out like men.

Men tend to admire toughness; they honor victory. A great deal of their activity centers around sports, either as a spectator or participant. Sports provide conversational topics which can be used to exclude most women. They also provide an opportunity to challenge or make claims about personal capabilities. The college sample was

Competition.

quite instructive. Several men wrote that they resented people who showed off their intelligence and there were at least twenty respondents who reported incidents in which they were "hurt" or embarrassed by someone in the classroom. On the other hand, virtually all wrote about socialization and friendships made through some form of sporting encounter.

Work vs. family and friendship

Men tend to feel obligations. Many said it was hard to make friends because they had family obligations and because work took so much of their time. Several of the married men wrote about the obligation they felt towards parents and siblings which took away time they would otherwise spend on recreation and friends. Many of the younger men showed similar loyalty to family. Only a very small minority felt an urgent need to get away from their families altogether.

Work was often given as a reason for being away from wife and children. Most professional and managerial men are intensely involved in work. Their involvement does not express dislike of their families, but rather their view of what it takes to withstand the pressures of the world. A surprisingly large number of male students were similarly involved in studies. Engineers, science majors, and accounting majors seemed particularly prone to avoid social contact in order to excel at work. Law and medical students seemed to block out thoughts of socialization almost entirely.

Most men, young and old, verbalized loyalty to mothers and sisters. Younger men wrote of finding (some day) an old-fashioned girl to marry. Most said they wanted an intense relationship with a woman, the purpose of which would be to start a family. Most did not seem familiar with symmetrical and parallel relationships, and one could not avoid getting the notion that their conception of marriage was entirely complementary. It did not seem likely that most respondents could handle a marriage with a career-oriented woman. Furthermore, a discernible minority of younger men seemed to seek contact with older women, almost as a mother substitute.

Responses Dealing with Women and Sex

Can men and women be friends? "Absolutely not! My wife is not my friend, she is my wife." "Can't live with 'em, can't live without 'em," sings Rowlf the Muppet. Actually, it never occurred to most men that women had any potential as friends. The question took them entirely by surprise. At the time of this writing, September 19, 1981, a news bulletin came over NBC Evening News reporting that seventy-five per cent of males report that their wives are not their friends.

Most men verbalized a desire for deep and intimate relationships with women who would help support, nurture and heal them, with whom they could share secrets and enjoy "good sex." The theme of "good sex" ran through most of the male responses, particularly those of college students. It was not clear whether the phrase had a common meaning. It appears, however, that there are two kinds of sex: "recreational" and "good." "Recreational" is casual, no strings attached; anything goes between consenting adults. "Good" is serious and requires a bond.

We did not find one single protocol in which the respondent did not discuss women sexually. Whatever else characterized relationships with women, sex in one form or another figured in all reports. An occasional religious person claimed to be uninterested in sex, but they still regarded women as a source of temptation.

Tim C., Student. When I think of a woman I admittedly think of what it would be like. Maybe I do this because I feel women are inferior and should be treated accordingly. Sex or sexually-related topics always seem to be the forerunner in conversation when it comes to women. I don't know why, but they are. I guess men are just born this way.

There was an interesting phenomenon with younger men. They sometimes sought out older women (and sometimes identified younger women as "older") in order to acquire mothering. Older women gave advice and sympathy. They listened. (It appeared that, in general, men defined the proper role of women as listener.) It was hard to explain the intense loyalty that these men gave to older women except in terms of "mother." They, themselves, were unaware of what they were doing. There was clearly no overt sexual content in these relationships unless one is Freudian enough to refer to an incomplete Oedipal transition.

Most men reported fantasies about particular women; they also declared that when they first met a woman they speculated on her sexual possibilities before they thought about anything else. (Some reported "X-ray" vision.) David Barash in *The Whisperings Within*, describes males as having a biological urgency to "sow their seed" in as many places as possible. This, he claims, is the way nature guarantees that the species will continue. E. O. Wilson regards humans as transitional creatures whose biology still concords with the needs of a hunting and gathering society. The idea that excessive offspring could be dangerous to survival in a world of diminishing resources does not seem to have any effect on male sexual behavior. The proportion of men who choose vasectomy is still very small. Men still expect the woman with whom they have sex to take the precautions against conception.

The following statement was constructed from the interview responses of two particularly representative men. Both are successful, one a self-employed professional, the other in a high corporate position. Both are family men married more than twenty years, one with four children, one with three. Both claimed they had never been unfaithful, although both have had opportunities. Both reported a good deal of sharing with their wives. During the interviews they were asked to build a definition of women and to explain relationships with them. By combining their ideas and altering them to conceal identity, we can approximate prevailing male attitudes in this extended answer to the question, "What is the typical man's attitude toward women?"

The Frenchman said that women were different from men and thank goodness for the difference. No matter how you slice it, when we meet a woman we think first about her sexual appearance. When I thought about getting married I didn't have any notion about sharing my life with a partner or any of that. I wanted to get laid. I was a twenty-one year old virgin and I didn't have the guts to do it with a lady of easy virtue, so I got married.

It was my duty to have a family. So I had a family. It was my duty to provide for my wife and family. So I provided for my wife and family. It was my duty to be with her in sickness and in health and for better or for worse, so when she was sick I was around and when I had emotional problems she stood by. After a while we discovered that we needed each other, that we trusted each other, that we probably couldn't get along without each other. We divided things up. She managed the money and the house and had primary responsibility for the kids. I provided; morning, noon and night.

I did the double-take when I was watching *Fiddler on the Roof*, the scene where they are moving away from the Cossacks and it suddenly occurs to the lead character to ask his wife if she loved him. "After twenty-five years," or something like that, she says, "you ask me that question? Haven't I proved it by what I do for you?" "Yeah," he says, "but it's nice to hear it once in a while, too." And so after twenty-five years they talked about love, and had a relationship that was more than sex and children and husband and wife and getting and spending and cooking and cleaning and repairing.

I don't know whether we can improve on that. As for best friends, you only get best friends when you go through tough experiences with people. No tough experiences, no friends, Well, there's no one you share more tough experiences with than your wife. When you watch a kid almost die, or you try to figure out how to save the house when you lose your job, then you have tough experiences. Being in love is maybe being friends with a woman, and it is just as rare as being friends with a man. Maybe we shouldn't talk about it so much because it hardly ever happens. I know there have been a lot of women I wanted to sleep with. But then I asked "why?" I'm more than an animal. I don't need the power trip. Sex is sex, but there is probably nothing like the love of a good woman. I believe that. But I am not sure that I know what it means, and I am not sure what it costs here, either.

Meaning assigned to the sex act

Most respondents dealt perfunctorily with the topic of the meaning of intercourse. They talked about sex, usually with a wink and a leer and then, "oh, come on, you know." The answers were then very succinct. "Feels good." "Makes you a man and her a woman." "What consenting adults do for fun." "What's the matter, aren't you getting enough so you have to read about other people doing it." In general, it appeared that men had a great deal of difficulty talking about sex. Through interviews it was possible to discover more about the meaning men assigned to sex.

Most men think of intercourse exclusively as their own pleasure. Few feel responsible for helping women to enjoy it. The topic embarrasses most men. The few willing to discuss intercourse as communication believed its main purpose was to intensify an already good relationship. The others talked of men's physiological needs and how women ought to meet them. They saw sex as primarily orgasmic, and felt they were entitled to sex on demand from their wives and girl friends, as payment for protection and income. Most seemed unable to see women beyond a sexual function or as wives and mothers. They found it awkward to discuss women in nonsexual terms.

Back in the 1940's, the joke was, "every man wants a deaf and dumb, blue-eyed Miss America nymphomaniac whose father owns a liquor store." With a few notable exceptions, male verbalizations confirmed that this view was still popular. A few respondents took exception however.

Professor Joe Wigley (printed with permission). I think most men just talk about it. There is this legend about a fraternity raffle in which the prize was a night in bed with Miss America. The catch was that the winner had to make a choice. If he took the night in bed he had to tell the world he refused the prize. On the other hand, if he went into the room where the woman was supposed to be (she would not be there), he could have a press conference and say anything he liked in the morning. The question was, which would you choose. According to this legend, the overwhelming majority chose the press conference and no sex. Which do you think you would pick?

Sexual intercourse is often used by men to enhance self-esteem. Claiming a sexual contact with a desirable woman has considerable prestige value. Physical beauty is important. Wives grow old and, hence, sexually undesirable. Furthermore, the double standard still prevails. Most men claim the right to have intercourse outside of marriage though they would deny the privilege to their wives. The paradoxical view of women as madonnas and "whores" still appears to afflict a majority of men. It was interesting, however, that older men seem less susceptible to it than the college age group.

The image of women

The prevailing attitude toward sex defines the image women have with most of the men with whom they must work. In the 1972 survey, over sixty per cent of the male respondents believed that if a man took a woman out and showed her a good time, he was entitled to demand sex. Thirty per cent of the women agreed. In the current survey, the male view remained the same, although the proportion of women dropped considerably. Many women are beginning to find identity without buying into males' definitions of them.

There is a resurgent minority of men who are beginning to renovate ancient religious superstition about women as instruments of the devil whose purpose it is to tempt men into sin. This religious fundamentalism poses a serious threat to women who have begun to assume major roles in business and the professions.

No matter how you look at it, it is difficult for a woman to be respected for her competency. The bulk of retail women's clothing, for example, tends to follow the prevailing fetishes in the underground pornography market. Designers emphasize sexual embellishments. We are not arguing for gunnysack garb, but it is clear that if men are trained to look for symbols and women have no choice but to wear them, the prevailing attitude that women are sex objects will be reinforced. Secondary sexual characteristics often clamor so loudly they drown out any other capabilities. It takes considerable effort on the part of a woman to establish herself as a unique personality, for males tend not to be interested in casual socialization with them. When a man is alone with a woman, sex is not only a real possibility; it tends to be the first concern. The current rape statistics testify to this, for many an unsuspecting woman who invited a sincere-looking young man up for a drink at the end of a pleasant evening was startled to find herself in a horizontal position against her will and without any recourse, since the courts tend to define the invitation in as an invitation to sex.

The authors' editorial comment is that men are at a real disadvantage when they permit their perceptions of sexual possibilities to obscure the fact that women are equally competent. It means ignoring the collaborative possibilities of more than half of the human race. When both men and women can overcome the stereotypic attitudes they hold about each other because of sex, they can go on to other relationships. Said one woman, "men sometimes use the word 'woman' as if it were a disease or a condition." She referred to the fact that so many men paid exclusive attention to her physical features rather than her skills. She was not upset about men regarding her as attractive, but she felt she was entitled to more. It is hard to escape the stereotype that when a man and woman work together they are also a sexual pair.

Feminism

Most men do not take the "Women's Movement" seriously. They believe that it is populated by lesbians and man-haters, but paradoxically, they see its main purpose as entitling women to be more available to them sexually. Hardly any are willing to accept the idea that women are legitimately seeking to redress social and economic grievances in society.

Bill Rubin, Editor. I think Women's Lib was invented by a couple of advertising men who were not getting all they wanted from the fairer sex. It sure has made "making out" a lot easier. I wasn't much of a stud in college. Now I am approaching thirty and I have a paunch and I am hardly romantic, but I have no trouble getting all I want from the girls in the office. They think that if they don't put out people won't think they are "Thoroughly Modern Millies." I don't even have to make the propaganda. There's a copywriter who wants to help me find myself so I can write the great American novel. Hell, I don't want to write a novel. There's a division supervisor in accounting who thinks I admire her for her mind and that's why she shares her body with me. Hell, I don't admire her mind or her body. I don't even think sex is much fun any more, but with this women's movement, if I don't indulge people will think I'm gay, or at least strange. I don't think Lib has really solved anything for either sex. But I still support the E.R.A.

Men fear being seen as gay. Those homosexuals who have made public their sexual preferences face continual discrimination and hostility from the bulk of the men with whom they must associate.

Most of employed men were very concerned about the entry of women into what had been traditional male domains. Some were not at all apologetic about their antagonism to women. Many verbalized the belief that women succeeded because they gave sexual favors to the "brass." The hostility toward women in managerial and professional positions was much more virulent than the hostility toward racial minorities. The conclusion seems to be warranted that women have really not gained very much in a generation of battling. Many men still see women's place as tending the hearth, suckling the young, and fulfilling the duty, "place thy hand beneath thy husband's boot."

Bert R., M.B.A. Student. Women are on the attack now and are being supported by all sorts of laws and social norms that say women should have to be accepted equally. This has to a certain degree put a lot of men on the defensive. While almost everyone believes in equal opportunity in theory, it is much harder to subscribe to it in practice when the source of one's identity and masculinity is being invaded by the sex that was just a few years ago not only not a threat but totally dependent on the male sex. Dealing with women that are as competent or even better at a job than a man must be a very bitter pill to take for men who

---

are socialized in this society. These women are a very real problem for some men, and so much attention has been given to helping the women adjust to their new roles, that the male point of view has almost totally been ignored. Who can blame the man who is fighting back?

There is a sense of tragedy in this point of view. There is no question about women's competency. Denying them the opportunity to work to their ability denies the society the services of competent people. The men who oppose their entry into the work force suffer the most from the inability of American industry to meet foreign competition. This may seem like a *non sequitur*. It is not.

Fred Kester, Economist. The major problem American industry faces is that we do not have skilled technicians, designers, financial people, and other professionals in the proportions that the Japanese and the Germans do. The Germans are using their women well. The Japanese are beginning to. We need to make room for women and minority groups if we are going to compete in the decades ahead. We are denying ourselves an important national resource by permitting the male conspiracy to keep them from important jobs.

The nature of intimacy

We have already discussed intimacy in detail. We have explored its most prevalent and obvious aspects. Two themes that cropped up in a large minority of the respondents are worthy of mention. First, to a fair proportion of the sample, intimacy meant the opportunity to do strange and unusual things to women. We found, for example, that about fifteen per cent of the respondents referred to sado-masochism and other fetish type aberrations. For them intimacy had no connotations other than sexual, and then, the sexuality was kinky.

A second bizarre theme was the emergence of a discussion of a kind of idealistic male bond as an example of intimacy, the camaraderie of soldiers at the front, for example, or of athletes (gladiators) after having decimated a large group of lions. Four of the interview subjects referred to that very special feeling you had for the man who was on your side during the brawl. The important finding was that in more than half of the interviews, the respondents said something to the effect that intimacy was something that could never really be known by a man and woman together, that only two men could really know what it meant to be intimate. (It is interesting to note that early in 1982, the film *Personal Best* applied this comrade theme to women, apparently in the effort to reinforce the normality of the idealized male–male relationship.)

What It Means to Be a Man

Sharing fears and emotions

Some contemporary scholars advocate that men and women should encourage development in themselves of characteristics by which the other sex is identified. Men would become gentler, more supportive, while women would become more competitive and assertive. It may well be that this is a hopeless goal at present, but it affirms the fact that very little of male/female personality is physiological or genetic; rather it is a function of pressure from society to conform to stereotypical expectations.

In an earlier chapter of this book we have shown you how important it is for men and women to form a relational bond in which they could share emotions and private feelings. Most men find it difficult to discuss relationships or to show intense emotion about other people. Men found it important to be able to define themselves as "reserved." The few that embraced the values of the Encounter Movement sometimes overdid disclosure bringing it almost to the point of prurience. In general, however, adult males had difficulty saying what was on their minds. The college sample appeared equally restrained.

Eric Dunnett, Office Manager. One of the sad things is that I can't talk to doctors. I don't like to complain. My Mom told me sissies cry and I remember that. She cried a lot, but she was a woman, you know. I had this problem with my backside and I couldn't sit down, and almost couldn't walk. I mean it hurt. But I'm a gym teacher and a coach and I couldn't let the kids know how much pain I was feeling. Then my wife talked me into going to the doctor and I couldn't do anything but point. He knew what it was and he took care of it but I've always worried if it was something not so obvious, how could I say where it hurt. Then I got depressed once and my wife talked me into going to a shrink and I couldn't answer him. He said he couldn't work with me and he gave me some Sinequan and sent me home. I can't even tell my wife what bothers me most of the time. She knows when I'm having a problem and she knows what to do, but I can't tell her about it. Maybe it would feel better if I could talk, but my mother said that sissies cry.

The paranoia of the executive suite prevents the sharing of feelings and fears. In the competitive world of work, anything you say can be used against you. Many of the people who talked to us told us how important it was not to let anyone "get something on you." Mistakes must be concealed even if they are costly. And several were concerned about "paper trails," making sure that there was a written record to show that you did things by the book. As you got nearer the top you found that there were more and more people worried about their closest allies doing them in.

Kirk Smith, M.D. I'm a psychiatrist myself, but I had a hell of a time overcoming my fears. I left private practice and went to work in the hospital and I had to become part of the political system. Everything I did professionally had to be considered politically. My boss was under attack and I knew if he went down I'd go down with him, so I used the network. I had a college classmate in charge in Washington, so I called him and he did me a favor and put a hit on the hospital administrator, and I got a promotion. All it cost me was my conscience about getting that poor bastard to lose his job.

My friend has a practice midtown and he sees a lot of executives and most of them are not in good shape. But he tells me that several of his patients have to be reassured that he doesn't sell secrets to their bosses. You know, when you have to live a life where you have nowhere to let it out, you will never make it: your heart will get you, or some other part of your body will fail. Your body sort of conspires to make you scream. I've had two coronaries and open-heart surgery. It came every time something big was at stake. I lost, but I never had to blame it on myself, I could always blame it on the illness.

Now I've found I don't have to compete with my wife and I can tell her some of my feelings and she won't use them against me, but even there, she can't hold off teasing me a little about some of the things I say. I don't ever feel secure. I'm talking to you because I don't think I'll ever see you again. You're like a bartender.

The role of sports and physical strength

This statement sums it up nicely.

Stan Lafferty, Machinist. Back when I was a kid I bought pulp sports magazines and there was this ad on the back about being a ninety-five pound weakling. It was some kind of muscle building course that would make you tough so you could beat up the guy who was messing around with your girl on the beach. I always wanted to take that course. I always wanted to be an athlete, but I didn't want to get hurt. I was always jealous of the football players because they got the best women and everybody respected them. They got better jobs, too. Nobody cared about my almost perfect grades. When I went to work for the company they moved a football player who barely graduated ahead of me, and you know, he did well. It made me wonder how much time I'd wasted on contemporary protest literature and the philosophy of radical sociologists. I don't miss Super Bowl Sunday. It's a ritual. The guys from the neighborhood get together. We get a case of beer. I don't even like beer. We eat like hogs and we curse and cheer. It's important. Even when you can't play, there are guys out there doing it for you. It makes you feel like a man because you're interested in them acting like men.

Locker-room talk, dirty jokes and the playboy philosophy

There is one theory of humor that says that people joke about the things they fear. Men joke about sex, going to the bathroom, women and minority groups. When men get together they share jokes. The jokes run in cycles, many of them repeated in each generation. The man who can tell jokes well is popular. People seek him out. He is like the court jester. But most men will try to tell jokes even when they do it badly, because the jokes enable them to talk about topics they fear and to hurt people they cannot hit in public. They can joke about impotence, but they won't really talk about impotence to each other or to their doctor. They can joke about

women and blacks but they can't talk about what they fear from women and blacks. They joke about terrible things that are happening to their bodies because they cannot talk about them.

Jokes are, and always have been, important to maintain sanity among men. Getting together in the locker-room, spinning yarns and telling tales, swapping jokes, talking about female anatomy and what should be done with it is like the meeting of the hunting pack. It happens on all socio-economic levels. It is our impression it is a very effective therapeutic procedure.

What "making it" means

Getting ahead must happen in two ways. The team must win and you must be an important member of the team. Men have a tendency to identify in a team way. In school it is important to run with a good group. It is important to work for a good company. America has to be "numero uno." During the late 60's and early 70's, in the "hippie" culture, men identified with groups who did particular kinds of drugs or who were into bizarre sex or music. Belonging to the winner is important.

In addition, a man must beat his enemies. Enemies are those who are not for you. The worst enemy is someone who claimed to be your friend who then turned on you or who took your money or your women (shades of the frontier). Men tend to identify with violent heroes. They admire TV gun-slingers even though they might not want their kids to watch. There does not appear to be a chance that pacifism will catch on with the typical male.

You have to have evidence that you have made it. The profit and loss statement will show it for your company. Your house, car, kids and wife will show it for you. Your wife must be sleek, well-groomed, sexually appealing, but totally loyal to you. Your kids have to make the team at school and win a scholarship to the proper college.

A great many of the men we talked to were apprehensive about their families. They felt that their kids weren't achieving or their wife was disgracing them. It was our impression that a lot of relationships broke up because the man felt that the woman was not carrying her share in the competition. These days it is a status symbol to have a career woman as a wife. But men are very ambivalent about this kind of woman. On the one hand, they want the double income and to conform to modern values. On the other hand, they demand a traditional family and unchallenged rule in the home. The fact that career women are gaining prestige is a hopeful sign. At least the premise of the capable woman has been established for some men. In general, the older men appeared to be most hostile to employed women: however, a few unthreatened men at the top were even-handed in their view of their male and female junior executives.

The question of what it takes to be a man is most difficult to resolve. The whole difficulty between men and women arises because of the traditional definition of what it is to be a man. There are a great many men who seek to be regarded as fair, competent, and considerate. Several verbalized their desire to improve their ability to relate to women. The pressure of the social myth is very heavy, however; most, at one time or another, slip into defining women by their biology.

Part of the definition of manhood seemed to involve the ability to dominate a woman. Women were often made scapegoats for vocational failure. The ideal of the symmetrical or parallel relationship seems almost utopian in the face of the consistent image of women as house tenders, bearers of children, and sources of sex. Men also defined female qualities according to prevailing media standards of beauty. Women who deviated too far from these norms were not considered desirable. On the other hand, women sometimes had an easier time on the job if they did not conform to male standards of physical attractiveness.

Greg Halloran. Look at that little twirp Kissinger. He's got women crawling all over him. Now, you can't tell me that those women see anything in that ugly little bastard besides his power. His old lady is taller than he is and younger, and I don't know what he makes her do in the bedroom, but I bet I could do it better. But Kissinger has power. He talks to heads of state and the women that walk along with him are looked on by their sisters as being really something. You know, women really hate each other, and they hate those kind the most, but there isn't one of them that wouldn't trade places. See, the myth is that women go for sex. Hell, they don't even know the difference: it's all the same to them, but what they want to do is brag about who gives it to them.

The speaker is thirty-five-year-old professional, an attorney for a large corporation, married (happily, he claimed) with two children. His wife, a part-time bank teller sat and listened to his responses without changing her expression. The interviewer asked for her comments. She had none. The interviewer could not resist speculating silently that she may have had some reservations about her husband's expertise in sexual matters. It is hard to explain why so many men were hostile and envious when they talked about women. It appeared to be the tip of an iceberg that would bear subsequent investigation. The expressions were surprising from a well-educated, affluent, middle class individual. This was not the kind of statement we would have expected: it was, however, characteristic of a large portion of the sample.

Chapter Summary

We have painted a somewhat dismal picture of male attitudes toward women and themselves. These are hard times in which to live. Some authorities (Daniel Yankelovich in *The New Rules*, for example) refer to them as transitional times in which people are struggling for new roles. It is hard to surrender what you have, and traditional male bastions are being assaulted not only by women and minority groups but also by machinery. Employment is no longer a reliable source of self-esteem.

It is hard to be a man in contemporary American society. Most men live under the constant fear that they will lose their jobs. They are compelled to compete. Those that slip outside the system are ignored or insulted. The mid-life crisis is no fiction. Many men are aware they have sacrificed a great deal of human content in their lives by their commitment to the job.

It is not strange that males are as hostile to and suspicious of women. Women are a threat. A competent woman is hard to compete with. Men have not been trained to regard women as potential allies. Therefore, men and women find it awkward to work together. Competent women are threatening to men. Most women still feel that they compete ineffectively. Some succumb to the male image. They either sell out as sex objects or they become hostile to other women. Much of the time the employed woman will reinforce male impressions by being a good secretary and preparing the coffee. It is simply too hard to stand up against the kind of pressure that is commonly imposed on women when they are in the minority. At the moment, women are easy to defeat, but they are there and some of them win because they are simply better than the men with whom they compete. They are doing well, and gradually, men are learning not only to accept them but to collaborate with them in productive, professional ways.

It is very hard to meet society's standards for manhood. Men are supposed to be strong and tough, able to meet challenges and solve problems. They may not admit weakness. They are models for the young, protectors of womankind, executives, fathers, and heroes, and at the ame time are expected to be understanding counselors and intelligent advisors. No one can live up to this image. Most men try hard and sincerely and many feel a great deal of pain as a result.

A major part of being a man is to relate to women in some way. The ways are ambivalent, paradoxical, and contradictory. A man loves his mother (with mother love), loves his wife (sex plus something else), loves any female (sexual intercourse). He may also love football and french fries. (Maurice Samuel used to say "a cannibal loves his neighbors.") Men like to look at women and at pictures of women. They buy a great number of magazines for that purpose.

Women are supposed to be gentle and supportive. They are supposed to understand subtle things, to heal and strengthen. None of these characteristics are vices. If men and women can share them as they begin to share the work space, the prospect will be very bright.

There are hopeful signs that men will be able to overcome their acculturation and welcome competent women into their vocational alliances. We can hope that the entry of large numbers of women may reduce the intensity of interpersonal competition as well.

There are new kinds of problems arising from what Betty Friedan calls the "second stage," young women who have been raised in a feminist ethic. They have essentially the same difficulty accommodating to their potential as mothers as their mothers had accommodating to their vocational potential.

Eventually it will work out. It already has for some. The important issue is, of course, that there must be choices that are equal for everyone concerned. Without equity for both sexes, we will return to some form of past subordination of women by men, and we will lose their talents. Women must have the right to choose their form of fulfillment, exactly as men have that right to choose. The negotiation necessary to accomplish this sort of equity is challenging and rewarding, for the end product is truly adult relationships and enriching intimate bonds.

REFERENCES FOR CHAPTER 9

D. Barash, *The Whisperings Within*. New York: Harper and Row, 1979.
G. Gilder, *Sexual Suicide*. New York: Quadrangle, 1973.
S. Hite, *The Hite Report on Male Sexuality*. New York: Random House, 1981.
D. Levinson, *The Seasons of a Man's Life*. New York: Knopf, 1978.
R. Lucas, *Men in Crisis*. New York: Basic Books, 1970.
J. Scanzoni, *Sexual Bargaining*. Englewood Cliffs, N.J.: Prentice-Hall, 1972.
D. Sabo, Jr., *Jock: Sports & Male Identity*. N.J.: Prentice-Hall/Spectrum, 1980.
H. Schoeck, *Envy*. New York: Harcourt, Brace, 1966.
A. Storr, *Human Aggression*, Forge Village, MA.: Murray Publishing Co., 1968.
L. Tiger, *Men in Groups*. New York: Random House, 1979.
E. O. Wilson, *On Human Nature*. Cambridge: Harvard Univ. Press, 1978.

10

THE WOMEN TESTIFY

Ruth B. pursues a full-time career as operations manager for a small company. In addition, she does nearly all of the housework and cooking for herself and her husband who teaches at the local college.

Gloria T. is a second-semester senior whose academic and work record have led to job offers from two of the "Big Eight" accounting firms. Her fiancé, also an accounting major, is still waiting for his first offer.

Sherryl K. is in the policy-making division of a state social service agency, Ed D., a senior colleague, offers to assist her in preparing a major proposal. She is not sure whether his motives are personal or professional.

Ellen N. and Barry H. work as a team to design marketing campaigns for a consumer services company. Frequently they stay late at the office to work on assignments and they make occasional out-of-town trips to present their work. Ellen realizes that her working relationship with Barry is one of the hottest gossip items with their colleagues in the company, but she doesn't know how to refute the gossip without appearing to "protest too much."

Shirley W. has been married for twenty years. Her youngest of three children has just gone off to college. Shirley married right after high school graduation. She would like to get a job but wonders what she can do.

You have, no doubt, known people who have faced similar issues. If you are a woman, chances are you'll encounter such situations in the foreseeable future and you'll need to decide how to define goals and balance priorities. The traditional images of women and men in our society seem to be changing.

The guidelines about the ways men and women relate to one another have become blurred. We have few reliable cues about what is expected of us. In general, interactions and transactions between men and women produce considerable anxiety, mistrust, and misunderstanding.

The purpose of this chapter is to report the issues contemporary women identify as salient to their choices of self-definition and their formation of relationships with other women and with men. We will not offer any techniques for managing relationships, nor will we define appropriate life-styles for contemporary women. The categories used in this chapter will differ from the previous chapter, because women view the world differently and have different priorities than men. Written reports from our survey are primary data for this chapter. In addition, information is drawn from the author's conversations with the numerous women who discussed their goals and conflicts with her. The chapter also reflects the personal experience of one of the authors.

Julia T. Wood, Co-author. At the time I write this chapter, I am a thirty-one year old tenured associate professor. I have been married (to the same man!) for seven years, and we have no children. I consider myself fortunate to have come of age during this time in our society, for I have not only observed major changes in women's roles, but I have been a part of many of them. To an extent, this chapter reflects my own views and my concerns as someone who works closely with hundreds of young women and men who are currently trying to settle their values and design their lives in a turbulent era.

Compared to most textbook presentations, you will find relatively little in the way of facts or theoretical propositions in this chapter. Instead, we will present you with a wide range of points of view representing possible orientations for women in our society. You will probably agree with some of these ideas, disagree with others, and be uncertain on many. Regardless of your present opinions, this chapter should provoke you to think about your goals in relationships. If you are a woman, you might discover some new possibilities for your relationship choices and formulate some responses to some of the questions raised. If you are man, you might learn something about women's changing perspectives on relationships, particularly those with men. This may help you understand something about new possibilities for future relationships. In the previous chapter we reviewed the range of issues facing contemporary men. Perhaps the most productive outcome from reading these two chapters would be some relatively open discussions between women and men. The picture presented in both chapters seems a bit bleak, but it's not a static picture. There are numerous possibilities for changing the current state of affairs. The issues identified here are real ones, raised by real people. You will need to face them at some time in your own life.

The chapter is divided into four sections. First we'll examine how women view friendships with each other and with men. Second, we'll look at women's expectations of romantic and marriage relationships. We will consider what women want to invest in their intimate bonds. Third, we'll explore some sticky issues that confront women in work settings, such as professional alliances, tokenism, exclusionism and sexism in the professional world. The final section of the chapter addresses the most basic question of all for women: what does it mean to be a woman in contemporary American society, and what does the future hold?

Women's Views on Friendship

Women consider friendship very important. They are conscious of it and are generally subtle in their awareness of who relates to them in what way. While some tend to associate with other women, either because of their status and prestige or that of their husband, the predominant reasons for association are recreation, personal support (consensual validation), and problem-solving.

Recreational friends change quickly. Most women strike up conversational associations quite easily and are usually willing to share time with other women who happen to be present at an event or gathering. Easy socialization provides women with an opportunity to conduct "tryouts" and arrange explorations with many of the women they meet.

Personal support is a second purpose for women's friendships. Women see friends as confidantes. Much more than men, they feel it is necessary to have very close friends to whom they can disclose intensely personal information and feelings. It appears that women

Women place priority on friendships with other women.

require consensual validation throughout their lives, though men are trained to abandon it as a sign of weakness early into adulthood. Women select confidantes who will listen to their disclosures and keep them confidential and share their own secrets in return. Confidentiality is considered very important. Women regard breach of confidence by former friends as the most serious form of betrayal. Because the information exchanged is so sensitive, most women have only one or two friends who fit into this category, most of them of long-standing. Women, much more than men, seem to retain long-term active associations with people from their past. They appear to exert greater effort to sustain their associations.

Topics of conversation with close personal friends center on personal fears and insecurities usually resulting from the prospect of an intimate relationship with a man, consideration of possible pregnancy, and uneasiness about work.

Alma W. I sometimes think that Susan and I have more to say to each other than we do to our husbands. We became friends during our second year at Vassar. We both were maids of honor at each other's weddings and godparents at the christenings of our children. When Susan moved to the West Coast we stayed in contact by phone weekly and we met in Chicago for three lovely days together each year. I was overjoyed when they returned to New York. My husband, Lou, says sometimes that Susan is more important to me than he is. He doesn't like Susan's husband, but he keeps a good face on it because he knows how important it is to keep Susan as my friend. I could say she was like a sister, but we have more going, I think than most sisters. We need each other very much.

Problem-solving is very important, both to working women and those who select more traditional orientations. The focus of this kind of friendship is on "checking things out" and getting ideas from others who have had experience. Topics of concern for working women include responses to sexism in the office, how to manage potentially compromising situations with male colleagues, discovering the norms of conduct and conversation, learning who can be trusted, and managing conflicts between work and home. Women who focus on a home-making career use these kinds of contacts to swap advice on husband and child behavior.

In deference to this need, a great many publications attempt to act as surrogate friends. Magazines addressed to women deal extensively with many of the topics that women share with problem-solving friends. In the most recent issues of several magazines addressed exclusively to women, the following topics were considered: how to dress to discourage sexist remarks in the office, how to convince male colleagues you have technical knowledge, how to modulate your voice to sound more serious, what to do about children who are failing in school, how to help your husband overcome his mid-life crisis, and how to make the transition from work to parenthood and back to the world of work.

In general, the respondents to the survey seemed to indicate awareness of the reciprocal nature of friendship. While the words "exchange" and "equity" were rarely used, virtually every written response expressed ideas which indicated the writer was aware of and responsive to exchange concerns. For example:

We have worked it out over the years how to take turns paying the check for our weekly lunches. When one of us forgets our money, the other pays, but we make sure we pay back almost instantly. I know it may sound a little petty, but it is a sign that in other parts of the relationship, the big parts where we both give without question, things will remain the same. We can always count on each other.

For as long as I can remember Louise has sat by my side while I filled out my income tax. She simply knows more about it than I do. But she is so naive about buying. So whenever she makes a big purchase, I am like the *Consumers' Report* for her. I help her figure out how to make the decision and when she thinks it is necessary, I go with her.

I can think of no major event in either of our lives that we haven't shared with the other.

In fact, the idea of exchange seems to be the primary criterion of judgment about whether or not a person is a friend. A person who does not return help or service or call on the other for it soon becomes suspect.

Andrea F., Student. Seems I was always unburdening on Kim. After a while it really started to bother me because I felt she wasn't willing to rely on me or trust me with things in her life. I started to feel I was the dependent one in the friendship. Then I learned she talked about her feelings and personal problems with Joyce. That was the end of our friendship. It was pretty clear she didn't regard me as a friend or she would have shared with me like I did with her.

This is an important consideration. Popular mythology has it that women are possessive about their friendships. The evidence in the written responses, however, is that what appears to be posses-

siveness is really responsiveness. Women seem more sensitive to the subtle nuances of friendships than men. They do not wish to be dependent. Many wrote about how it made them feel strong when the person they relied on also relied on them. The conclusion is that most women build their friendships in order to strengthen each other. Their friendships are much more reliable and stable than the alliances men build in the office. While there may be considerable jockeying around in developing stages of women's friendships, once the relationship is mutually affirmed, the chances of its survival are very high.

Friendships with men

Women do not agree about friendship between men and women. Most women seem to believe that it is *possible* for men and women to form friendships that have no sexual overtones. However, this possibility is seldom realized in actual experience. According to most respondents, sex is most often an unarticulated but dimly present issue in their relationships with men. While sexual invitations and comments may not be made directly, awareness of sexuality seems almost inevitable in female-male interactions.

Sexism takes many forms. Men may compliment appearance or hold open doors, light cigarettes, provide assistance with coats, pull out chairs at the table. They may offer verbal assurances that they have no sexual motives. (According to many women this is one sure sign that they have at least considered sexual possibilities.) Several women admitted that they sometimes slipped into flirtatious behaviors when interacting with attractive men. Most troubling was the recurrent complaint that men often exhibit an unnecessarily protective stance toward women, very often acting as if the woman was a child.

Mildred S., Corporate Junior Vice President. Mike and I went to MBA school together, so we've known each other for ten years now. We always get together at conventions to talk and catch up. But if he doesn't stop patronizing me, I simply am going to end the association. At the last convention I presented a paper, and some very tough questions were posed by the audience. Before I had a chance to respond, Mike jumped to my defense and began answering the questions. I resented that. I am completely able to fight my own battles. I don't need him to come to my rescue and I resent his assumption that I do. Furthermore, I really got angry that he did that in front of my professional colleagues because it made me look like a poor little girl who can't make it without assistance of a big, strong man.

Greta T., Secretary. Joe tried to start his car and it wouldn't start. He stormed into the house and called the garage and the garage told him that nobody's car would start on a morning like this and it would be two hours before they could come. I smiled, put on my coat, went outside, pulled my car out of the garage next to his, opened both hoods, took the jumper cables out of my trunk (he didn't even know I had them), fastened them to my battery, hooked the cable onto his battery and carefully grounded the other, and started his car for him. I had waited twelve years for this and he damn well looked at me differently after that.

It is very difficult for many men and women to avoid responding to each other according to our entrenched sex-role expectations. Nonetheless, most contemporary women seem to want to avoid this kind of orientation and many expect men to monitor sex-stereotyped attitudes.

On a different note, most women do believe that it is possible and desirable to be friends with a romantic partner or husband. Almost all college-age women and a majority of older women think a good romantic relationship must include friendship. They expect husbands and lovers to enjoy joint recreation, to provide personal support and assistance in problem solving, and to share confidences. The issue of reciprocity was important here, too. Most women are troubled when their male partner fails to disclose personal feelings or problems and refuses to rely on the woman'a strength in times of need. Traditional male socialization advises men that personal disclosures are both risky and a sign of weakness. Men are commonly somewhat reticent about seeking assistance with problems. It is hard to maintain real intimacy, however, unless there is mutual sharing, and most women are sensitive to their mates' reluctance to confide in them.

Betty J., Clerk. Sometimes I feel like screaming, "Kevin, tell me what's bothering you. I want to help. I want to know. Don't keep shutting me out!" But I know there's no point. He won't talk to me or anyone about his worries. So they eat him up. Then, too, his strong silent style does damage to our marriage. He locks me out of big parts of his world, and I don't know him as fully as I want to. And I'm beginning to feel uneasy about unburdening my feelings on him, because I think he has enough problems of his own. It's awkward because he gives me no way to return. You know, men are as trapped in their sex roles as women are.

The problems encountered in developing a complete exchange with a man may account for the special status women give to friendships with other women. Even among women who report successful non-sexual friendships with men, there are special dimensions and values to their relationships with other women. There is a natural kinship between women who embrace compatible philosophies on the way they live their lives. The support they exchange is particularly important considered against the backdrop of uncertainty experienced by women attempting to make it in the world of work, where they are, at the moment, an unwelcome minority.

Most women report that there are some issues that can only be discussed with other women, issues men simply cannot understand. Some of these topics, for example, are the emotional aftermath of rape, the meaning of sexuality, how to fend off unwanted advances, how to cope with subtle and blatant sex discrimination, how to reconcile career and home responsibilities, and whether to have children. Men do not seem to understand these issues except on an intellectual basis. They are as mysterious to men as male concerns about the team and competition seem to be to women. The conclusion is that there are some topics on which men and women *have not yet developed dual perspective for to do so would mean revising both their roles and expectations.*

The unique content of talk between women is paralleled by a specialized style of relating. Women see each other as more expressive, supportive, nonjudgmental, and openly caring than men. Friendships between women employ communication that is distinctively warm and provides a special sense of security. As one woman explained, "with my women friends I don't have to worry about how I express myself or whether they'll disapprove of something I've done. With men, even ones I'm very close to, there's always the need to keep my guard up a little, to make sure I come across effectively." The expectation of security in relationships fosters so much trust in women that they are confused by office politics. A major problem for women who work with men is their inability to compete effectively on their own behalf.

Brenda P., Production Supervisor. I don't think there are three men in the company who are as good as I am. But no one knows it. Every time I get up to talk, they come at me. It isn't a sexist thing. They hassle each other, too. But they can handle it, and I can't. They mangle each other and then go off to the bar to have a drink, and if somebody attacks one of them, they all gang up on him. When they hassle me, I'm hurt. They all learned how to fight when they were little boys and I learned how to be a nice little girl. I know that if I don't learn to compete the way they do, I won't advance in this company, no matter how good I am, but I don't want to be one of those tough, hard women you run into from time to time. It's a real problem for me, and I don't have anyone to talk about it with.

In summary, women seem to attach more value to their friendships than men, but they are less able to manage strategic alliances and competition. Most women believe that their friendships with men would be improved if men could learn to disclose more effectively. Women build their friendships on an exchange of private information, mutual support, and shared cooperation in problem-solving.

Women's Views on Romantic Relationships

Women still believe in romance and almost all (heterosexual women) think that personal fulfillment must include satisfying romantic relationships with men. Other than this there are few generalizations that can be made about romantic ideals. Some authorities, Shere Hite, for example, equate romantic tendencies with fantasies. There is no doubt that many women engage in fantasies about how "it could be" with the right man. Many are attracted to literature that tells romantic stories.

Marlene M., Media Research Consultant. The soap operas depend on the romantic tendencies of women that stay home during the day. It is a generalization based on a stereotype, but it seems to work. The soaps get loyal audiences and the advertisers sell their products. The women viewers seem to love to watch the complicated male/female relationships get acted out. Many of them identify with particular characters. Many of them identify scenes from their own lives. It is hard to say whether this is good for women or not. There are some authorities who believe that life imitates art and that at least a few women try to get their own lives to be like soap operas. The prevailing opinion, however, is that soap operas are a good antidote to the relatively mundane and routine lives most housewives lead. This sort of identification is not confined to women. We find men making the same kind of identification with cowboy and cop heros and with major sports figures. In general, the media cater to stereotypes. They feed them and engender them to the point where those who identify with them are trapped.

There are three fairly distinct points of view on the issue of romantic relationships that can be identified: traditional, independent and dually-oriented.

Traditional women

The feminist movement notwithstanding, many contemporary women hold traditional views of the male-female relationship as well as of the female roles within these bonds. Many of these women have strong religious commitments which support their traditional views. They regard men as dominant, women as subordinate. They believe men should be allowed to make the major decisions and control how the relationship operates. They seek a complementary bond, where the woman is consistently subordinated. The roles are defined and secure. They have no ambiguity about their responsibilities. Within the arrangement, they are allowed considerable leeway to develop their own social contacts, usually through organizational volunteer work, the church, and the school.

Women in this group identify themselves with their husbands and their children. They acquire self-esteem through the accomplishments of their husbands and children. They form their opinions (at least the ones they say out loud) based on their husbands' points of view. They regard physical attractiveness as very important and work very hard at it. They spend a great deal of money and time on hair styling, shopping for clothing, and most recently on staying trim.

They are also considerably concerned about child rearing. Conversation between women in the traditional group very often takes the form of comparing notes on behavior of husbands and children, sometimes sharing problems and seeking support in those areas. It is important to them to have a man as head of the household. Furthermore, the man should be older and more intelligent, ambitious and competent, both on the job and in the home. Task roles are clearly divided into man's work and woman's work.

They expect men to provide for them and take care of them. If they work, they regard it as temporary, a way to add to the income when needed but not the source of esteem or fulfillment. Their primary goals are to have children, and to stay home and rear them properly while their husbands pursue the traditional male obligation to earn an income. Women within this group serve as the primary audience for media information on how to enter the world of work, for increased life spans confront them with many years when child-rearing can no longer be their focus. The problem of re-socialization faced by the past-middle-aged traditional women represents one of the most serious femal crises. On the other hand, the security offered in the traditional arrangement has considerable appeal, even for women who are making it in their career.

Ilene C., Homemaker. I know my ideas aren't exactly "in" today, but what I really want is to have a marriage built on shared faith and to have three kids and keep up a nice home for all of us. I think my role is to raise the children to be moral people and to make the home a place of peace. It's impossible for a woman to take a job and still do what she should for her family. And I think family life is the foundation of our whole society. It has always been the woman's place to preserve that.

Traditional women seem a bit mistrustful of women who are career-oriented. Some think a career is all right for those who choose it, but they resent being regarded as second class women because they chose the role of mother and home-maker. Others regard professional women as "not quite real women." Many women in middle years regard younger women in the office as real threats to their marriages.

There are two serious issues here. The first, expressed eloquently by Betty Friedan, is that a great many young women are discouraged from choosing a career as wife and mother, even temporarily, because of a previling norm that real satisfaction can only be found on the job. The second is that a great many women who choose the role of wife and mother do not prepare themselves to do something after the children are grown and have moved away from home. Many of the respondents in the survey were aware of these issues, and some of the younger ones had already begun to grapple with them. On the other hand, a great many of the older respondents displayed a kind of "double-take" in their responses as if to say, "why didn't someone warm me about these problems?" Consider the following two reports:

Caller on the Donahue Show (22 July 1981) (Paraphase) I'm forty years old and I've been married seventeen of those years. Ever since the children started school I've wanted to work part-time. But each time I brought up the idea, my husband talked me out of it. He wanted the all-American life with me at home to take care of him and the children. So I always gave in, because I wanted to be whatever he wanted. I built my life around his values. Three weeks ago he told me I'd been right all along. He said he'd realized women are more interesting when they work outside the home. His mind was changed by a thirty-two year old woman in his office who he says can relate to him in ways I can't because I'm just a housewife. He's filed for divorce.

Corinne J., Administrative Assistant. When I was twenty-five I was going with a guy named Marvin. Marvin was kind of a dud. He wanted to get married. I didn't. We had some sexual relations for a while. We sort of kept each other busy. I kept working and my mind was on my job and getting ahead, and Marvin sort of drifted off and I heard he got married. About six months ago I ran across him. He told me about his wife and showed me pictures of his children. He seemed very happy. I am not. I am forty. I have gone as far as I can go with the company, and I don't seem to be able to make a lateral move. I am entirely alone. I want children and I am too old. Somebody should have told me this could happen.

Traditionally women have not perceived many choices for themselves. The few careers open to women demanded great dedication, and there was still a social stigma attached to spinsterhood. To an extent, this is happening to young career women as well. There is a tendency for the popular media to confront women with an "all or nothing" demand for complete success in what they try. As we will show later on, it is difficult, if not impossible, to be totally successful at both career and home-making. The responsibilities can be balanced but one must give way in part to the other.

Traditional beliefs are not necessarily good or bad, nor are the alternatives. The problem seems to lie in the fact that insufficient information is available to women about their choices. The decisions with which they are confronted are extremely complicated. A man remaining at home to care for children is exceedingly rare, something to feature on the "Real People Show." Women who allow themselves to slip into a life choice because of someone else's definition face the loss of their self-esteem and the inability to control their own lives.

Independent women

Independent women stand in stark contrast to traditional women. They are committed to personal autonomy, fulfillment in a career, and equal relationships with men. Independence is an important concept for these women. They express confidence in their ability to care for themselves both economically and emotionally. They are generally committed to a feminist ideology and seek support by association with others who believe as they do. They feel little need for approval beyond their social group.

Careers are the central feature of independent women's lives. They enjoy the challenge and self-esteem that comes from performing successfully on an important job. Second, they cherish the financial independence that a career provides. They do not want to rely on a man for money and they resent having to account to a man for how they spend their incomes.

Jennifer C., Paralegal. I just can't see myself having to ask my husband for money to buy clothes or to go on a trip or whatever. That's dependency with a capital "D." I won't have it. I make a good salary and I don't want to have to check with anyone about how I spend it. I will never get into a relationship where I have to count on somone else's generosity to get what I want. It reminds me of a kid asking her father for an allowance.

Independent women do not necessarily reject the idea of a marriage, provided that it is genuinely egalitarian. They repudiate complentary relationships and, within the marriage, demand full equality. Hard choices, like what to do if one partner is transferred, are often resolved by turn-taking or divorce. For these women, long-term intimacy is an option but not a necessity. They will take it only on their own terms. One limitation lies in the fact that most men are not willing to participate in this kind of relationship: hence, their pool of choices is limited. Another potential problem is adopting an extremist position that denys the opportunity to review other options.

Georgia R., Marketing Director. Marriage? Sure, I believe in it, in general anyway. I'm beginning to think it will never work out for me, though. I'm thirty-seven now and I wouldn't think of marrying any of the men I've dated in the past four years. Most of the men I meet are intimidated by my achievements and my self-reliance. They realize I don't need them, that I'm perfectly able to take care of myself. That's very damaging to the typical male ego. But, to answer the question, yes. I would like to marry a man who's sufficiently successful and competent not to be threatened by a woman of equal competence. Unfortunately, that's an endangered species of male.

Georgia may be right about the scarcity of men who will commit to a truly egalitarian relationship with a woman. According to married independent women a genuinely balanced relationship is still largely in ideal, not a reality. Many report that their husbands verbalize liberal views but fail to live up to them in practice. There are imbalances in basic household tasks and sex-linked expectations, as well as the assumption that career conflicts should be resolved in favor of the husband.

Grace B., Teacher. I thought we had really freed ourselves of traditional sex-role stereotypes and that we had an equal marriage. Then we decided we wanted a child. It was a mutual decision. But Greg insists that I take off a few years from my job when we have the child. He won't even consider taking time off from his work or having each of us take a one year leave-of-absence or having both of us work part-time. He thinks taking care of a baby should be my responsibility because I'll be the mother. And he thinks it's more important that his career not be interrupted. Some equality! The strange thing is that I sort of feel the same way.

It is very difficult for women and men to overcome centuries of sex-role training. Grace and Greg cannot easily cast aside deeply-rooted values that surround such issues as parenting. It is even more difficult to handle these issues in the face of contemporary pressure to "preserve the family." It almost appears that "preserve the family" is the secret code for "keep women in their place," somewhat like the relationship between "law and order" and racism. But the ambivalence is extraordinarily difficult to overcome.

What is worse is the disillusionment that comes when an independently oriented woman marries in the expectation of finding equality only to discover that her husband is not willing to comply once the relationship has been made permanent. Very often, the woman finds herself surrendering her position reluctantly to preserve the marriage. On rare occasions, it is the reverse.

Sara J., Ph.D. When I got the offer of the professorship, I was amazed that Jim gave up his job to come with me. "I'll get something," he said, "I'm competent." But there was no job for him in the little college town. He was "overqualified" for everything available, and "under-credentialed" for major positions. Back in the city, he had a management job. Here, there was nothing he could do. When the baby came, he stayed home and cared for Joseph. He was a good father. I could see that he was becoming bored and bitter, but he didn't say anything and he did not get in the way of my career. I can't tolerate seeing him thwarted like this. I am giving up my position so we can go somewhere where Jim can get a job. I guess it's my turn to stay home.

It is hard to tell where this relationship will go. Sara is not sure of her role and neither Jim nor Sara wish to constrain the other excessively. There is strength in the dual perspective each displays, so they may be able to maintain their bond despite problems.

Because many independent women still feel the pull of traditional values, it is not surprising that a number of them feel threatened by more traditional women, just as traditional women feel threatened by independents.

Alicia M., Retailer. I went to my ten year high school reunion last month, and that was one bad scene. Most of my classmates were married and had children. The talk among the women was about their husbands and children. I tried to talk with some of the men, but they made it clear I didn't fit with them. So I went back to the women but they really made me feel like an oddball. Like, Ann asked if I had a family and I said "no." She said, "too bad, you're missing what life is all about." Sharon asked if I felt I was a "real woman, not having children." The message was clear. Those women didn't consider me one of them. I had disgraced my sex by not marrying and having kids. If I'm really honest with myself I have to admit that part of me feels that way, too. Sometimes I think I really might be happier with a family than with my career.

Alicia's report is not atypical. Suspicions run both ways. Single women mistrust those who are married. They resent them because they have families, but they look down on them because they are not employed. Married women resent the career women because they feel their status challenged. They see career women as potential predators on their men. Life is particularly difficult for the divorced or widowed woman who is newly separated from an intimate relationship. Many such women report that they are cut off by many of their married friends. They also report that it is common for their friends' husbands to make advances, offering themselves to "satisfy their needs." The formation of networks of divorced women is a recent phenomenon, evidencing how women rely on each other for mutual support.

Harriet H. I did my duty for seventeen years. I kept the house, produced and tended three children, entertained captains when he was a lieutenant, majors when he was captain, and colonels when he was a major. Since his promotion it has been generals all the way. I kept the glassware shiny and the silverware polished, and learned to be a gourmet cook. "Good, *old* Harriet," he would say, "you can always count on her for a good dinner." Then he walked out. Just walked out, leaving me with a sixteen year old and a twelve year old and an eight year old, and no income and no training. He started a divorce because he found a general's daughter to marry, and when my lawyer went at him for child care payments he acted like he had nothing to do with producing those kids. To make things worse, my neighbors, the other colonels' wives, turned their backs. I didn't exist. One of the captains' wives told me that the gossip was that with a figure like mine they didn't want me near their husbands. I won't tell you what it was like getting sympathy from those husbands. I took my kids and went to visit my old friend, Irma, who never got married. She helped me find an apartment and a job. Last month Irma announced her engagement, a triumph, she said, a forty year old, a bride for the first time. I met her fiancé once. I am not invited to her house any more. We are still friends, but she comes to see me or we meet downtown.

The relationship that women have with their friends is strong and sustaining except when one women perceives another as a threat to a husband or job. It is hard to get data about competition between women. Hardly anyone talks about it, although many allude to it. A few respondents who could be classified as independents talked about how some women, when they reach the top, hurt other women. Middle-aged women indicated young single women and divorcees as potential seducers of husbands. It seems that distrust of those whose choices or opportunities differ is fairly common. The distrust may reflect the general insecurity with whatever choice a woman has made, and regret for what was sacrificed in order to make it. Whatever the reason, women seem uncomfortable in dealing with other women who are unlike them.

Dually oriented women (superwomen)

A third group of contemporary women endorse a mixture of traditional and feminist values. These women seem to have the most difficult of all positions, because they constantly juggle competing priorities and attempt to reconcile conflicting values. Frequently pulled in two incompatible directions, they try to meet competing demands and suffer frustration and guilt about those not met.

Wendy P., Ph.D. I'm a tenured English professor at the university and I'm also married. I love my work, the teaching and the research. I also love my husband and I want to do things with him. It seems to me I wind up feeling guilty about neglecting one or the other all of the time. If I'm in my den working, I feel I should be out talking to Jake or doing something with him. If I'm working on a meal with Jake, I feel I ought to be in my den doing research. It's a constant "no win" situation. We both want children, but how in the world could I juggle a third responsibility?

Wendy speaks for a great many women who have both traditional and independent goals. They want the stability and comfort of family, yet they want, equally, the personal and material rewards of full-time careers. They cannot abandon the traditional values with which they grew up, but neither can they be satisfied with just those of the contemporary social world. For many, life becomes a series of trade-offs in which one set of values dominates in one moment and another set of values rules in the next. For these women, ambivalence is a way of life.

Most women in this group consider long-term intimacy an important aspect of their current or future life. They want an enduring relationship with a man. Furthermore, the majority of these women seek a parallel relationship blending complementarity and symmetry. Within their marriages they tend to assume many traditionally female responsibilities such as shopping, cooking, and planning social engagements, and their husbands do conventionally male chores such as yard work, cutting fire wood, and maintaining the car. Their independence is evident primarily in career pursuits and participation in major financial decisions in the marriage. As individuals, they strive for a more feminine self-presentation than do independents, but a less subordinate role than that assumed by traditionals.

Superwoman.

For women in this group, particularly those already married, the most troublesome issue is children. According to the women surveyed, there is a strong desire for at least one child. Most dually-oriented women think that having a child is an essential part of a complete life. However, many are painfully unsure of their ability to cope successfully with the obligations of motherhood in addition to those imposed by their professions and marriages. They feel that if they have a child they should suspend their careers temporarily in order to stay home during the first few years. Yet they think this is an extremely high price to pay; for some it is too high to deal with.

These women are caught between two worlds, and they live daily with the tension of trying to reconcile competing demands. They can enjoy aspects of both the traditional and independent world, yet they cannot have all that is possible in either system. Often, however, they put extraordinary pressure on themselves to attain perfection in both worlds. Discussion of the "super-woman" occupies many pages in current women's magazines.

Even more stressful is the situation faced by a great many women who must work in order to make ends meet, even though they may not want to. Women in the lower middle class often take factory or clerical work simply because it is impossible to live on one income. They do not espouse independent values, and they are very uneasy about the consequences of their working on their families. Rising unemployment makes these women even more vulnerable. Their families have committed to a life style which requires two incomes. If they or their husbands are laid off, their families can literally come apart.

Cora W., Assembly-line Worker. My mother stayed home with us kids. There were five of us and we all grew up all right. Bert went to college and works as an accountant at the X Co. here in town. My husband, Len, works for X Co. also, as a machine maintenance man. My two sisters are married to shop foremen and they don't have to work, and my kid brother is in college now. He wants to be a doctor and all of us kick in to make sure he makes it. Len gets about $1100 a month without overtime. The best he ever did was about $1500, but he can't keep that up too long. I took a job on the production line and I make near $4.50 an hour, but it's seasonal, so I average about $6000 a year. We need it to make out with the mortgage payments and the car and parochial school for the kids. I got three kids, and me and Len would like another one, but it's hard. My mother comes over to be with the kids when they come home from school and when she's sick the neighbor takes them, and sometimes I have to call in sick when one of the kids has a fever or something. I ought to be home with them. I want them to grow up to be good kids like we were. I want them to go to college. But they won't go to college unless we have more money and that means I have to keep on working. I don't think there's another way.

The problems of the Coras of the world rarely get consideration. Most of the literature written for women deals with those who are college-educated and career-bound. There are literally millions of women caught in a trap where they are compelled to be independent against their will. They do not understand or endorse such independence and they must assume responsibility beyond anything they had ever bargained for. They *do* raise good kids and they keep a "nice" house and their husbands usually stay with them. But it is a hard life with few rewards in between, other than knowing that they are doing their best to sustain their families and their feminine role given economic pressures.

There is conflict between the possibilities that women have about the way they will spend their lives. The male possibilities are easier to deal with because they contain fewer options. Perhaps, if men could see more options for themselves, possibilities for choice would expand for women, or these choices would be easier for them to make. The male role is clearly defined as worker, and it remains so. It is unusual for a male to assume household or child care obligations. Thus, most women are locked into situations where they must, in the words of Lewis Carroll, "run just as fast as they can to stay in the same place." Figuring out a way for women and men to crystallize mutually satisfying goals remains a crucial interpersonal issue for our generation.

The following statement comes from one of the author's co-workers who read this chapter in manuscript form. Her statement makes the point that choices of life-style and self-definition need not be static, that in the course of a lifetime each of us may sample diverse options.

Dianne Luce, Secretary. In my life I have so far been in two different categories. When I was at home with my children for eleven years I was happy being the traditional woman. Now that circumstances have put me in the dually-oriented woman category I am happy with that and find it a challenge to juggle all the demands made on me and still find time for myself. I may, at a time in the future, find myself as an independent woman, although I see that only if something should happen to my husband. That's what makes life so interesting. I'm glad to live in a time when women are free to make these choices. I think most women are glad to be able to sample the different life-styles. It gives more insight and tolerance into the way people choose to live. I don't think our society accepts as easily men who might also want to sample these life-styles. In this way, women are more fortunate.

Women's Views on the World of Work

How women view work is a broad topic that involves a number of issues. The first that must be resolved is why women work. There are a variety of answers. A great number work for the same reason men do: they have no choice. Women who head households, who have to support children, or whose husbands' earnings are not high must work to maintain a consistent income level. However, many of them look forward to a time when they will not need to work, for their jobs are not that satisfying. Nevertheless, for most of them, being employed is a permanent economic necessity.

There is an increasingly large number of women who work in a quest for personal fulfillment. Their counterparts are the men who seek professional careers or highly skilled occupations. Having a job or career for these women is a way of contributing to society, enhancing self-esteem, and assuring personal independence. Among college students and younger working women, there was still a third reason for working—to have personal status. They felt that society tended to view traditional women with contempt.

Susan M., Sales Representative. Actually, I don't like working. It's boring. I'd rather be home with the children and taking care of the house. But if you are *just* a housewife today, you're nothing. People think you're lazy or that no one will hire you. It used to be that women who worked were the strange ones. Now it's the other way around.

Susan and women like her have discovered the great male secret: that most work is boring. There are as few exciting and challenging careers open to women as there are to men. There are only a few professional artists that get hired; only a few account executives or general managers. The supply of good jobs is limited and both men and women compete for them. The bulk of men and women do routine technical and clerical work; they are bureaucrats or paper shufflers. In the early days of the woman's movement, simply breaking with the tradition was fulfilling. Once it became commonplace for women to work, however, they began to learn some of the bitter facts, not the least of which is that they get paid less than men do. Despite all of the pressure from the female community and from the government, the pay differential between men and women persists. Furthermore, women are still shunted off toward routine or menial jobs, and most, however well-qualified, have a hard time moving up.

Arlene McK., Employment Agency Owner. I must tell women work is a perpetual blind alley. Most men know that. When men come they ask first about benefits and days off. I don't handle the best jobs. I place shop foremen and clerks and secretaries and people who do routine things. But I handle about eighty-five per cent of the placements in this market. There's a specialized agency in town that handles top placements. They rarely talk to women. There's little anyone can do about that. It isn't really discrimination, it's credentials and experience. Men have them. Women

---

still persist in taking general college courses, liberal arts, or even general business. Or they prepare for "socially useful occupations" that don't pay much and will pay even less with government budget cuts. Socially useful jobs are dull and no one gets fulfilled working with the wretched of the earth. The best job I can put women in is secretary. Good secretaries start at about $15,000 these days. Social workers go for $9,200, but the young girls want to be social workers because they think it carries prestige. Computer operators, Telex operators, programmers, technically-trained women, I can place at good wages. I don't care if they have college degrees or not. But women think they can't have any identity without a degree. I don't think I can eat identity. I've been at this employment business for nearly thirty years and I hoped that when women got into the market they would be less silly than the men, but they aren't.

Those women who get into a potentially fulfilling career track, need to figure out how to handle the politics of working in situations where they are outnumbered by men. It is somewhat sad to have to think in terms of combat or competition, but it is a fact of vocational life. Advancement is competitive. There are only a few top jobs and shrewd executives manipulate their people so that competition will bring the "best" to the top. It is a circular kind of reasoning, but best often means "best competitor."

Women have great difficulty learning to compete. They have not been trained in forming alliances. Many report that they cannot get access to the informal networks in organizations. They are rarely supported by a mentor who can ensure them information, recognition, and opportunity. Men who compete with them often have the support of an older and more powerful executive.

Women are understandably less skillful than men at using informal socialization as a means of forming alliances because their efforts to socialize are often misinterpreted as sexual offers. Furthermore, "old boy networks" do exist and they systematically exclude women. There is no way to pass a law to keep men from congregating at bars and simply stopping the conversation when a female colleague comes near. Without connections to the network, women lack the information they need to compete well. To be locked outside the system is a severe professional handicap. Furthermore, many women report that their male colleagues have techniques of insulting them and making them feel out of place. Sometimes women feel like they have crashed a stag party when they come near a male grouping.

Nola K., Junior Partner, Law Firm. I can't prove it's deliberate, but I really cannot believe the men don't realize how offensive their conversation is to a woman. It's almost as if they are deliberately trying to make me so uncomfortable that I'll leave their territory. What really burns me is their off-color humor only gets heavy when a woman joins them. It's their way of excluding us.

The men cannot be blamed for failing to move over to let their competitors get ahead. The man who makes way for a woman or anyone else loses his chance to get ahead. Hence, women are left to their own devices exactly like everyone else. There is, of course, the possibility of forming or joining a women's network, but since women are in the minority in most places, this really has limited pay-off. Furthermore, most men place a stigma on women's groups. Said one respondent, "they think a women's association is either a glorified coffee klatsch or a radical feminist group, and either perception is professionally suicidal."

Membership even in a strong women's network cannot compensate for the advantages of participating in mainstream networks dominated by men. Other minority groups seeking to enter the vocational world have found the same sort of problem. Laws against discrimination can do little or nothing about the tacit affiliations that men have been using for generations to support each other. Men are as disappointed as women when they do not advance in their careers. They cannot, therefore, be expected to surrender their important protections, and very few of them do. Some women, however, have excessively optimistic expectations and become distressed when confronted by male exclusion.

Some women report gaining a modicum of acceptance through an association with a supportive male colleague who performs functions as basic as introducing them around, attesting to their competency, and filling them in on the personality quirks of the people in the executive suite. Career women generally resent and resist paternal over-protectiveness, but courtesies normally extended to by men to their young male counterparts are very much appreciated.

James R., Manager. I'm getting disgusted with some of my colleagues who say they favor equal opportunity for women and who claim to have no biases against women as colleagues. The same men who give lip service to these ideas seldom make the slightest effort to make a newly-hired woman feel at home in our company. It's not that women need *extra* help, mind you. But they do need the same amount of assistance that any other new employee gets. They need to know who's who around here and be invited to some of the informal get-togethers. All these self-professed liberals around here are very good at screening women out simply by ignoring them.

There are no ready answers to the problem of being excluded, but women seem unusually surprised by it. They seem to feel that getting the job is the big problem. They are protected by law in seeking their job, but not so much in keeping it and advancing or being comfortable with colleagues. They are on their own, and forced to compete at a disadvantage to their male counterparts.

A second major problem confronted by working women is how to deal with male colleagues who sex-type them. More complex than sexual advances, sex-typing is a process by which women are defined as fitting into one of four sex-related roles: mother, sex object, pet, or iron maiden. (Rosabeth M. Kanter, *Men and Women of the Corporation*. New York: Basic Books, 1977.) Though these roles are quite different, each one defines a career woman primarily as career*woman* rather than as *career*woman. A woman defined as mother is supposed to support and nurture her male colleagues, but she is not supposed to exercise other professional prerogatives like criticism, decision-making or reprimand.

Tara P., Assistant Director, Training and Personnel Development. Just tell me why I'm always the chair of the social committee and why I'm assigned to counsel the new trainees each year. Any man on this staff could buy cake and coffee for social programs just as easily as I can. Any man could listen to the problems of new employees. I get those jobs because I'm the only woman here. If I'd wanted to be a mother, I wouldn't be here at all.

A woman defined as a sex object is expected to be glamorous and to "decorate the office." She is supposed to be available for seductions. A pet, on the other hand, is treated as cute, but essentially helpless. People like her because she presents no threat. Women who accept the roles of sex object or pet are non-threatening and, therefore, generally acceptable.

Helen R., Radio Station Program Director. I am damned sick of being shown off as the only women executive in the company. Any time an important client visits, my boss marches him (and it's always a man) down to my office and introduces me as "our little Helen who shows just how much a girl can do." One of these days I'm going to act the part and wag my tail!

The iron maiden is seen as non-female, a "bitch," who is harsh, tough and unfeeling, "castrating," everything a woman should not be. No doubt there are women in industry who have compensated for some of their adversity by becoming very tough. On the other hand, the iron maiden role is another way of keeping women typed so that their ability to compete is materially reduced. Once a woman gets a reputation for being a tough bitch, her chances for advancement are materially impaired. Men who are well-disciplined and tough are viewed with respect. The same qualities in a woman are treated with contempt.

Evelyn Z. I'm the supervisor of this department. But some of the men I supervise just cannot accept the fact that their boss is a woman. They act like it's some sort of attack on their manhood to take assignments from me. And they really go up the wall when I have to criticize them or point out inadequacies in their work. They have their ways of letting me know they don't accept me as their superior. The other day, for instance, I called in someone and told him off for turning in a very sloppy report. He said, "I guess I just forgot how neat and tidy you ladies like things." Last year we got funds to redecorate the offices, so like all the other supervisors, I asked my subordinates to state their preferences for colors in carpet and paint. One man sent me a memo saying that he'd trust my judgment since women are so much better at interior decoration. Oh yes, they have their ways of letting me know they think my position is a joke.

Being seen stereotypically is a persistent problem for working women. Part of the problem comes from women seeing men stereotypically. There is at least some reason to believe that part of the reason women are seen as sex types is because they see men as sex types. Some women slip into the roles expected of them because of an acculturated tendency to regard men as potential romantic connections. The cross-stereotyping feeds mutually and persists until someone breaks the circuit. Each individual needs to find strategies to break through and declare individual identity.

There are no sure-fire tactics for responding, nor is there any permanent way to end sex-typing. It starts up anew with each new encounter. Women have, however, come up with a variety of strategies to use. Here's a sampling of those reported by the women we surveyed.

Redirection. My standard ploy is to reroute a conversation any time a man treats me as a woman, not as a colleague. If a man makes a big deal about how much an outfit shows off my figure, I say, "thanks, now lets get on with that report." Sometimes it takes several times, but they generally learn.

Response in Kind. When men make some remark about how I look, I wait until a bit later in the conversation and come back with, "my, that's a lovely tie," or "you really look cute in those tight pants." I try to make it as irrelevant as his remark. They get bewildered but they stop.

Confrontation. I tell any man who patronizes me or hits on me that he's out of line. I explain that I understand exactly what he did and that I will not tolerate such behavior. Then I tell him either to treat me as a colleague or stay clear. They usually respond with a put-down, but the next time they stay on the topic of business.

Ignoring. I try to overlook the subtle put-downs and come-ons. I figure an aggressive response would just add to the problem.

Humor. The most effective tactic is to kid a man out of a pass or put-down. For instance, last week, one of the customer reps came to my office for a file and said something about nice it was to do business with such a foxy lady. So I smiled and told him that foxes can be vicious if attacked. That was the end of that. Sometimes it works, sometimes it doesn't.

Definitive Movement. You know how men put their arms around you and play housepet with you. I don't tolerate that for a minute. I stiffen my body and move away. I don't say anything about being married, I just act as if I had been touched by something really repulsive. They call me cold fish around here now, but they don't touch me and they don't make remarks.

Gender Negation. I'd rather be thought unfeminine than unprofessional, so I de-emphasize my female qualities. I conceal my figure and keep my hair short. I wear glasses instead of contacts and I simply don't respond to their jokes. By now they accept me.

Acceptance. As long as I know I'm doing my job I just let them think and say what they wish. I don't argue about being asked to take notes and get coffee at meetings. Sure, I resent it, but those men aren't going to change no matter what I do.

Withdrawal. I try to do my work and avoid interacting with men who treat me as a sex object. I'm outside the network, but they leave me alone in other ways, too. It's easier this way.

Redefinition. I refuse to accept the norms. I can hold my own at the bar and I know about power plays, but I reject those codes of conduct. My conduct must set an example of how I think the game should be played. I think I and other women have an obligation to try to change things.

Litigation. I heard that there was a rumor out that I was having an affair with one of my supervisors. I told my husband about it and we simply paid an attorney to send a letter threatening a slander suit. Word of that got around, and I am no longer a topic of conversation.

Feminism. I may not be able to do much alone, but I can join groups that can defend me collectively. Feminism is more than a hysterical game, it is a potent political movement.

Counter-attack. I can play hardball. When a man makes a pass at me, I aim for his ego. The other day one of the senior partners let his hand rest on my knee while we were lunching. I very calmly told him that if he didn't move his hand I would kick him where it would make him a permanent eunuch. He moved his hand. A man once propositioned me and I told him I couldn't take any more disappointments. I don't win many friends, but men leave me alone.

None of these strategies is infallible. Men have a great number of rejoinders available. It is unfortunate that women have to worry about this kind of self-defense, but men must also deal with put-downs from their competitors. The act of competing, even if the competition is not effective, sharpens personal identity which helps to dampen stereotyping.

There is one last problem which threatens women at work. Sexual relationships in the office place everyone involved in jeopardy. People do not cast off their sex roles because they have gone to work. They attract each other, and when they link up, each places their future in the hands of the other. Intimacy means a sharing of secrets and vulnerability. Men know how to use compliant women as sources of information and unwilling allies. Furthermore, tempting a potential competitor into a liaison cuts down the number of obstacles to advancement. By the same token, it appears to some women that sexual politics is an easy way to advancement. The admonition we offered earlier, about avoiding close friendships with work colleagues, still is the best advice. It goes double for sexual involvements.

Brenda K., Ph.D., Employment Counselor. There are far too many women who give in to the role assigned them. Probably the worst problems are women who *do* use sexual favors to get advantage in their company. They really betray other women because they set off expectations. People tend to stereotype and if it gets around that a woman is being easy, it makes life very difficult for other women. A second problem is the woman who gets to the top and then uses her power to persecute other women. It is like they do not want a female competitor near them. They exploit and they damage. A third problem is the women who makes it and then cops out and goes to the vine-covered cottage to have babies. That just confirms the stereotype. You know, I think a woman who has a child has an obligation to that child and I think the woman who works her way to the top has an obligation to the rest of us to stay there and not plant the notion that we are unreliable colleagues. Well, I don't know what to do about these things. I warn women, that's all. But men do not have these problems.

What It Means to Be a Woman in Contemporary Society

This is the most interesting issue of all, and it resulted in the most diverse responses. As you've found in reading this chapter, women are not of one mind on the meaning of womanhood in contemporary American culture. Despite the range of views expressed by the women we surveyed, three themes consistently emerged: choice, frustration, and responsibility.

Choice

The first theme is freedom or choice. Women, particularly between nineteen and thirty, seem especially aware of their alternatives for self-definition. No longer is there a single, narrow view of what a woman is or should be. Only in the past twenty years has society broken away from the assumption that women are defined by their reproductive capacities and by their associations with men.

Anne F., Saleswoman. The other day I was talking to my neighbor, a woman in her late fifties. She asked when Joe and I planned to start our family and I told her we hadn't even decided whether we wanted children. At first she seemed a little surprised, but then she looked really thoughtful and said, "I wish I'd had that option. When I was your age, it was expected that a woman would raise a family. We never questioned the idea. Yet, I had a lot of big plans for myself, and they all got pushed aside for the family. There just wasn't any choice for women in my day."

The traditional view of women still prevails in many segments of society, but there are alternatives to it. Contemporary women seem to recognize they have alternatives, even when choosing them promises hard work and much difficulty. Pressures against deviating from the traditional view are heaviest in families that adhere to conservative and fundamentalist religious values. For them, the meaning of womanhood carries a number of religious connotations. In spite of these pressures, however, the society offers women the choices. Each must deal with her own values and commitments to society in coming up with an answer that works for her.

Debbie R., Commercial Artist. I'm not sure I ever want to get married. I like being on my own, and I haven't ever met a man I'd want to stay with for very long. It's too confining. I'm really glad this is 1981 so I have the choice to live alone without having people call me a wierdo or a spinster.

There are some problems ahead for Debbie. She may very well change her mind about marrying. Most women do. If she does remain alone, she may be seen as peculiar. Chances are her married female relatives will pressure her about being a "spinster." Having a choice is not without its perils. Furthermore, not all women rejoice in having increased alternatives for self-definition.

Frustration

Frustration represents a second theme of contemporary woman-hood. A number of women, particularly younger ones, feel frustrated by their options. They have a surplus of choices and very little guidance in how to choose. They do not know the implications of the choices, what problems they will face and what they must give up. Once again, men experience less conflict for they cannot evade the responsibility to seek a career.

Betsy W., Senior Majoring in Sociology. I know a lot of women think it's great to have alternatives like career or family or both or whatever. But to me its just confusing. I don't know what I'm supposed to do with my life. At least the women of my mom's generation knew what was expected. The rules were pretty clear and all a woman had to do was follow them. Maybe it was confining but it was also easier. I just feel lost, like I have no guidelines for deciding what I want to be. I'm really worried I'll make a wrong decision and blame myself for the rest of my life.

Betsy's is not a solo voice among women. Many of our respondents echoed Betsy's sense of insecurity. The responsibilities imposed by choice are most evident in the decision of whether to have children.

Jean D., Social Worker. I'm thirty-three right now, so I'm facing the big decision. I've been working for nine years and I'm advancing well. I like being a career woman, meeting responsibilities, and gaining respect from others through my work. I'm just afraid that if I have a child I won't devote as much time and energy to my work. Yet I think maybe if I don't have one, I'll regret it when I'm forty or fifty. And I have to decide soon since it's risky to have children after thirty-five. How to you figure out something like this?

Family is not the only problem. Women who have chosen a career track are sometimes confronted with very tough choices. A major problem is reconciling the "perfect career opportunity" with the "perfect mate."

Thelma F., Resort Agent. Roger just accepted a great job offer in Chicago and I think he was right to do it. He's got a fabulous salary and position. The problem is that I don't have any offers from Chicago, and I don't expect any since my line of work is not big in that region. I'm going to have to work in the Gulf area and I have good offers in Texas and Florida. I have to decide what is more important, the career I prepared for or Roger. I guess when we got married I expected everything would fall in place. I guess it hardly ever does, and I don't know what to do, except I'm going to lose either way.

Few women will be able to live up to the media image of the superwoman who has it all, career, marriage, family, happiness, fulfillment, success. Most will deal with a sequence of trade-offs. The intriguing thing is that women are now being confronted with choices previously denied them, the same choices that have been the cause of stress and strain in men for generations. Not all women will make sensible decisions, just as not all men manage to think things through productively.

Responsibility

The third consistent theme in contemporary women's definitions of themselves is responsibility. The most fundamental responsibility is to personal identity. Each individual woman has to struggle to define herself. Self-esteem is more than a fuzzy word, and vicarious self-esteem through husband and family is no longer universally accepted as legitimate. The female community is so fragmented that there is no choice a woman can make that will not be applauded by some and treated with contempt by others. There is no universal woman's point of view. Perhaps there never was, for certainly there were women who rebelled against prevailing norms in every generation. In view of today's situation, being a rebel is the one option that is denied contemporary women. There is nothing to rebel against, for virtually every point of view has a following.

Beth C., Personnel Counselor. It is very exciting to be a woman today and I mean that. There are so many challenges and options for us that it seems impossible for us to look toward the future without a tingle in our hearts. But for every tingle in the heart there is a knot in the stomach. I think I want to blame someone for making me decide between or figure out how to coordinate all the things I want. It seems women are in a no-win situation. Whatever choice we make, someone will put us down for it. The guidelines that we follow are up to us. That is something that we are not used to. We are a society accustomed to rules and are at a loss when there are none. But really, who is "society?"

The last line in Beth's statement is provocative. She appears to be realizing that just as individuals are shaped by society, so is society created by individuals. It is a reflection of the activities and values of those who comprise it. One of the genuine excitements of living in this era is the knowledge that the paths we choose, the directions we chart will influence the evolving fabric of society-at-large.

Responsibility to other people is another aspect of the issue. No one can make a choice that does not affect someone else. To maintain a loving relationship with a man requires commitment. Violation of that commitment even for something of greater value does injury. While women have been freed from social pressure, they have not been freed from conscience, and a great many women suffer great anxiety about who might be hurt by the choices they make. A number of them hurt themselves rather than do injury to someone to whom they are committed.

Saddest of all, most men do not understand the agony of the choices with which many women are confronted, so they do not understand the magnitude of the sacrifices often made on their behalf. Men cannot be entirely faulted for concentrating on their own concerns. It is clear to most men that a major share of their self-esteem comes from success on the job. While he is free from real concern about choosing to bear children and keep a home, all of his eggs are in one basket, and to "make it" in the world, he must be single-minded in his dedication to his occupation. Increasing alcoholism rates as well as concern about the male mid-life crisis both testify to the pressure that working men, on all levels of employment, feel in their day-to-day existence. When women enter the world of work they do not trade one set of concerns for another, they simply buy into the concerns which already exist. The facts of occupational life do not change when a woman takes a job. Many women who entered their occupations or professions with excitement and hope find themselves as disillusioned as their male counterparts once they face the frustration and boredom of working for pay, struggling for advancement and, in these days of declining economy, simply fighting to stay employed. We can expect reaction by women as more and more of them enter the labor force in jobs competitive with those traditionally occupied by men. We cannot predict the form the reaction will take. It may result in humanizing work, it may result in women taking on the defensive nuances that men have learned to employ in order to survive on the job.

Basic issues like assuming the burden of maintaining the home sometimes present irreconcilable conflict. Couples skilled in sensitive and persuasive communication have the best chance of working out an equitable arrangement. We must remember, however, that an arrangement made by a couple that permits both to work on the job of their choice does little to alleviate the state of affairs in the world of work. Many couples will resolve their problem at home only to face other frustrations outside.

Elaine V., Public Relations Director. People say I'm lucky to be married to a man like Alan. My friends envy me because we share all the work around our house. Alan does most of the cleaning, and he can do some really good cooking too. Once, when he was laid off for three weeks, he took over all the chores. If we ever have children, I think I can count on him to do half of the midnight feedings when I decide to stop nursing. But it is not a matter of luck. It was hard work to get things settled. I had to convince Alan that I worked hard all day, just like him, and I was entitled to a fair share of relaxation. I made that clear before I married him, and I held to it even when I was tempted to give. I'm glad I found a man who understands fairness, but I wouldn't have married him if I hadn't been sure he would cooperate with me in working things out.

Responsibility for handling the details of life in the twentieth century is also important. Today's women should understand the rudiments of car repair and appliance maintenance just as men should be able to handle the details of a household. There are enough single parents and single person households that it is no longer possible to think in terms of man's work/woman's work.

Responsibility for learning about finances is also an important issue. The widow unable to manage her fiscal problems has become a cliché. The issue, however, is more than a cliché to the woman who confronts it. Therefore, it follows that today's woman should be responsible for making sure she is educated enough to make informed choices about her own welfare. She must be equipped to choose single life, if that is her preference, so that she is not forced into marriage simply because she cannot cope with details of living. She must be skilled in mothering even if she is educated as a professional of the highest order; otherwise the choice to be a mother will have painful consequences.

Chapter Summary

What does it mean to be a woman in today's society? Many things to many women, but for all of them, it involves choice, frustration about making choices, and responsibility for how the choices made characterize situations.

There is no longer a universal image of womanhood in American society. Miss America is likely to be a feminist, and Supreme Court justices may have husbands. Life for the American woman is paradoxical, threatening, and filled with opportunities to rejoice in becoming potent and powerful without sacrificing the her own female values, whatever they may be.

These past two chapters provide the basis for productive discussion between men and women, and perhaps a basis for making decisions on how to improve the way men and women communicate with each other socially, professionally, and intimately. In the final chapter we will offer some methods couples can use to analyze their relationships and make decisions about how they wish to change.

REFERENCES FOR CHAPTER 10

J. Bardwick, *In Transition: How Feminism, Sexual Liberation, and The Search for Self Fulfillment Have Altered America.* New York: Holt, Rinehart and Winston, 1979.

B. Friedan, *The Second Stage.* New York: Summit Books, 1981.

E. Goodman, *At Large.* New York: Summit Books, 1981.

N. Henley, *Body Politics: Power, Sex, and Nonverbal Communication.* Englewood Cliffs, N.J.: Prentice-Hall, 1977.

S. Hite, *The Hite Report.* New York: Macmillan, 1976.

R. Kanter, *Men and Women of the Corporation.* New York: Basic Books, 1977.

A. Rich, On Lies, Secrets and Silences: Selected Prose, 1966–1978. New York: W. W. Norton, 1979.

11

HUMAN COMMUNICATION AND HUMAN RELATIONSHIPS: SUMMING UP

Sometimes I wonder if men and women really suit each other.
Perhaps they should live next door and just visit now and then.
—*Katharine Hepburn*

There is an ancient premise that in the absence of truth, people make their own by talking with one another and finding ways and means to do the best they can for everyone concerned. This is the principle on which democracies were built. We have already pointed out that when people form intimate relationships, they have created a mini-government. We also pointed out that by talking together, people can anticipate problems, react to problems and solve problems. It should take little stretching of the imagination to accept the principle that intimate couples, good friends, and people who like each other, or live near each other, or work together, can build their own "truths" by talking and trying to find ways and means to do the best they can for everyone concerned.

In this final chapter we'll summarize and extend the ideas we have presented. We will review, briefly, what we have presented, make some suggestions about ways to apply theory to real life, and finally look at some of the implications for relationships between men and women in the future.

The Value of Interpersonal Communication

The basic theme of this book is that skill at interpersonal communication is fundamental to successful human existence. Communication skill is more than just a "nice extra" in your life. There are a great many human problems that simply cannot be solved unless people understand what other people are saying so they can figure out what *they* believe and how to respond appropriately.

People use communication to form social systems that enable them to do together what they cannot do alone. They manage their lives and they find ways to feel secure. They develop ways to identify acquaintances, allies, friends and enemies. They organize systems to bring people together and protect and educate children. They build institutions to educate and acculturate children to make them adult members of society. They develop complicated procedures for trading so that people can exchange work for money, which they can exchange for goods and services. All of these systems are included in our private relationships, as well. We establish all kinds of fragile human networks and maintain them through interpersonal communication.

Public networks in which we communicate according to generally accepted norms are called *interactive systems*. They furnish order and security for people who live in a particular culture. Private relationships in which people communicate according to rules they have worked out exclusively for themselves are called *transactive systems*. These kinds of relationships are devoted to providing satisfaction and confirmation of each partner's worth by the other partner. We participate in both kinds of systems simultaneously. We function in both according to explicit and implicit rules. Some rules are clear and publicly stated. (Don't talk during the performance.) Others are clear but rarely expressed publicly. (Don't carry on personal disputes in public). There are a great many ambiguous rules (Be charming at the cocktail party without appearing obsequious) and situations for which there are no rules (What if I am trapped in an elevator with *his* wife). These cause considerable difficulty in our human relationships. In interactive systems, there are methods and procedures for resolving such difficulties. By the use of laws, which are subject to enforcement and are backed up by the courts, misunderstandings and violations can be handled with some degree of equity. In private relationships, there are no outside agencies to resolve conflict. When there is a problem between transacting partners, they must deal with it themselves.

All relationships have features in common. Identification of these common features enables us to work out the particular details required in unique relationships. The common features function as "heuristics" which means they provoke us to think in new ways, in this case about our own relationships and those around us. Relationship systems consist of structure and content. Structure refers to common features and style while content refers to what is said, its purpose, and its effect. The structure of relationships remains constant. The norms of public association, the etiquette of social situations, and the rules of doing commerce are generalizable. The content of relationships is unique to the place, time, and people who are relating, and it changes often during the life of a relationship. Understanding relationship structure helps us be more effective in working out relationship content. For example, if we know that every relationship must have a means of making rules, of carrying them out, of resolving conflict, and so on, then we have a way to diagnose our problems and make our plans. When there are disputes about content, the structure of the relationship provides both protection for the disputants and a method to follow in resolving the conflict.

Skill at interpersonal communication assists your efforts to live a productive and satisfying life. Understanding of interpersonal communication will help you set realistic goals for yourself and find effective ways to seek them, with the help of others. Communication skill gives you maximum control over your own life. It is difficult to overestimate the value of this skill; it is a primary tool of survival.

A Perspective on Human Nature

Our perspective on interpersonal communication is based on our understanding of human nature. First and foremost, we believe that *the distinctive quality of human beings is our ability to communicate.* Because we can communicate we can reflect on ourselves and exert our personal will to define ourselves, to direct our activities, to seek cooperation from others, and to work together for mutual accomplishment. Reflection allows us to profit from our mistakes and plan for the future.

Because we can use symbols, we are aware of ourselves as individuals and we can influence who we become. We can decide how we wish to be seen by others, we can set goals and plan to influence others to see us the way we want to be seen. Through our dealings with others, we gain confirmation of ourselves and our ideas. We are constantly subject to similar activity by those around us who gain confirmation of their identities from us.

Individuals cannot impose their wills on each other. They must be persuasive. They must attempt to convince each other to accept proffered identities and goals. We can control our own communication, but there is no way we can automatically gain cooperation from other people. We can intimidate and threaten them, we can use force, or, if we live in civilized society, we can solicit their cooperation in helping us attain our goals by offering them our cooperation in seeking their goals. In order to be confirmed as a person by others, we must confirm others as persons.

In many ways, we act like merchants in our dealings with other people. We offer what might be useful to them and solicit from them ideas, services, sentiments and confirmation in return. A good bargain is when two people exchange in such a way that they both gain. When one person gives much and gets little, the relationship is not satisfying. We seek "equity" in our relationships, a "fair shake." To be effective at seeking security and satisfaction means that we must help others achieve security and satisfaction.

The mythology interferes

We are not always intelligent in the way we go about making our relationships. In fact, human relationships have been plagued with myths which have interfered with the formation of arrangements which can ensure mutual security and satisfaction. Most of us are sensitive to superstititions like "step on a crack . . ." or "don't walk under a ladder." We tend to reject decisions based on hunches and question the accuracy of predictions by soothsayers and fortune tellers. Yet, we make a great many decisions about our interpersonal relationships on beliefs that have no substance in fact. Many of us spend considerably more time finding accurate information about the household appliances or cars we buy than the people we select as friends. As a result, friendships and even intimate relationships are often plagued by disappointment and disillusionment.

Some of the things we believe about our private relationships are myths that have been passed on through the generations and supported by the media to the point where people accept them as facts. One of the major contributions of research done on interpersonal communication has been to refute many of these myths. We will review some of them here before proceeding to some recommendations for how you may analyze and review your relationships.

First and foremost, *many humans refuse to admit that they have the ability to control the way they behave toward others*. They also will not admit that they are at least partly responsible for the relationship problems they have. Very often, when people have relationship difficulties, they define them as diseases (neuroses) and seek a cure (therapy). It is, however, a myth that all relationship problems are the result of sickness. As a matter of fact, through effective communication, a great many relationship problems can be solved, and many more can be prevented in advance.

Furthermore, it is important to try to manage human relationships. They cannot be permitted to happen spontaneously. It is a myth that *skilled communicators are born and not made, and that it is manipulative to try to plan effective communication.* People must control what they say to make it serve a useful social purpose. No one has the right to hurt another person or to demand attention for themselves through the use of purely expressive communication. Perhaps the most important finding by marriage and family counselors is that people need to *learn* to relate well to one another. Sometimes it requires methods unique to particular relationships, but these techniques and training are available for people who wish to work it out.

Human relationships do not "just happen." People choose their associates for some reason, good or bad, and then work things out over time. If you make choices based on personal appearance without checking beliefs and behaviors, you risk disappointment. There is absolutely no evidence to connect personal appearance with any particular attributes of personality. The same holds true for people who select others because they "look familiar." Many decades of psychoanalytic research have demonstrated that it is dangerous to select friends because they look like your parents, an ex-mate, or some other important person in your life. Society has a built-in mechanism for testing whether or not relationships will be rewarding. Conversation and some experience in interaction should provide useful information on which you can base decisions about whether to intensify a relationship. There is no substitute for what you can learn from experience accompanied by reflection. However, we all have to be careful not to focus too intensely on ourselves. Attention to other people and their needs is essential to successful relationships. There has been a great deal of concern among human relations specialists about the possible effects of narcissism on relationships. Awareness that relationship must be a reciprocal arrangement involving two or more people will help you guard against becoming so preoccupied that your own concerns impair your dealings with others.

Another influential myth is the notion that if you can get to know all there is to know about someone you can have a perfect relationship. *It is very rare that you will get to know very much about anyone.* Such a state is reserved for only those very few intimate relationships you will make during your life. Even then, a great deal will be reserved, hidden even from the most intimate connections. To disclose a great deal to someone with whom you have limited experience is to set yourself up for betrayal. Giving away information doesn't automatically get information in return. Disclosure, when appropriate, may enhance understanding and intimacy. However, premature or indiscriminate disclosure seldom results in such benefits; often such behavior may cause embarassment and rejection.

The most damaging myth is expecting too much, asking for the impossible, confusing the desirable with the doable. Expecting perfection is a guaranteed route to disappointment and frustration. Couples that seek the perfect two-career marriage may miss out on some delightful intimacy in their urgency for perfection. Couples that seek perfection in sex, perfection in child rearing, or perfection in anything make it impossible for themselves to find reasonable gratification. Similarly, it is not reasonable for friends to expect each other always to be available and to provide substantial time and energy on demand. The myth of perfection has a serious affect on interpersonal relationships, for success at relationships requires constant and serious effort all the time. Anything that deters couples or individual partners from making that effort is subversive of their relational culture. Furthermore, to think primarily of "actualizing yourself" keeps you from thinking about your partner's concerns as well as the mutual good. By keeping focused on the exchange aspects inherent in rhetorical communication, you can improve your relationships to the maximum, but never to perfection.

Relationships Serve Human Goals

To avoid falling into the trap set for you by the myths, keep focusing on the notion that *relationships do not "just happen"*. People construct them to meet individual and collective goals. Humans, by nature, pursue many goals which require many different types of relationships. We all want pleasant people with whom to work and pass the time of day. To do so, we work out ways to form casual acquaintanceships with people we encounter regularly. We establish various types of friendships for recreation, solving personal problems, gaining support and confirmation, and exchanging information. We discuss professional matters or cooperate on tasks with our colleagues. Finally, we commit to an intimate bond, and when we want to ensure an extended future of transaction with a person for whom we care very much. All of these relationships arise out of our personal goal-seeking. *If we are aware of our goals then we can make informed choices about whom we approach and why and how we approach them.* Lack of thought about objectives can result in careless, sometimes counterproductive behavior. Furthermore, it is important to consider the possible goals others may have for approaching you. If you can accept the idea that sometimes you may seek your own goals at the expense of others, you will find it easy to believe that others may sometimes not have your interests uppermost in their minds. Generally, this is not because of malice but simply because all of us become preoccupied with our own concerns. Awareness of others, however, is the most effective way to meet our own needs.

Jeannette E., Receptionist. I used to think the men in this office were just plain sexists, but I'm not so sure any more. They always make passes at me and come-on to me. The other day I was complaining to Marie about this and she said it was my own fault. She said I invited them to see me as a woman, not as a professional. She said I sent messages that invited them to do what they did, and that she didn't have any problem at all. She showed me that I used a softer voice and smiled when I talked to the men and my clothing advertised my figure more than necessary. She said my heavy cologne was suggestive. At first I was really angry at Marie, but in retrospect, there is a lot of truth to what she said. I just wasn't aware of what I was doing, I guess because I wasn't sure what I wanted from these men, so I wasn't very careful about how I came across.

Jeannette's problem was that her goal of forming professional associations was not conscious and definitive enough. It was undercut by a less conscious goal of engaging in male-female courtship behavior. Had she been sure of what she was after, she could have monitored her behavior to do a more effective job of seeking it.

Forming relationships involves choices and responsibilities

Our relationships are what we make them, no more, no less. If they are based on realistic understandings of everyone's goals, then relating partners build their connection on the choices they make individually and collectively. You can choose to invest time, energy, and thought, or you can let inertia and luck control your life. You can work to keep important relationships going, and to revitalize them from time to time, or you can let them stagnate through benign neglect. You can choose to emphasize your partner's strengths in order to strengthen the bond, or you can emphasize weaknesses and create dissatisfaction and a negative climate. You can let your partner know how much you value the relationship, or you can keep your partner guessing by taking him or her for granted. You can choose to deal directly with problems or you can ignore difficulties and hope for the best. All of the active choices you make require reflection, determination, and skillful communication.

Choice also implies responsibility. We are responsible for how we build and maintain our relationships. We cannot escape our personal responsibility for the way we act and respond to other people.

It is crucial to acknowledge personal responsibility so that you can make thoughtful choices about the kinds of relationships you want and select effective ways to try to obtain them. The psychologist, Timothy Leary won considerable distinction with his theory that people tend to evoke behavior that is the counterpart of what they present. For example, a person who appears helpless attracts helpful or dominating behavior. A person who appears directive usually draws submissive behavior, and so on. The logic is not quite as simple as it appears, but in general, we do ask for certain types of behavior from others and we generally get what other people think we are asking for. If we act like we wish to be excluded, people will exclude us. If we act like we wish to cooperate, we evoke cooperative behavior.

Above all, you must recognize that other people have exactly the same obligations and privileges you do. Unsuccessful efforts may be due to your lack of skill, but they may also be because the person at whom you directed your efforts simply did not want a relationship or did not know how to participate in building one. You cannot blame yourself for not getting what is impossible to get. Neither can you blame the other person for not wanting a relationship with you. There usually is nothing personal. Some people have all the relationships they can possibly handle and simply are not available. Some people may not even be aware you are seeking their attention. Checking for those possibilities is one reason for taking time in early stages of relationship development.

Successful relationships are built on reciprocity

To survive, a relationship must meet some of the goals of everyone concerned. There can be no relationship if everyone does not benefit in some way. The more equal the perceived benefits, the stronger the relationship. All partners must make an effort to retain equity in the relationship, and that means adapting both to changing external conditions and changing internal goals and commitments in other to keep the relationship satisfying.

People decide whether or not to stay in a relationship by considering the balance between rewards and costs (effort vs. outcome) incurred in an association. If the rewards are greater than or equal to the costs, the relationship is considered satisfactory and probably will be maintained, unless there is an alternative which promises more rewards or lower costs. This may seem like a cynical position, but it is an accurate description of what happens. People who have control over their decision-making do an effective job of analyzing and assessing their relationships.

There are limitless possibilities for exchange. Each of us seeks particular kinds of rewards in our various relationships and each of us has a variety of capabilities to offer others. Likewise, each of us defines costs in unique ways; a cost to one person may be a reward to another. Thus, the content of exchange is varied, unique to each relationship. *The important point is that exchange must go on. Its particular nature is decided by the people in the relationship.*

A great many casual relationships are built on trade-offs like lending garden tools or providing specialized assistance. One neighbor may be able to help with plumbing emergencies, the other may share a snow blower. College students share clothing, cars, labor around the dorm room, and help each other on exams and papers.

Equity means "a fair share." It is the basis of all relationships. People may differ on what constitutes a fair share, but we all want it. If one partner feels he or she is not getting "enough" of a share, resentment arises. Virtually all relationship problems arise from the feeling one partner or the other has that the relationship is not operating fairly.

Carla T., Student I was very flattered when Theresa began spending time with me. She was the most attractive girl on the dorm, the prettiest girl I had ever seen. She was popular and powerful. She had boy friends coming out of her ears and she belonged to all the important campus organizations. She really had her act together. When her parents were on campus she invited me to go to dinner with her, and I got lots of dates just because I caught the spill-over of the guys she just couldn't fit in to her schedule. It took a while before I caught on to the little favors she would ask me. Like she would give me a very sloppy English theme and ask me to "clean it up," and sometimes, when I was going to the library, she'd hand me some cards and ask me to get her some notes on something or other. By the end of the first semester, I was doing most of her work. We were supposed to study together for the two courses we were in together, but we never did, but she sat next to me during the exams and she was the most skillful copier I ever saw. I finally got mad and asked her not to copy any more, and she got mad and gave me one of those "after all I've done for you" speeches, and that ended our friendship. When she found I didn't think her company was worth all the work I had to do to get it, she simply moved on and found someone else.

Information is a most important type of exchange in intimate relations. Couples exchange a great deal of personal information during the intensification stage of their relationship. Much of it is sensitive information, public disclosure of which could be not only embarrassing but injurious to self-esteem.

It requires a great deal of trust to share private feelings and thoughts with anyone. It is extraordinarily painful when confidences are betrayed. You can experience a great sense of relief by confiding some of the things people commonly conceal: feelings of inadequacy and impotence, feelings of lack of self-worth, fear of rejection, embarrassment at affection, guilt feelings, the urgency to be punished for some real or imagined offense, depression and despair, pessimism about one's future or the future of a loved one, fear of sickness and death, dependencies, feelings of loneliness and isolation, conflicting feelings about loved ones, desires to control and dominate, the discovery of intolerable personal characteristics, feelings of ugliness, and the desire to avenge oneself and do harm to another.

Many of these feelings have irrational bases. Most people eventually turn to professional help when these feelings overwhelm them. But an intimate relationship with a person willing to exchange in this dimension can do a great deal to make a hurting person feel whole again.

Exchange may take a great many forms: time, affection, material goods, services, money, knowledge, sexual intimacy, status, and so on. The important point is that in every relationship, from casual to the most intimate, there will be some form of exchange. As long as the relating partners can count on the relationship and believe that it provides equity, the relationship will survive. It will survive until the balance shifts, or a more rewarding alternative is seen.

Relationships are nourished by dual perspective

We have stressed the importance of dual perspective, the ability to affiliate your viewpoint with someone else's. Dual perspective develops as you recognize that another person's goals, values and ways of interpreting experience can be synthesized with your own in order to benefit both of you. When you integrate the other's idea into your own, you confirm the other's importance. You also increase your effectiveness, because your talk is purposive rather than expressive. Your communication demonstrates concern for the other and involves him or her in your goal-seeking, even as you involve yourself in his or hers.

Dual perspective is the basis for all interpersonal communication; by extension it is a cornerstone of all human relationships. Only when we are considerate of others' perspectives can we contribute to healthy relationships. Without consideration there are no relationships, only individuals in proximity. Dual perspective implies both awareness of others and willingness to treat them and their ideas with respect. One of the people we interviewed seemed particularly skillful at developing dual perspective.

> I am seventy-one years old this June and there is no place in these United States where I am more than one hundred miles from bed and board with good friends. Now I've had some friends that were more than brothers, about two or three. Two of them are dead now, but Leland is still living in Grant's Pass and I

make sure I see him two or three times a year. He's in a wheel-chair, but I can still move around and I won't sit still til Mother Nature makes me.

Since I've retired, I'm free to come and go as I please. The places are dull now. I don't care so much for scenery any more. But the people never get dull. During my work years, I was a trouble shooter for the company and I can still work when I want to or have to. I can earn a buck with the smaller companies as a consultant because I understand their problems and what they need. That's how I feel about people too. I'm welcome all over, I guess, because I listen to their concerns and sense what they need. I can't give them money, but I have a lot of kind words and a few helpful tricks up my sleeve.

I try to keep moving. Ben Franklin said that fish and guests stink after three days. If my wife was still alive, she'd be with me. She travelled with me all the time when she was alive. We were glad to be together. She enjoyed people too, and we enjoyed each other. But I can still make a new friend because I know how to listen to what they say and ask them good questions about it. You know, that may be the secret; that good question tells the other person that you've heard him and that you want to know more.

Old men are a dime a dozen these days, but I think I'm worth more. My friends are all ages and I have something for them. A good ear, a kind word, some shared experience, a funny story, and a good healthy respect for the way they live, whether I'd live that way or not.

Dual perspective is not an all-or-nothing quality. It exists in degrees. With our casual acquaintances we have only limited access to their frames of reference, so we are constrained in the extent to which we can adapt to them. That is why we keep most of our relationships in public where we can all be bound by rules and norms that we hold in common. In public situations, everyone wants to be seen as a good conversationalist, an intelligent person, and a decent human being. It's easy enough to respond to this kind of goal-seeking through exchange of attentiveness and thoughtful talk.

When we listen to new acquaintances we pick up information that permits us to adapt more specifically the next time. At the minimum, we can keep ourselves from using expressive communication in public interactions. It is not appropriate to say whatever comes to your mind. Spontaneity is often an excuse for inconsideration. Public communication should be designed to address the interests, goals or values of listeners. It is rude to speak without taking others into account or just because you "want to." Even with strangers and casual acquaintances, we can employ a minimum degree of dual perspective to make interaction mutually rewarding.

We have more opportunity to develop high levels of dual perspective with our intimate partners. As a result of extensive intense communication with our intimates, we gain detailed understanding of how they define themselves, what they value, what they hope to achieve, and what they expect from others. We learn their sensitivities, how they respond to a wide range of situations and events. The greater our dual perspective, the more carefully we can adapt our communication to demonstrate a genuine respect for our partner. Dual perspective is reciprocal. The more effort you make to appreciate someone else's ideas, the more they tend to appreciate yours. Whether in casual, social, professional or intimate relationships, your success is based on guiding your communication with dual perspective.

Relationships develop over time

Our final premise is that human relationships evolve. They are dynamic, always changing. To sustain a relationship there must be a great number of adaptations made over its life. There will be alterations in rules, roles, goals, and exchanges. Relationships must flex to meet changes in the outside environment, as well as individual changes in the partners. Change is a constructive natural phenomenon in relationships, for it is a safeguard against stagnation. Change

You should live so long.

is a problem only if partners do not acknowledge it or do not revise their behaviors to adapt to it.

The evolving character of human relationships underscores the importance of dual perspective and responsibility. Dual perspective is important for it sensitizes partners to change in each other. Responsibility is important for it motivates partners to modify their behavior to adapt to the changes. Hiding and ignoring are irresponsible ways of responding to the necessity of change.

A Perspective on Intimate Bonds

We have, in this book, emphasized intimacy as the primary form of human relationship. We have done so consciously. It is our most important form of association, and it is least understood. Public relationships have engaged the interest of countless authorities. You can find any number of reliable references to understand public social behavior. Private relationships, however, have evoked a great deal of opinionated writing, but very little systematic attention.

The distinguishing feature of intimacy is relational culture, the private ways of transacting that define a particular bond. Norms, rules and roles are socially defined for public relationships. They can be discovered. In private relationships they must be developed. To do so requires intense commitment to the construction of a way of being together that provides mutual security and satisfaction. While success at public interaction requires skill at sensing the rules, success at private transaction requires skill at making the rules. As lifestyles come together and partners learn about each other, they develop for themselves a bond within which they relate as a unit, a couple. By communicating effectively to adapt their relational culture to meet changing needs, they sustain their bond.

Relational cultures each have unique content. But they are alike in their form. Every intimate bond requires the partners to deal with nine basic issues. The way they deal with them will vary widely, but the issues remain the same. Following is a summary of the issues we have discussed in previous chapters.

(1) *By what means does the couple make decisions?* Is it a complementary, symmetrical, or parallel relationship? Does one member feel deprived of a share in decision-making? Does one member feel too much responsibility? Is there conflict about particular issues, that is, is the couple sure who is responsible for what? Is one member seeking specific revisions? For what reasons? What exchange is the person seeking revisions willing to make for extended privilege? Does one member feel he or she made a bad bargain to begin with?

(2) *Who does the work?* What do the partners define as the work that

needs to be done? Do both members fulfill their share of the bargain? Do they do the work they agreed to do? If the work is not done, how do they make up the deficit? How is the work supervised? Is there some conflict about who has responsibility for doing what? Does one partner feel that he or she is doing more than a fair share?

(3) *How are problems handled?* Is there a regular system by which one partner can alert the other to a problem? Are grievance aired through argument, reasonable talk, pouting and sulking, or what? Is there a regular time and procedure established for airing grievances? Once grievances are aired, how are they resolved? Does one party make all the decisions? Do they sweep the disputes under the rug or do they struggle to resolve them? Are third parties ever involved in disputes? What effect does this have?

(4) *What is the nature of the exchange?* Who does what, under what circumstances, for whom, and with what return? Does one partner feel he or she is giving too much? Is there some arrangement for postponing return on favors or for getting "advances" on assistance? Must exchanges be made on the spot, or is there a way of deferring them til later? Are there new commodities (new sentiments for example) that must be introduced into the relationship? How are inequities handled? Who notifies whom under what circumstances about problems in equity? Then what happens?

(5) *How does the couple become aware of outside circumstances that might result in changes in the relationship?* Is there a time for them to share personal experiences and describe new pressures and challenges? What sources of advice do they have about problems that affect the relationship from the outside? What counsel and support do they expect from each other?

(6) *What is the nature of their ritualization?* Do they observe ceremonies and rituals? Do they engage in regular gift exchanges? Are satisfying verbal sentiments exchanged? Are there ways to memorialize important events?

(7) *Is there a procedure for revising and modifying policies?* Is there a regular policy about private space and time? Is there a regular review of the common attitude on where to live and how, getting ahead, goals for the future, children and family, etc.?

(8) *How are external people handled?* What is the nature of the relationship with parents, extended family, old friends, friends exclusive to one party, newcomers? What is the image the couple presents to the world? Is there a regular review of their socialization practice? Do they experiment with new social forms and with new people? How are discussions about new people and other external relations handled?

(9) *Is there a regular review of the CLs and $CL_{alt}s$?* Is there some effort to monitor goals and the extent to which they have been attained? Are alternative goals regularly considered? Do partners air their examination of external alternate relationships? Do they review the influence of work and hobbies on the relationship?

This kind of analysis represents a form of trouble shooting. People can use it to review their own relationship, and researchers can use it to describe how people carry on their intimacies.

Sylvia A., Guidance Counselor. I am not a possessive woman. I have my own career and I have always respected Jim's right to his career and to his privacy. But when he began to work with Nola, I became very concerned. For one thing, we had never, in seven years of marriage, failed to eat dinner together. All of a sudden, Jim began phoning me and telling me to eat on my own, that he was going to grab a sandwich with Nola because they were on a project. It was never clear to me what the project was or what kind of work Nola did. She was more than a secretary, that was clear, but there had never been a female engineer in Jim's firm and it never occurred to me that they would hire a woman. After about three weeks in which we ate dinner together only twice, and weekends were continually disrupted because Jim was working, I decided to inquire. I was certainly not going to hang on to a relationship that had outlived itself. If Jim wanted Nola, he could have her, but I wanted to know so I could make arrangements to protect myself economically and emotionally. So I asked.

Fortunately, I asked gently. It turned out that Nola was not only an engineer, she was the new chief engineer. She was in charge of a major project and she had Jim's promotion in the palm of her hand. She had selected him because she wanted him to take over the project when she moved on to the next task assigned her. As a matter of fact, their relationship was tense, threatening, challenging, and entirely non-sexual. Jim brought Nola home to dinner. She was good-looking, incredibly tough, and actually rather pleasant. We had no trouble getting along and she made it clear that her intentions for Jim were honorable. In fact, Jim and I laughed later about how much I acted like an aggrieved father defending a daughter's honor. It was a real role-reversal and we were actually happy about it. Jim got his promotion. We are enjoying the money and I just wrote a Christmas card to Nola who is setting up a new project in Bogota.

Every relational culture includes understandings about how to deal with basic issues. Sometimes the understandings are explicit, worked out through careful talk. Sometimes they are implicit, inferred from previous behavior. Sometimes they are assumed, often erroneously. Whatever the source of the understandings, they represent the basis of equity, and thus, the crux of satisfaction in an intimate relationship.

Partners have the ability to reconsider and revise their understandings, their expectations, and the ways they transact. Some of the most effective marriages we know include regular check-up conferences in which partners review their rules and amend the "constitutions" of their bond. In this way they retain mutual control over the nature and quality of their relationship.

Applying the Theory

In this book we have directly contradicted some popular conceptions of relationships. People generally try to avoid thinking systematically about their relationships. We have pointed out that they seem to think it is either impossible (you cannot analyze something as complex as a human relationship) or undesirable (you shouldn't try to scrutinize a relationship). They also seem to think it is unethical to try to do something about relationships (it's manipulative). People almost seem to think relationships are magic and that analysis of them will break the spell.

We believe that avoiding analysis is irresponsible and potentially dangerous to everyone concerned. When people avoid analysis they prevent themselves from accepting personal responsibility for the quality of their relationships. They put themselves in position to blame someone else for what happens. We are quick to ascribe public problems to faulty decisions, defective policies, or poor judgment. However, people mostly refuse to take a similar approach to their private relationships. They prefer explanations such as luck, fate, or vibes. (Some even prefer "scientific" explanations that suggest that everything is caused, motivated or conditioned by outside forces.)

We believe that planning is important in all relationships. Most people reject this idea. They believe that important and fragile relationships cannot be planned. They must happen because that's the way things are. It takes considerable planning to keep intense private relationships on course and of high quality. They are much more difficult to manage than public relationships, because so much more is at stake and there are no social forces like courts or mediators to handle problems. Everything that happens in a private relationship, good or bad, can be ascribed to the decisions made by the partners and the way they are implemented.

Planning together permits development of dual perspective, sharing of goals, synthesizing of concerns, and generation of satisfactory ways and means of transacting that the partners are able to handle. The opposite of planning is spontaneous, expressive communication which often becomes self-centered and self-serving. Planning is much better suited to the requirements of successful transaction.

We elected to take a rhetorical approach in this book. We selected it over the idealism that has permeated the bulk of the writing in the area of interpersonal behavior. We prefer the rhetorical position because it places responsibility in the hands of individual humans. Rhetorical responsibility proceeds through effective communication, and it relies upon the three main characteristics of human beings: symbolizing ability, self-awareness, and the ability to make and implement personal decisions.

We admit that it is usually easier and more comforting not to assume responsibility for what happens to us. It is consoling to believe that nothing is our fault. We prefer to blame others and to believe in a person or system that will "cure" our relationship illnesses. Phrases like, "we just grew apart," "the magic is gone," "I guess we no longer meet each other's needs," "it's not special anymore," "she/he is not the same person I married," reflect this sort of irresponsibility. Partners do *not* grow apart or cease to be special because of whims of fate. *It is because they have chosen, consciously or unconsciously, to let their relationships falter.* We contend that it is preferable that you be aware of what you have decided so that you can manage it more effectively.

Using CL and CL$_{alt}$

We have used the concepts CL (comparison level) and CL$_{alt}$ (comparison level of alternatives) as a basic criterion for relationship analysis. CL refers to a comparison of what is happening to what you think should happen. Given that you have set realistic goals and are not dreaming the impossible dream, an analysis of comparison levels gives you a sensible idea of how satisfied you are. Application of CL$_{alt}$, examining and comparing alternatives to what is going on, provides you with a basis for deciding how important your present relationship is and how badly you want to stay in it or leave it. Monitoring on this basis helps you respond to the requirements of the growth stages. To do this kind of analysis, you will need to review some of the "possibles" you can derive in relationships with others. We offer you a list of possibilities with the admonition that it is only a partial list, and you must make your decision about what you need. Once you have identified a confirmation, quality, service, or sentiment you need, you must ask:

1. What are the chances I can get it from my present partner?
2. What do I have to do in order to motivate him or her to provide it?
3. Is it worth it to me to seek it?
4. Is there anyone outside the relationship that could provide it?

5. How do I know?
6. What would I lose by moving outside the relationship to attain what I want?

This kind of analysis requires a the use of a cost-benefit analysis of your exchange. Generally speaking, it is best done in conversation with your partner. Examination of outside possibilities is not threatening if they are dealt with directly. It is when one partner is looking outside and the other is not aware of it that trouble starts in the relationship. Honest admission of the outside possibilities usually results in effecive adjustment of the present relationship, largely because people tend to idealize people and situations on the outside. Their attraction vanishes when subjected to logical review.

Some Possible Qualities to Check in Performing a CL, CL$_{alt}$ Analysis

1. I need someone to tell me that I am a good person.
2. I need someone to tell me I am a competent person.
3. I need someone to tell me I am an attractive person.
4. I need someone to tell me I am a (fill in our own quality) person.
5. I need someone to give me advice about _____.
6. I need someone to listen to my private thoughts and feelings about _____.
7. I need someone to share the following kinds of work with me. _____.
8. I need someone to give me time.
9. I need someone that I can count on when I am depressed, in trouble, or confused.
10. I need someone to help me enjoy myself.
11. I need someone with whom I can share my hobby or recreation.
12. I need someone who can give me good sex.
13. I need someone to help with the expenses.
14. I need someone who can give me ideas about _____.
15. I need someone who needs me . . . The list can go on and on.

To take control and responsibility for your relationships, you may consider the choices open to you at each stage in relational evolution. Chapters 6, 7, and 8 explained the process of development. They provide a foundation for making informed choices about your actions and responses to others' actions. We can review these stages by highlighting the choices open to you in each of them.

Stage	Choices Open to Individuals
Individuals	Do you seek additional relationships? What purposes do you have for relationships? What are your criteria for interaction partners?
Invitational Communication	Who is available for interaction? How do you declare your public identity? How do others available declare their public identities? How do available others respond to you? Is a desirable person interested in further contact? Are you interested in further contact?
Explorational Communication	How much personal information should you reveal? How do you respond to the others' disclosures? Are you satisfied with the other's response to you? Is there a basis for a future relationship? Should you end, stabilize, or escalate the relationship?
Intensifying Communication	How do you declare your private identity? How does the other respond to your declaration? How do you respond to the other's private identity? Is an intimate relationship desirable with this person? How will you and the other define your relationship?
Revising Communication	Do the rewards of this relationship outweigh the costs? Are you willing to make changes in your personal style, behaviors, expectations, etc. to continue? What rules and roles will the two of you establish for your relational culture?
Bonding Communication	Do you want to commit to share your future with this individual?
Navigating Communication	How do you organize your bond? How do you deal with external influences on the bond? How do you initiate changes to keep the bond viable? How do you maintain a steady state of intimacy?
Differentiating Communication	Do you wish to allow increasing separation of lives?

Stage	Choices Open to Individuals
	How will you deal with issues underlying differentiation?
	Can anything be done to reduce the costs of transaction?
	Can anything be done to increase the rewards of transaction?
Disintegrating Communication	Do you wish to violate the relational culture?
	How do you respond to infractions by your partner?
	Can costs of transaction be reduced or rewards increased?
	How do you deal with apathy and anger?
Stagnating Communication	Do you see attractive alternatives to your bond?
	Do you want to work at revitalizing this bond?
	What is the value of maintaining this stage?
	What are the costs of staying in this stage?
Terminating Communication	How do you safeguard your interests while ending the bond?
	How do you deal fairly with your ex-intimate?
	How do you define your future relationship?
Individuals	How will you alter your standards, expectations and behavior the next time around, or will there be a next time?

This chart does not include all of the choices people can make as they move through the stages of relationship. However, it makes the point that choice-making represents the basis of success and satisfaction at each stage. It confronts you clearly with the issue that decisions are in your hands. You cannot blame failure of the relationship in the stagnation stage on your partner alone, if you have not made the effort to deal with some of the questions you face.

To apply the rhetorical approach to interpersonal communication you must think of relationships as sequences of choices. This perspective gives you maximum control over what happens to you in any kind of relationship you seek. The other person has responsibility, too, but if you are sophisticated in interpersonal communication, you can help the other person understand choice-making and get him or her to cooperate with you in working through issues.

Perspectives of Contemporary Men and Women

A final issue we addressed in this book is the difference between men's and women's perspectives on human relationships. Changes in our society, have required men and women to face new possibilities and new problems in the way they relate to one another.

The data we gathered about men and women did not reveal universal answers to our questions about how men and women view themselves and each other. We were, however, able to identify some trends and groupings based on responses to key issues. Men and women are caught in conflicting value systems. Many are reluctant to choose and others do not know how. But success at relationship building depends on a secure orientation to these major issues.

Men face the traditional challenge of masculinity: to be strong, self-reliant and dominant in relationships. Yet, a growing number of men would like to be released from the pressure, and be able to choose a more gentle, less stressful, more cooperative mode of relationship not only with women, but also with other men. A great many men who succeed at achieving the goals of masculinity reach mid-life shaken and ready to change to a less combative style. It may be even more difficult for them to change after so many years of playing the expected masculine role.

Similar ambivalence is displayed by men confronted by new choices in selection of intimate partners. Many men seek women with traditional qualities: physical attractiveness, dependence on men, deference to and support of mates, dedication to home and family. Yet many men are attracted by competent, career-seeking women, who are self-reliant and independent.

Contemporary women are no less confused in their expectations for relationships. Many are unable to choose who they would like to be. They strive for perfection in many areas: traditional feminine qualities and the qualities of the independent woman. They face an equally difficult challenge in deciding on an orientation to their mates. Should they remain dependent in their romantic relationships, or is it possible to work out relationships based on the principles of equity?

This is a time of great ambiguity in relationships. It does not appear that the role of women will revert exclusively to a traditional one, nor that the strengths of traditional values will be entirely abandoned. Further, it does not appear possible, in the foreseeable future, to expunge some of the worst effects of traditional values on both men and women. Therefore, women and men will continue to be confronted with hard choices and great difficulties in forming lasting relationships. They will, however, have opportunities their parents never dreamed of.

We offer this book to help you to face these choices. We ask you to recognize and celebrate your human abilities to self-reflect and make choices, and we urge you to assume your share of responsibility in building and sustaining relationships. We offer you new possibilities and some guidelines and advice for achieving them in cooperation with others. We also urge you to remember that both your strengths and limitations are built into you as an individual, but within those limitations, you have the ability to make choices for yourself and for the common good.

This book is not a comprehensive guide to interpersonal behavior, but a first step toward understanding yourself and others. We believe that we all have the capacity to improve the way we relate to others, and that such improvement is imperative if we are to survive the social changes that lie ahead of us. The understandings you have gained from this book should enhance your ability to build and sustain satisfying relationships throughout your lifetime.

REFERENCES FOR CHAPTER 11

R. Brain, *Friends and Lovers*. New York: Basic Books, 1976.

R. Farson, "Why Good Marriages Fail," in R. Kostelanetz (Ed.), *The Edge of Adaptation*. Englewood Cliffs, N.J.: Prentice-Hall, 1973. Pp. 108–117.

R. Laing, *Self and Other*. New York: Pantheon Books, 1971.

W. Lederer, *Marital Choices*. New York: W. W. Norton, 1981.

APPENDIX A

A NOTE ON RESEARCH THE ORAL AND WRITTEN INTERVIEWS

When we first conceived the idea for this book both of us thought it important to find ways to demonstrate how theory works in practice. We wanted to show readers how various principles are applied by everyday people as they conduct their relationships. We decided that we would need examples from the lives of people like those who would read the book and like those people who read the book might become. Thus, we designed a two-step research process.

First, we surveyed nearly 4,000 people asking them to respond anonymously in writing to a series of questions about their relationships. Next, we interviewed a smaller number of people to explore in greater depth some of the issues that recurred in the written responses. Our intent was not to conduct a rigorous, scientific opinion poll; those have been done and we have drawn upon their findings in this book. Rather, we wished to supplement the insights from existing research with a human-oriented investigation that would result in greater understanding of the issues.

The results of our study did increase our understanding of the many ways people view their relationships and the alternatives from which they choose their behavior toward others. Further, the results provided us with examples that personalize and dramatize the information in this book. Throughout the text we included excerpts from the responses we received. In general we do not identify the authors, since we guaranteed them anonymity. We altered names and occupations so that no individual can be identified. Occasionally we used statements from real people with permission. We regard each excerpt as a rich source of ideas for analysis and discussion of issues critical in interpersonal communication.

The Questions for the Study

Since we sought to understand personal viewpoints and unique relationship choices, we judged it inappropriate to rely on a standard questionnaire which might artificially limit responses. We did not want to restrict our respondents in any way, nor to bias them toward conventional answers and ideas. Instead, we designed six general questions to stimulate extensive, descriptive answers. Apparently we succeeded, for the length of written responses averaged just under six typed pages. Following are the six questions:

1. Describe your best friendship. How did you meet your best friend? What do you do and talk about when you are together? What makes this person your *best* friend? Why do you think this person considers you a friend? Describe how your friendship started, developed, and changed.
2. Define friendship. What do friends do for each other? How important is friendship to you? Describe the different kinds of friends you have.
3. What are your views on marriage? How important is marriage to you? What makes a marriage "good"? What roles do you see for spouses in a marriage? What alternatives to marriage would you consider? How important is it to you to have an intimate and exclusive relationship with someone of the opposite sex?
4. What are the possibilities for relationships with the opposite sex? Can they be friends? Colleagues? Co-workers? Is sex ever absent as an issue in relationships with the opposite sex?
5. What is the meaning of sex? What purpose and value do you attribute to sex?
6. What does it mean to be a woman/man in America today? Describe how you personally feel about your goals, joys, problems, responsibilities, and concerns as a woman/man.

The same basic questions were used for the oral interviews, although respondents were helped by questions to discuss their ideas thoroughly. We attempted to follow our respondents' interests and to emphasize in the interviews what they wanted to talk about. We used one more source of information; casual public conversations. By listening to people "shoot the breeze," and participating in talk with them, we learned quite a bit about their biases and interaction styles.

The Respondents

We wanted responses from a wide range of people, so questionnaires were given to students and institutions willing to let their employees respond. Of adults we asked to respond, over ninety percent of the men, and ninety–five of the women agreed. In fact, they seemed eager to get their ideas on the record. College students were often asked to respond as part of a communications course, but they were provided with anonymity and the option not to respond if it violated their principles in any way. Students responses were solicited under the protection of standard university regulations for the protection of participants in studies. They were provided with a detailed description of how their responses would be used. They were also told to omit items not relevant to their lives or in which they were not interested. In some cases, the student questionnaire was broken down into detailed questions, all open-ended, but more particularized.

Following is a summary of our respondents.

	Men	Women
Employed, professional, managerial	345	111
Employed, blue collar	141	48
Employed, clerical	58	118
Housepersons	0	310
Teachers	24	35
Professors	33	8
College Students	1243	1361
Totals	1844	1991

Our sample represents people of various races, religions, and ethnic backgrounds. Our major oversight was a lack of respondents from the "poverty class." We have no doubt that the opinions of the very poor would differ in some important ways from those expressed by our respondents.

The interviews, naturally, were more limited in number. We interviewed twenty-five men and thirty-four women employed outside a university setting (we considered homemaking a form of employment). We also interviewed approximately fifty students from our classes willing to talk with us after the class had ended and the grades were in. We repeat, this set of respondents should not be regarded as a sample. They were willing to respond and their demography varies in some ways from society in general. On the other hand, they are very much like the people we know and you know.

General Conclusions from the Study

From the answers to our questions we were able to piece together a detailed picture of how women and men relate to each other and to members of their own sex, how they form social and intimate relationships, and what they think about these relationships. We learned what our respondents considered major problems and some of the ways they tackled these in their lives. Where relevant, we compared our findings to those of an earlier study conducted by Phillips (Gerald M. Phillips and Nancy J. Metzger, *The Study of Intimate Communication*. Boston: Allyn and Bacon, 1981). That study concentrated on same-sex friendships although there were some items about female/male relationships.

We do not believe our findings represent a set of fixed values. What we have is an up-to-the-minute review of what a broad sample of people are willing to admit they believe. There are some important differences between this report and the earlier one that lead us to conclude that human relationships are in a constant state of change and that *individual choices continually shape social norms.* We find, however, that both men and women in public tend to defer to what they think are important social norms in their private relationships. Thus, their private business is influenced by what they think is acceptable in society. On the other hand, we find that their private choices have had an important influence on broad social norms.

We find the issues remain the same, though the possibilities for handling them change. People are concerned with love, marriage, family, fair treatment, satisfying personal goals, getting ahead, just like they always were. Our most important finding is the urgency for equity in relationships, a growing consideration for women and men alike.

Our most important finding is that human beings have the ability to make personal decisions and they do so in most remarkable ways.

We were startled both by the antiquated attitudes of some of our respondents and the remarkably creative ways in which others were responding to contemporary issues and pressures. Quite clearly, both women and men understood they were restricted to some degree by their physiology, by their physical location and environment, by long standing social codes and mores, and even by chance. On the other hand, there was no doubt about the willingness of a great number of our respondents, of all ages, to experiment with new and productive ways of handling their relationships. By presenting their ideas to you we offer you the opportunity to influence your own life. It is important for you to know that you are not a creature of the "fates and furies," that human beings have considerable capacity to change the world and the lives they live. This is the excitement and the challenge of our era.

APPENDIX B

THEORIES ABOUT HUMAN RELATIONSHIPS

Interpersonal communication as a scholarly discipline combines the efforts of representatives of many fields. This appendix offers you a way to evaluate the information they have produced. To explain even the most accepted ideas would require a whole book. In these pages we offer you a sampling of ideas and with each, references to current books or articles from which you can obtain additional information. The central questions scholars address are these:

• Which aspects of interpersonal communication behavior come primarily from genetics and physiology, and which ones come from social training, education and acculturation? Given that interpersonal communication behavior is some combination of nature and nurture, what aspects can be changed by what means?

Robert Ardrey, *The Territorial Imperative*. New York: Atheneum, 1970.
David Barash, *The Whisperings Within*. New York: Penguin Books, 1979.

David Riesman *et al.*, *The Lonely Crowd*. Garden City, N.Y.: Doubleday and Co., 1950.

Lionel Tiger, *Men in Groups*. New York: Vintage Books, 1970.

E. O. Wilson, *On Human Nature*. Cambridge: Harvard University Press, 1978.

• In the social aspects of interpersonal communication, which behaviors stem mainly from responses to environment and which ones stem from adherence to social rules generated by human activity?

D. Hewes, "Interpersonal Communication Theory and Research: A Metamethodological Overview," in B. Ruben (Eds.), *Communication Yearbook II*. New Brunswick, N.J.: Transaction-International Communication Association, 1978. pp. 155–169.

• To what extent can interpersonal communication behavior be used as a way of discovering internal mental processes and intrapsychic activity? To what extent is the internal mental processing that underlies interpersonal communication behavior an orderly process, and to what extent is it generated from unconscious or preconscious mental activity? How does interpersonal communication develop socially?

Michael Argyle, *Psychology of Interpersonal Behavior*. Baltimore, Penguin Books, 1967.

Eric Berne, *What Do You Say After You Say "Hello"?* New York: Grove Press, 1972.

Robert Carson, *Interaction Concepts of Personality*. Chicago: Aldine Press, 1969.

Jay Haley, *Strategies of Psychotherapy*. New York: Grune and Stratton, 1963.

Karen Horney, *The Neurotic Personality of Our Time*. New York: W. W. Norton, 1937.

Timothy Leary, *Interpersonal Diagnosis of Personality*. New York: Ronald Press, 1957.

Samuel Novey, *The Second Look*. Baltimore: Johns Hopkins Press, 1968.

• Are people trainable in interpersonal processes? Given a long tradition of formal training in public speaking and oratory, can formal training be similarly applied to interpersonal processes? Given that people can be trained, is training most effective when it emphasizes performance skills and stresses responses to others in encouraging social milieus, or when it attempts to condition responses of individuals to changes in social contingencies?

Ron Adler, *Confidence in Communication*. New York: Holt, Rinehart and Winston, 1982.

Robert Golembiewski and Arthur Blumberg, *Sensitivity Training and the Laboratory Approach*. Itasca, Ill.: F. E. Peacock, 1970.

Sidney Jourard, *The Transparent Self*. New York: Van Nostrand, 1971.

Robert Mager, *Goal Analysis*. Belmont, Calif.: Fearon Publishing, 1972.

Bruce Maliver, *The Encounter Game*. New York: Stein and Day, 1973.

Gerald M. Phillips, *Help for Shy People or Anyone Else Who Ever Felt Ill at*

Ease on Entering a Room Full of Strangers. Englewood Cliffs, N.J.: Prentice-Hall/Spectrum, 1981.

Carl Rogers, *On Becoming a Person.* Boston: Houghton, Mifflin, 1961.

• What relationship does the work carried on by psychiatrists and psychologists to treat abnormal or distressed people have to the activities of normal people in an ordinary social world? Can the study of people with exceptional problems be applied to the understanding of ordinary interpersonal communication?

Roger MacKinnon and Robert Michels, *The Psychiatric Interview in Clinical Practice.* Philadelphia: W. B. Saunders, 1971.

Abraham Maslow, *Motivation and Personality.* New York: Harper and Row, 1954.

Richard Rabkin, *Inner and Outer Space.* New York: W. W. Norton, 1970.

Jurgen Ruesch, *Therapeutic Communication.* New York: W. W. Norton, 1973.

Paul Watzlawick, Janet Beavin, and Don Jackson, *Pragmatics of Human Communication.* New York: W. W. Norton, 1967.

• To what extent must we understand non-verbal communication behavior in order to understand interpersonal communication behavior? Can non-verbal activities be codified or must they be studied entirely in the individual case?

Edward Hall, *The Hidden Dimension.* Garden City, N.Y., Doubleday, 1966.

Mark Knapp, *Nonverbal Communication in Human Interaction.* New York: Holt, Rinehart, and Winston, 1972.

Albert Mehrabian, *Public Places, Private Spaces.* New York: Basic Books, 1976.

• What is the influence of various "points of view" endorsed by scholars of Speech Communication? Specifically, what are the contributions of symbolic interactionism, exchange and equity theory, situationism, rules theory and constructivism?

Robert F. Bales, *SYMLOG.* New York: Basic Books, 1980.

H. Blumer, *Symbolic Interaction.* Englewood Cliffs, N.J.: Prentice-Hall, 1969.

Donald Cushman and Robert T. Craig, "Communication Systems: Interpersonal Implications," in Gerald Miller (Ed.), *Explorations in Interpersonal Communication.* Beverly Hills, Calif.: Sage Publications, 1976.

Jesse Delia, "Constructivism and the Study of Human Communication," *Quarterly Journal of Speech.* 63, 1977. Pp. 66–83.

Sally Jackson and Scott Jacobs, "The Structure of Conversational Argument: Pragmatic Bases for the Enthymeme," *Quarterly Journal of Speech.* 66, 1980. Pp. 251–265.

George Homans, *Social Behavior: Its Elementary Forms.* New York: Harcourt, Brace, Jovanovich, 1974.

Gerald M. Phillips, "Rhetoric and Its Alternatives as Bases for Examining Intimate Communication," *Communication Quarterly.* 24, 1, 1976.

Julia T. Wood, *Human Communication: A Symbolic Interactionist Perspective.* New York: Holt, Rinehart, and Winston, 1982.

• What are some good general books from which a reader can get an overview of theory?

Dean Barnlund, *Interpersonal Communication*. Boston: Houghton, Mifflin, 1968.
Ellen Berscheid and Elaine Walster, *Interpersonal Attraction*. Reading, Mass.: Addison-Wesley, 1969.
Murray Davis, *Intimate Relations*. New York: Free Press, 1973.
Erving Goffman, *Relations in Public*. New York: Basic Books, 1971.
Kurt Lewin, *A Dynamic Theory of Personality*. New York: McGraw-Hill, 1935.
Gerald M. Phillips and Nancy J. Metzger, *Intimate Communication*. Boston: Allyn and Bacon, 1976.

The above list is not exhaustive, but it will start the interested reader on an investigation of the exciting ideas that have been offered about interpersonal communication behavior. There is a great deal that remains to be done before we even scratch the surface in this study. However, interpersonal communication is so intrinsic a part of our lives that we must understand it if we are to have any success in making and sustaining relationships.

• *Sociobiology is a contemporary synthesis of ideas that underlies our theoretical view on interpersonal communication behavior.* Sociobiology is a new area of study which attempts to synthesize what we know about human biology with our knowledge of human social behavior. Its goal is to discover the latitude of freedom we have in our social behavior given our physiological limitations.

The fundamental premises of sociobiology are that all animals, including humans, seek (1) to preserve their species, (2) to develop a secure world (homeostasis), (3) to find a place to fit in with others of their kind, and (4) to keep stimulated through sensitivity to the world. Language enables us to maintain personal identity. It is the basis for the games and arts from which we derive stimulation, and for the honors and awards from which we derive status, or territorial fit. Our governments are a symbolic way to make our rules orderly and permanent (homeostatic). An unique feature of human social behavior is urgency for *personal* survival and identity. Our symbolic capability enables us to develop personal identity. Self awareness means that individuals have a special concern about *personal* survival, security, satisfaction, and status. This makes it very difficult to draw general conclusions. So much of our behavior is specifically adapted to our own needs that often we must concentrate on applying some very general understandings to individual cases. This is what led us to *rhetoric* as a basis for understanding interpersonal communication, for rhetoric seeks to understand and modify the *particular case*.

Humans use symbolic communication (verbal and non-verbal) to make themselves more secure and satisfied, to struggle for status and power, and to serve the social interest. Every human relationship involves political, social and economic, as well as personal issues. Each person seeks to maximize pleasure and reduce pain. People succeed to greater or lesser degrees as they recognize shared interests and concerns. People exchange symbols in order to make decisions about who is in charge, who should do what for whom, how everyone can feel safe, and how disputes should be settled. In addition, language is used for both personal and social pleasure; in the fields of music, art and theater individuals' produce for personal expression and satisfaction.

People feel secure when they believe their problems are solved or manageable and they are satisfied when they believe they are accepted and loved. When humans fail to accomplish their goals, they feel unsatisfied and unsafe. They become anxious. Much of what humans do with each other can be interpreted as a defense against anxiety, an emotion some authorities believe is the most painful experience humans can know.

Ineffective communication is a main source of anxiety.

- If you cannot set specific goals for your communication behavior, you become anxious because you aren't sure what to do and you cannot tell whether you have accomplished what you should.
- If you cannot discover ways to win cooperation from others, you become egocentric and demanding in your goalseeking, causing it to result in rejection, frustration and anxiety.
- If your communication is poorly planned and executed, the best intent will not facilitate success. Inept communication results in loneliness, boredom and ineffectuality, prime sources of anxiety.
- If you are not aware of the effect of your actions on others, you will not be able to adapt to their behavior. Consequently, you will look awkward and act out of phase. Your efforts to solicit relationships with others will be thwarted and anxiety may result.

The sociobiological orientation explains why we seek protection from harm and the security of affection. All people obtain their most important rewards from other human beings. Once we discover how valuable other people are to us we begin to seek secure relationships with them. Interpersonal communication is the method we use to achieve these relationships.

Relationship skill depends on understanding and experience. You must understand both the *possibilities* and the *probabilities* in relationship behavior. Interaction or social activity is characterized by rule-following behavior which can be estimated in probabilities. Transaction or private activity contains endless possibilities for people to develop personal rules, which are designed to accomplish maximum satisfaction.

Private relationship behavior is motivated by personal goals. Public relationship behavior is controlled by general agreements. If you understand both what is possible and what is likely, you can set goals realistically and not let wishful thinking distort your estimate of situations. This is a rhetorical process that is fairly logical, but not completely so; it is personal, but fully responsive to others, not entirely capricious, but filled with surprises.

We've now identified some of the best respected theories about human relationships. Each theory offers an explanation of how and why relationships are formed and how people operate within them. Each suggests a point of view about the nature of the humans who are relating. Each provides some valuable insights into interpersonal behavior, and many of these are reflected in the rhetorical position employed in this book. You should now have sufficient awareness of theoretical options to make an informed choice about your own position as well as to define areas you wish to study further.

AUTHOR INDEX

A

B

C

D

Davis, M., 117, 128, 140, 147, 176, 206, 304
Delia, J., 303
Duck, S., 147

F

Fair, C., 35–36, 37
Farson, R., 292
Fitzpatrick, M. and Best, P., 176
Freud, S., 26, 47, 48
Friedan, B., 269
Fromm, E., 37, 60

G

Gilder, G., 235
Goffman, E., 304
Golembiewski, R., 302
Goodman, E., 269
Goodman, P., 23, 37

H

Haley, J., 302
Hall, E., 303
Hart, R. and Burks, D., 19, 60
Hart, R., Carlson, W. and Eadie, W., 19
Henley, N., 269
Hewes, D., 302
Hite, S., 235, 245, 269
Homans, G., 303
Horney, K., 19, 302
Hutchins, R., 29–30

J

Jackson, S. and Jacobs, S., 303
Jennings, L., 13–14
Johnson, W., 10, 19
Jourard, S., 302

K

Kanter, R., 260, 269
Knapp, M., 117, 147, 206, 303

L

M

N

P

R

S

Sabo, D., 235
Satir, V., 112
Scanzoni, J., 235
Schoeck, H., 235
Sheehy, G., 112, 117, 147
Slater, P., 25
Socrates, 6
Storr, A., 235
Sullivan, H., 7, 25

T

Terrace, H., 61
Thiabaut, J. and Kelly, H., 88, 89, 112
Tiger, L., 214, 235, 302
Toffler, A., 14, 37, 104, 112

W

Watzlawick, P., Beavin, J. and Jackson, D., 112, 302
Weaver, C., 80
Weiss, R., 207
Wilson, E., 223, 235, 302
Wilson, J. and Arnold, C., 80
Wood, J., 61, 80, 117–18, 147, 177, 207, 303
Wood, J. and Phillips, G., 61
Wynn-Edwards, V., 96, 112

Y

Yankelovitch, D., 14, 37, 234

SUBJECT INDEX

A

B

C

Communication (*continued*)
  focus, 5–6
  and human development, 121
  importance of, 6–13
  in contemporary life, 13–15
  relationship, 97
  social, 73–74
  social issues, 23–31
  value of, 272–73
Communication apprehensives, 69
Communication climate, 168
Communication strategies, 166–68
Comparison Level (CL), 88–90, 100, 124, 136, 138, 144, 164, 186, 192, 284, 287–88
Comparison Level of Alternatives (CL$_{alt}$), 89–90, 101, 124, 136–37, 138, 144, 164, 191–92, 284, 287–88
Competition, 24–25, 213, 220–21, 252, 258
Complementary relationships, 98, 151–53, 249
Complications
  in deterioration, 203–206
  in growth stages, 143–46
  in navigation, 173–75
Conflict, 195, 202, 256
Conformity, 24
Consensual validation, 32, 213, 239, 240
Cooperation, 24–25

D

Decreased involvement, 192
Dependence, 76–77
Developmental approaches, 116–122
Differentiating communication, 192–94, 289–90
Disclosure, 11, 32–33, 74, 79, 239, 240
Disintegrating communication, 195–97, 290
Dual perspective, 51–54, 59–60, 94, 95, 99, 133, 134, 245, 280–82
Dually-oriented women, 253–56

E

Equity, 279
Euphoria, 131–36
Evoked negative identity, 187–89
Exchange, 242, 244, 279–80, 284
Expectations
  idealistic, 182
  individual, 180–83
  in intimate situations, 65
  of a partner, 183–85
  in social situations, 64–65
  unrealistic, 181

Explorational communication, 129–31, 288
Expression, 5–6

F

Family, 221–22
Feminism, 249
   male attitudes toward, 226–28
Friendship, 75, 211–18
Frustration, 265–66

G

Generalized other, 95
Goals, 9, 66, 276–83
   goal centered, 15
   goal seeking, 9–10
   goal setting, 68
Group dynamics, 3
Guilt, 204–205

H

Human nature, 273–76

I

I, 91–96, 107
Identity, 6–7, 109
IFD disease, 10, 46, 164, 183
Incompatibility, 174–75
Independence, 155
Independent women, 249–53
Individual, 24, 117–18, 123, 199–200, 289, 290
Ineffectiveness, 8
Intensification, 133
Intensifying communication, 131–35, 289
Interaction, 16–18
   strategies in, 73–75
Interactive systems, 272
Intimate communication, 168–71
Invitational communication, 124–28, 289
Iron maiden, 260–61

J

Joint identity, 143

L

Leisure time, 30–31
Listening, 72
Locker-room talk, 231–32
Loneliness, 8

M

Making it, 232–33
Male attitudes, 291–92
　toward feminism, 226–28
　toward friendship, 211–22
　toward sex, 224–25
　toward women, 222–24, 225–26
Me, 91–96, 133
Mentor relationship, 218, 258
Monitoring, 44, 67, 166–68
Myths, 10–13, 274–76
　of sexual quality, 122

N

Navigation, 150, 158, 185, 186, 193, 289
Navigational communication, 289
Nonverbal communication, 70

O

Old-boy network, 220, 258

P

Pair-identity, 134–35
Parallel relationships, 157–58
Personal freedom, 156
Personal support, 239–41
Persuasive communication, 51
Phatic communication, 126
Physical strength, 230–31
Pleasure, 25–27
　sexual, 27
Power, 151–52, 205–206
　balanced, 154–55
Premature commitment, 145–46
Problem solving, 241–43
Purposive communication, 47–51, 59

R

Rebound relationships, 204
Reciprocity, 53, 244, 278–80
Recreational friends, 239
Rejection, 76
Relational change, 159–65
  in individuals, 159–62
  in social systems, 163–165
Relational culture, 84, 92, 102, 107–11, 121, 140, 171, 185–86, 195–97, 201
  fatal ruptures in, 186–187, 283, 285
Relational deterioration
  extrinsic factors, 189–92
  intrinsic factors, 185–89
  reasons for, 180–85
Relational structure, 150–58
  changes in, 158
  complementary, 98, 151–53
  parallel, 157–58, 233
  symmetrical, 98, 154–57, 233
Relationship quota, 87–88
Relationships
  common features in, 273
  definition of, 84
  developmental approaches to, 116–22
  developmental patterns in, 119–20
  growth stages in, 122–43
  standards for, 87–90
Responsibility, 54–57, 176, 266–68, 277–78
Retribution, 146
Revising communication, 135–41, 289
Revitalizing communication, 171–73, 185
Revitalizing rituals, 172
Rhetoric, 5–6
Rhetorical perspective, 40–60
  ethical issues, 58
  self-reflection, 43–45
  symbolicity, 41–43
  will, 45–47
Ritual, 284
Roles
  women, 22, 227
  sex, 104, 266
Rules
  social, 11–12

S

Segregation, 27
Self, 6–7

U

Unequal effort, 173–74
Unilateral terminations, 204–205
Unrealistic expectations, 144–45
Unrequited love, 143–44

V

Violence, 25

W

Will, 45–47, 274
Women's Movement, 100, 226
Women's network, 259
Women's views, 291–92
   on friendship, 239–46
   on friendships with men, 243–46
   on romantic relationships, 246–56
   on the world of work, 256–63
Work, 221–22